Mastering Crypto Assets

Martin Leinweber
Jörg Willig
Steven A. Schoenfeld

Mastering Crypto Assets

Investing in Bitcoin, Ethereum, and Beyond

Published by John Wiley & Sons, Inc., Hoboken, New Jersey.
Published simultaneously in Canada.

For general information on our other products and services or for technical support, please contact our Customer Care Department within the United States at (800) 762-2974, outside the United States at (317) 572-3993 or fax (317) 572-4002.

Wiley also publishes its books in a variety of electronic formats. Some content that appears in print may not be available in electronic formats. For more information about Wiley products, visit our web site at www.wiley.com.

Library of Congress Cataloging-in-Publication Data is Available:

ISBN 9781394205394 (Cloth)
ISBN 9781394205417 (ePDF)
ISBN 9781394205400 (ePub)

Cover Design: Wiley
Cover Image: © istock_onespirit/Getty Images

SKY10061351_112923

Contents

Acknowledgments

Writing a book is an endeavor that can never truly be claimed by one individual, and this work on crypto assets stands as a testament to that sentiment. From the initial inklings of an idea to the final full stop, countless hands and minds have shaped, refined, and enriched the narrative. We stand on the shoulders of many.

Our collective journey was made all the more rewarding with our colleagues at MarketVector—Thomas Kettner, Emre Camlilar, Guilherme Brandao, Bilal Baig, and Eunjeong Kang—your combined expertise and collaborative spirit were integral. Working alongside you has been both a pleasure and a privilege.

The authenticity and depth of our book are heavily indebted to our interview partners. Jan van Eck, Fred Thiel, and Peter Brandt, your willingness to share your experiences and insights has added invaluable layers to our narrative.

To our guest contributors, Matthew Sigel, Marco Manoppo, Gregory Mall, and Rohan Misra, we extend our gratitude. Your keen analysis and unique voices enriched our chapters, providing readers with varied and nuanced perspectives. Token Terminal (Aleksis Tapper and Rasmus Savander), Marcel Kasumovich, and Timothy Peterson, your contributions further solidified our book's place as a comprehensive guide in the world of crypto assets.

Our sincere thanks to Digital Asset Research, CCData, and Figment. The data and insights you provided were pivotal, helping us to ground our discussions in fact and offer a well-rounded and informed view on our subject matter. Special recognition goes to Doug Schwenk from Digital Asset Research; Charles Hayter, James Harris, and Jimena Leon from CCData; and Joshua Deems, Benjamin Thalman, Chris Wilson, Colton Campbell, and Ivan Szeftel from Figment for their invaluable assistance and contributions to our project. Your expertise and support greatly enhanced the depth and credibility of our research.

And to the unsung heroes of the written word, our editors Bill Falloon, Barbara Long, and Purvi Patel. Your expertise and engagement transformed our collective thoughts into a cohesive, accessible, and engaging read.

To all those named and the countless unnamed who supported us on this journey, we offer our profound gratitude. In the ever-evolving landscape of crypto assets, together, we have crafted a beacon for the curious and the seasoned alike.

Preface

In today's fast-evolving financial landscape, traditional portfolio allocations are being reassessed, redefined, and restructured. The monumental surge of interest and involvement in digital assets, especially since 2020, has been nothing short of transformative. While the foundations of our financial systems and investment philosophies remain deeply rooted in time-tested practices, the emergent world of crypto assets demands our attention.

Mastering Crypto Assets endeavors to bridge the familiar with the revolutionary. For the institutional and professional investors, this book is not just an exploration but also a guide—navigating through the intricate corridors of blockchain technology, understanding the taxonomy of new-age digital assets, and integrating them into traditional portfolios.

In the recent past, we've witnessed significant institutional participation in cryptocurrencies, particularly Bitcoin. But beyond the news headlines and the volatile price graphs, lies a deeper transformation. Digital assets, we believe, are more than just fleeting phenomena. They are shaping up as foundational elements of modern financial portfolios. However, the question often remains—how does one integrate, categorize, and value these assets?

Throughout the chapters of this book, we take readers through the annals of Bitcoin's history, the innovations and myths surrounding it, and its burgeoning significance in the era of Web 3. Our approach to understanding crypto goes beyond just Bitcoin. We explore a range of digital assets, from DeFi apps to distributed computing platforms and delve into the valuation methodologies that are shaping crypto investments.

Investment philosophies have always been a blend of art and science, and nowhere is this more evident than in the realm of crypto assets. Valuation in this domain can be complex, and in some cases, esoteric. But armed with the right tools, methods, and perspectives, it can be navigated effectively.

It's important to note that our exploration is neither an endorsement for an all-crypto portfolio nor an outright dismissal. Our conviction lies in understanding the unique risk/return characteristics and finding a harmonious blend within traditional asset classes. And for those bound by restrictions, we provide alternatives and workarounds.

Index investments, a staple in asset management, also find a new frontier in the crypto space. How do traditional index models translate in this new realm? What are the nuances and intricacies of constructing a robust digital asset index? These are questions we grapple with, providing insights and answers.

As you journey through the book, you'll not just hear from us. We've been privileged to engage with leading influencers in the crypto and traditional finance industry—individuals at the forefront of this digital revolution. Their interviews, insights, and analyses further enrich the discourse.

What does the future hold? While no one can predict with absolute certainty, we can equip ourselves with knowledge, insights, and a balanced perspective.

We invite you to embark on this journey with us—to understand, to question, and to find your place in the vast and exciting world of crypto assets.

1 Introduction

> "There's no room for facts when our minds are occupied by fear."
> Hans Rosling

Technical Innovation: From Vision to Everyday Life

Innovative ideas often meet skepticism as people tend to adhere to what they already know. This pattern was evident with inventions like railroads, automobiles, the World Wide Web, and cell phones.

The Railroad Revolution

When the first railroad was introduced, citizens expressed apprehension about the potential effects of high-speed travel on the human body. They assessed the opportunities and risks of this new development differently, leading to initial hesitation. However, as time progressed, people began to realize the benefits of a rapidly evolving transportation network.

The Dawn of the World Wide Web

In a similar vein, the World Wide Web, an information system on the Internet, conceived by British physicist Timothy Berners-Lee in 1989, faced initial mockery. Today, this network has become a cornerstone of our daily life, playing a critical role in our economic system.

The Evolution of Computers

The transformation of the computer serves as a prime example of technological progression from a novel concept to an essential part of our everyday life. In 1949, Edmund Berkeley introduced the first real personal computer in his book *Giant Brains, or Machines That Think*. Within the subsequent 10 years, as many as 400 of these machines, named "Simon," were reportedly sold.

Despite the modest capabilities of early hardware, tech-optimists even back then envisaged the vast future potential of computer technology. The ensuing rapid technological enhancements sparked an exponential surge in computing power that lasted for decades. Concurrently, the theoretical foundation expanded, and software development burgeoned into a new industry, spawning increasingly powerful applications. The advancement was so profound that it ultimately decoupled end-users from the intricate technical processes behind applications. Today, anyone with a smartphone can access and utilize its myriad applications.

Tech advances didn't stop at personal devices. The commendable efforts of developers and engineers have also revolutionized the financial sector. Digital workflows and transactions are now the norm, paving the way for integrating crypto assets into our everyday lives—a small leap technologically, but a giant stride in practical terms.

Regulatory preparations are already underway, and these digital assets promise extensive opportunities for investors and users, focusing on cost savings, instant settlements, and full transaction transparency. But, technology won't rest on these achievements. Future technical feasibilities might include generating secure digital tokens representing proportional ownership of tangible assets, like real estate or artwork. This progression could unlock entirely new possibilities for investors.

Inevitably, crypto assets are poised to drive fundamental changes in various sectors, including capital markets. But, as we approach this new era, it's crucial to critically assess this technology and foster open discussions about the emerging structures. Such dialogues should consider both the potential risks and benefits, alongside the strengths and weaknesses of existing systems.

As history has shown us—from the advent of railroads, the worldwide web, to the humble personal computer—those who dare to innovate, adapt, and optimistically face the future unlock limitless potential. Crypto assets are more than a fleeting technological trend; they represent an evolution in our financial systems, promising transparency, efficiency, and opportunities beyond our current imagination.

Let's learn from our past, harness technology's power, and face the future of crypto assets with optimism and open minds. Our journey is just beginning, and the possibilities are as vast as our willingness to explore them. Let's step into this new age together, eager to create, innovate, and redefine our world.

2 Bitcoin—A Brief History

"Breeding homing pigeons that could cover a given space with ever increasing rapidity did not give us the laws of telegraphy, nor did breeding faster horses bring us the steam locomotive."
Edward J. v. K. Menge (1930)

The year 2009 unfurled as a time of significant change and notable events across the globe. It bore witness to the cessation of Sri Lanka's protracted civil war, and simultaneously, the World Health Organization alerted the world to the swine flu, declaring it a global pandemic. Zimbabwe's political leaders made a valiant attempt to stem the tide of hyperinflation by introducing a revamped Zimbabwean dollar. The realm of sports saw Tiger Woods bidding adieu to his illustrious golfing career, while Cristiano Ronaldo basked in the glory of being crowned the world footballer of the year. A remarkable achievement in the annals of space exploration was etched with National Aeronautics and Space Administration (NASA) propelling the Kepler space telescope into the sun's orbit. Concurrently, Slovakia embraced the euro, thus aligning itself more closely with its European neighbors. The People's Republic of China underscored its commitment to modernization by making Hanyu Pinyin the official Latinized transliteration of Chinese. In the meanwhile, as the Great Financial Crisis cast a long shadow across the world, several stock markets hit their nadir, marking a pivotal period in global economic history.

The intertwining of these historic happenings formed a background against which the anonymous developer launched the Bitcoin network on January 3, 2009. Indeed, the nascent Bitcoin network was given life amid the turbulence of the most severe financial market crisis witnessed in the last century. The bold maneuvers made by central banks during this crisis—characterized by substantial interventions in the capital market— were not merely stopgap solutions, but marked a significant shift in the financial landscape that continues to be felt to this day.

These radical interventions have created a ripple effect on the free price discovery mechanisms, skewing incentive structures and pushing market participants to grow accustomed to frequent interest rate cuts and a steady upsurge in bond purchase programs and loan securitizations. The prevalence of low and even negative interest rates has consequently put traditional capital market valuation methods to the test, rendering them less relevant, and in some instances, downright misleading.

In the wake of these unconventional market conditions, enormous risk positions materialized, justified solely on the premise of low interest rates, lending an illusion of economic viability. However, with the recent uptrend in interest rates, the veil has been lifted, and the detrimental impact of these precarious positions is gradually coming to light. Such an intricate and tumultuous backdrop underscores the relevance and potential resilience of Bitcoin and other crypto assets in our evolving financial landscape.

Moreover, with each valve of the financial market being successively shut, the global currency market, boasting a daily trading volume exceeding $6.5 trillion, has emerged as the final regulator of pressure. Although central banks hold considerable sway over price movements, their capacity to influence the most pivotal element—the public's trust in a currency—remains decidedly limited.

Since the dawn of the financial crisis, the persistent market interventions by central banks, coupled with the astronomical sums of money in play, have dealt a severe blow to people's faith in the enduring stability of numerous currencies. This gradual erosion of confidence has effectively shaken the bedrock of the global financial system, thereby highlighting an urgent need for alternative solutions.

With the birth of the Bitcoin network, a novel asset class was ushered in, paving the way for the development of a potential alternative. Nevertheless, it is essential to recognize that this reality of a burgeoning first crypto asset did not occur in isolation, but rather, was preceded by the tireless efforts of numerous pioneers who blazed the trail.

2.1 From the Fuel Card to the Trustless Payment System

The introduction of a functioning, decentralized payment system faced not only technical obstacles, but also the challenge of convincing people of the benefits of digital payments. Skepticism toward cashless payments was high in the beginning, and it took some innovative approaches to change people's minds. In the 1980s, a lot of cash was stolen from gas stations in the Netherlands, so the owners put in place a way to pay without cash. The owners wanted to lower their personal and financial risk, so they started accepting credit cards, which customers liked. At the time, this was a big deal because it was not something people usually did.

The advent of Flooz, the first-ever virtual currency, in 1998 marked a significant milestone. Its operational mechanism bore an uncanny resemblance to the familiar bonus point systems we know today. Users were rewarded with Flooz for their online purchases, and these could then be redeemed on affiliated websites. Each Flooz held a value equivalent to a single U.S. dollar. Nevertheless, akin to many analogous ventures, Flooz could not amass the critical user base necessary for long-term viability, and thus, fell, casualty to the collapse of the initial internet boom around the turn of the millennium.

In contrast, there were ambitious projects that took a big shot, as early as the 1980s. One of them was David Chaum's concept of a blind signature system,[1] which he patented in 1988. Chaum, a well-known computer scientist, had already set a milestone in the history of encrypted digital communication with his paper "Untraceable Electronic Mail, Return Addresses, and Digital Pseudonyms." Although the patents did not explicitly refer to digital currencies, the methods developed by Chaum were elementary building blocks of crypto assets.

In 1989, Chaum completed the development of a protocol for a digital currency, which he named eCash. The use of this currency was implemented by Chaum's company DigiCash. This concept incorporated many of his discoveries, such as the "blind signature," a technique for authenticating the sender of a message without disclosing the content, which is a crucial component of well-known crypto protocols.[2] However, DigiCash and its digital currency did not achieve enduring success. The emergence of e-commerce was just beginning, and despite the exceptional technical execution, the user base could not be sufficiently expanded. In terms of technology, eCash bore similarities to PayPal. However, the reliance on banks authorized to utilize eCash proved to be particularly troublesome. The established connection to the existing financial system circumvented legal complications like money laundering prevention. But this feature did not make eCash more appealing to users as the linkage to existing systems meant it could not be regarded an autonomous monetary system.

---

1 The patent is available at https://www.chaum.com/patents/US4759063.pdf.
2 See Chaum (1983).

In 1998, DigiCash declared bankruptcy. Nonetheless, David Chaum's efforts were not fruitless. His developed concepts and practical testing laid the groundwork for future advancements. Above all, the requirement for a central authority and dependence on the existing banking system were obstacles that needed to be surmounted in the future. The centralized nature of the eCash system and ongoing regulatory challenges made it evident to all digital currency advocates that a sturdy and independent monetary system must be structured in a decentralized fashion.

Roughly a decade after DigiCash's inception, Wei Dai, a Chinese hardware developer, devised the digital currency B-money.[3] In his paper, Dai outlined a protocol that presaged numerous facets of Bitcoin. For example, he articulated the possibility of using the computational exertion required to resolve a mathematical issue as a proof-of-work mechanism, while appropriately rewarding the participating machine for the computational task undertaken. Dai also mentioned the use of a shared accounting system (distributed ledger), with entries collectively verified and approved. Although his protocol never advanced beyond the conceptual stage, it significantly impacted later developments. In tribute to Wei Dai, the smallest unit of Ether, the *wei*, was named after him.[4]

Another significant forerunner in the realm of digital currencies is Nicholas Szabo, who hails from Hungary. In 1998, this computer scientist devised the bit gold protocol, an immediate antecedent to Bitcoin that already showcased fundamental components of its successor.[5] The essence of the bit gold protocol lies in the proof-of-work concept, which Szabo adapted from Adam Back's work. A year earlier, Back had developed a corresponding algorithm designed to circumvent spam messages and protect networks from distributed denial-of-service (DDoS) attacks.[6] This concept limits the unrestricted communication of network participants by mandating that previously completed work is a prerequisite for the acceptance of a transmitted message. Consequently, DDoS attackers or spam message senders would face computational expenses for

---

3   You can find Wei Dai's text on B-Money at http://www.weidai.com/bmoney.txt.
4   Ether is the native token of the Ethereum network.
5   See Szabo (2021).
6   Distributed Denial of Service attack: In a DDoS attack, attackers deliberately cause the unavailability of a service or server by making an enormous number of requests.

each request or message dispatched, rendering such attacks costly and unappealing.

The proof-of-work concept is as straightforward as it is inventive. Network participants contribute computing power to resolve mathematical problems. Once a computer has discovered a solution, it can relay the information to the network. As the computer has demonstrated its work through problem-solving, an entry can be recorded in the network's public directory. Each subsequent entry becomes part of the following task to be tackled. This process results in a continuously expanding chain of entries that is virtually immutable due to the enormous computational effort expended. This chain, containing all transactions that have ever occurred on the network, forms the foundation of the globally distributed decentralized accounting system, known as the distributed ledger.

Szabo's contributions to the development of a decentralized monetary system are remarkable. However, with his bit gold protocol, he was unable to satisfactorily resolve the double-spend problem. This issue pertains to the challenge of preventing the same monetary unit from being spent more than once in a decentralized money system. For instance, if a buyer pays for a music download and can access the service before the transaction is conclusively settled, the same monetary unit could be employed to pay for another service or simply transferred to a different address. The solution to this complex problem remained elusive for the time being. However, if Satoshi Nakamoto were to claim, akin to Newton, that he stood on the shoulders of giants, then Szabo would undoubtedly be one of those giants.

2.2 Enter Satoshi Nakamoto

> "If I have seen further, it is by standing on the shoulders of giants."
> Isaac Newton

The subsequent major advancement was Satoshi Nakamoto's Bitcoin protocol, outlined in a white paper as a peer-to-peer payment system. This protocol amalgamates various elements from its predecessors and, as a blockchain application, resolves the double-spend issue. Transactions occur directly peer-to-peer among network participants, without a central authority or centralized accounting. All the important information for each transaction is kept in data blocks that are linked one after the other to make a chain of blocks called a blockchain. The individual blocks are linked using a cryptographic hash function, with each block containing transformed information from the preceding block. As this process persists throughout the entire chain, no single block can be altered or removed.

Most of the network's computational power converges on a single, valid chain of blocks. Consequently, a continually expanding series of transactions is generated, with the majority representing the accurate history of all transactions. The network autonomously manages the creation of new entries, verification of transactions for consistency with transaction history, and updates. A central authority or a third, verifying party is rendered unnecessary. Data storage is also unconventional, with the entire blockchain existing on each network node (full node). Instead of centralized data storage, data is redundantly maintained within the network. Although this approach results in a larger total volume of stored data compared to centralized storage, the redundancy ensures robustness as failures of individual network nodes do not impact data security.

October 31, 2008, is a significant date, as it marks the publication of the Bitcoin white paper titled "Bitcoin: A Peer-to-Peer Electronic Cash System."[7] It remains unclear whether the pseudonym Satoshi Nakamoto represents an individual or a group of developers.[8] While working on the paper and two months prior to its publication, Nakamoto registered the domain "bitcoin.org." Ownership of this domain was promptly transferred to several individuals who were not part of the core Bitcoin developer group, thereby minimizing the risk of centralization in the decentralized project from the outset.[9]

On January 3, 2009, amid the most significant financial crisis since the 1930s, the Genesis Block marked the inception of the Bitcoin blockchain. This block is the first-ever created on the Bitcoin network. With the mining reward for creating the block standing at 50 Bitcoin, the first 50 Bitcoin were also generated alongside this initial block.

The timing of the network's launch was not coincidental, as the global financial system was on the brink of total collapse. One detail sheds light

---

7   The paper is available at https://bitcoin.org/bitcoin.pdf.

8   See Frisby (2014).

9   See Champagne (2014).

on Nakamoto's motives: a short text message included with the creation of the first block of the Bitcoin blockchain. This message quoted the headline of a January 3, 2009, article from the British newspaper *The Times*, which reported on then-finance minister Alistair Darling's plans to inject hundreds of billions of British pounds into British banks as part of a renewed bailout. The brief text read, "The Times 03/Jan/2009 Chancellor on brink of second bailout for banks." For Nakamoto, the Bitcoin network symbolized an alternative to the prevailing centralized monetary system, functioning as a bank-independent, peer-to-peer mechanism for global payments.

2.3 Bitcoin and Blockchain: A Closer Look

Bitcoin, as the native token of the Bitcoin network, represents only one form of cryptocurrency. Thus, the most well-known cryptocurrency is not synonymous with blockchain technology, but rather its most recognized application to date. While the following discussion pertains specifically to Nakamoto's invention, the principles outlined here are also applicable to other crypto assets.

The Bitcoin system comprises several components. First is the client software, which anyone can install on a computer. Computers running this software create the nodes of a distributed network, enabling communication between them. Alongside the installed client software, each network node maintains a complete version of the current blockchain containing all Bitcoin transactions that have ever occurred.

The network rules are defined in the Bitcoin protocol, with the client software implementing these encoded regulations. Among other things, these rules determine how new Bitcoins are created, who receives them, and how network transactions are verified. Mining computers function as the distributed network's accountants, collaboratively maintaining a decentralized, redundantly stored ledger. Miners are rewarded with newly created Bitcoins for their contributions to upholding an accurate and immutable ledger, and they can also collect transaction fees.

The utilization of blockchain technology and the economic incentive system for miners enable decentralized and independent verification of all ownership and transfers within the network. Bitcoin transfers between two participants occur directly on a bilateral basis. Transactions cannot be reversed in the case of errors or disputes, rendering Bitcoin transactions final. The independence from any third party and the finality of executed transactions are the fundamental differences between blockchain-based and conventional transaction systems.

Contrary to standard financial transactions, where the involved individuals or organizations must identify themselves via ID cards or unique IDs, the Bitcoin network does not require such identification. To carry out a transaction, one merely needs a private key[10] and a Bitcoin address.[11]

However, Bitcoin does not provide the anonymity it is often claimed to offer. Cautious users may attempt to obscure the transparency of their transactions, but the achievable degree of anonymity within the network is frequently overestimated. According to Cornell University researchers, even basic web trackers and cookies embedded in numerous websites can enable Bitcoin transactions to be traced back to an individual. In over 60% of the cases studied, a clear connection is possible.[12] It is not difficult to imagine how effortless it would be to attribute most transactions to executing individuals if sufficient data could be systematically aggregated. Law enforcement agencies have already managed to convict criminals based on Bitcoin transactions linked to the offenses committed.[13]

2.3.1 Primary Areas of Utilization for Bitcoin

Ironically, due to technical limitations and unavoidable transaction costs, Bitcoin is not well suited for many small transactions, contrary to Nakamoto's original vision of a "peer-to-peer electronic cash system." However, Bitcoin has inspired other projects that are better suited for this purpose.[14] Although the Bitcoin network could potentially facilitate everyday payment transactions, its strengths lie elsewhere.

---

10 A private key is a 256-bit string. In the hexadecimal system, it has 64 characters accordingly. An example of such a key is: 1b9cdf53588f99cea61c6482c4549b0316bafde19f768 51940d71babaec5e569.

11 Depending on the format, a Bitcoin address consists of a 34- or 42-character string in the hexadecimal system. An example of an address in the old P2PKH format is: 1MbeQFmHo9b69kCfFa6yBr7BQX4 NzJFQq9; an example of an address in the most modern Bech32 format is bc1qc7slrfxkknqcq2jevvkdgvrt 8080852dfjewde450xdlk4ugp7szw5tk9.

12 See Goldfeder et al. (2017).

13 See Manager Magazin (2021).

14 The Bitcoin Lightning Network is a second layer payment protocol built on top of the Bitcoin blockchain that enables faster and cheaper transactions by routing payments through a network of channels between users. It aims to solve the scalability issues of the Bitcoin blockchain by enabling instant micropayments without the need for confirmation on the blockchain.

In recent years, the benefits of the Bitcoin network have become particularly evident in two applications. The first is large-scale cross-border transactions, which can be executed quickly and with minimal bureaucracy using cryptocurrencies. These transactions are inexpensive and carry no settlement risks.[15] The cost and duration of a transfer remain the same, regardless of whether one transfers a single Bitcoin or 10,000 Bitcoin, or whether the transaction is between neighbors or people in different hemispheres. The internet knows no borders, and initiating a transaction of any size is as simple as sending an email. Settlement systems and intermediary organizations are not required, and transactions are settled instantly. Bitcoin either remain with the sender or are already with the recipient. There are no intermediaries, and consequently, no associated risks.

Furthermore, because Bitcoin is becoming less inflationary and even deflationary over time, it is seen as a central bank-independent investment with no risk of interest rate change or default.

2.4 The Fundamentals of Bitcoin

While blockchains and Bitcoin have been around for over a decade, institutional investors have only started paying close attention in recent years. The dramatic rise in Bitcoin's price and the resulting headlines in 2017 brought crypto assets to the attention of broader segments of the population for the first time. Private investors were primarily attracted by the high price gains, while professional investors were initially more interested in the potential applications of blockchain technology in the financial industry.

The new technology contains disruptive elements that can bring significant process improvements for financial companies, particularly asset managers. However, a mature and scalable blockchain-based system also challenges the need for traditional intermediaries and the costs inevitably associated with them. To address the relevant questions, a basic understanding of Bitcoin terminology is necessary.

---

15 *Settlement risk* refers to the danger that a transaction is not settled at all or not settled on time because the counterparty fails to fulfill its obligations by the settlement date, even though one's own obligation has already been met.

Bitcoin is currently the best-known use case of a blockchain. The blockchain is the central component of the Bitcoin network, but it is not synonymous with Bitcoin. Blockchain applications can serve various purposes, and the entire Bitcoin system consists of several components beyond the blockchain. Nakamoto's payment system is a relatively simple special case of using a blockchain. The brilliance of the Bitcoin system lies not solely in the blockchain, but in the intelligent combination of various existing technologies into an efficient whole. The strengths of the protocol lie in its simplicity and focus on the essentials. The simpler a system is, the fewer points of attack it offers.

In the following section, we will cover the basics of blockchain and the Bitcoin network. For those interested in the technical side, numerous books provide detailed descriptions of the structural features of Bitcoin and cryptocurrencies. Readers with prior knowledge may choose to skip this section.[16]

2.4.1 The Concept of the Blockchain

"We have a golden opportunity to digitise and standardise processes across the industry. The blockchain technology is there and if we succeed, it will lead to huge cost savings that will benefit not only supply chain actors like Maersk, but also customers and consumers worldwide."
Lars Kastrup, Head of Sales for TradeLens at Maersk

At its core, a blockchain is a distributed database that can be shared by multiple users on a network. Data is not stored in a central instance but redundantly on each individual computer that is part of the network. Individual data, which in the case of the Bitcoin network is transaction data, is combined in blocks. These blocks are then linked forming a growing chain that contains the complete and unalterable history of transactions. Various technologies such as the Internet, cryptographic methods, and hash functions are used to make this possible.

A blockchain can be crafted with varying architectures. Public blockchains, like that of the Bitcoin network, are universally accessible, welcoming anyone to join the network and utilize it fully. In contrast, a private blockchain mirrors the functionality of an intranet, necessitating user authentication and potentially allowing for the manipulation

---

16 See Bashir (2020); Schär (2021); and Voshmgir (2019).

of all mechanisms, from mining to individual entries, through a central authority. Consequently, private blockchains embody a structure that is decentralized yet centrally orchestrated. Permissioned blockchains, a hybrid of private and public models, make up the third category. Ripple (XRP) is a prime example of this category. There is no definitive delineation of good or bad blockchains—their appropriateness is contingent on their intended application and additional parameters like data privacy. Each blockchain variant caters to a distinct objective and satisfies different requirements, with their merits and shortcomings varying based on the context in which they are deployed.

2.4.2 Cryptography: An Indispensable Part of Bitcoin

Cryptography is a branch of cryptology that deals with methods for encrypting data. Although all historical Bitcoin transactions are unencrypted and can be viewed by anyone, encryption algorithms play an indispensable role in ensuring the security and authenticity of transactions in the network. The Bitcoin network uses a classic asymmetric encryption method with private and public keys. Examples of asymmetric systems include the RSA (Rivest-Shamir-Adleman) and the ECC (Elliptic-Curve Cryptography) algorithms used in Bitcoin.

Asymmetric cryptography increases the security of communication in untrusted networks in a scalable way. Cracking a sufficiently long private key is practically impossible. Only the person in possession of this key can initiate transactions in the network and send Bitcoin from one address to another. Releasing a transaction with the private key simultaneously ensures the authenticity of the sender. Therefore, the importance of the private key in the network cannot be overstated. Anyone who has the private key to a particular address on the network can freely dispose of the Bitcoin associated with that address. No further proof of identity or ownership is required. Without this key, on the other hand, nothing works. This procedure may sound complicated, but it is completely taken over by the user's wallet software. The user's only task is to securely store and manage their private key, ensuring it is not lost or compromised.

2.4.3 Hash Functions in the Context of Cryptography

Hash functions play a crucial role in the functioning of the Bitcoin network and other blockchain systems. They are mathematical functions that assign a unique output (hash value or "hash") to a given input value while fulfilling specific criteria:

1. Irreversibility: It should be computationally infeasible to determine the input from the output.

2. Unique output: No visible similarities between slightly different inputs: even a small change in the input should produce a completely different output.

3. Unique input: Each input should produce exactly one hash value, and two different inputs should always produce different hash values.

4. Fixed-length output: The result of a hash function should always have the same length, regardless of the length of the input.

5. Fast computation: A hash function should be quickly computable for practical use.

A Hash Function at Work

SHA-512 is a cryptographic hash function that is part of the SHA-2 (Secure Hash Algorithm 2) family. When you pass a text, such as the following Richard P. Feynman quote, through the SHA-512 function, it will produce a fixed-length output (hash value) that is unique to that input.

The quote:

> "I would rather have questions that can't be answered than answers that can't be questioned."

When hashed using the SHA-512 function, it would produce a hash value like this:

2f7557c54d6041a02c32f4b4a0a9aeb4d4ea1b09d8b6f7c6f39d6d-
fdb86d5a2a8f9a0e1d5e7d02a1e8a3d58e2cdff53b6e70e89a9e-
6bea9246d3c487efd3d3cd

When you remove the final period from the quote, you get the following text:

> "I would rather have questions that can't be answered than answers that can't be questioned"

Passing this modified text through the SHA-512 function will produce a completely different hash value, even though the change in the input is minimal. Here is an example of the hash value for this input:

3c6b8cb6d9a6f95a38b766e6df8a6b058d6c63ef76368c1e7a9c7d5b-1732c1e2e40b1f7c45c1b5765b5ae5e5d3e3f8a3fdaa7d93b2210902c14e82d4e4c4a734

As you can see, the hash value is entirely different from the one generated for the original quote with the period. This sensitivity to even the smallest changes in the input demonstrates the effectiveness of hash functions in maintaining data integrity and ensuring that tampering with data is easily detectable.

Hash functions are probably among the most underrated building blocks of blockchain technology. They play a critical role and form the backbone of many cryptographic algorithms and systems. The corresponding feature box provides an example of such a function at work.

2.5 The Driving Forces behind the Rise of Bitcoin

"It might make sense just to get some in case it catches on. If enough people think the same way, that becomes a self-fulfilling prophecy."
Satoshi Nakamoto (2009)

Bitcoin, the world's first decentralized digital currency, was created in 2009 by an unknown individual or group of individuals using the name Satoshi Nakamoto. It operates on a peer-to-peer network and allows for fast, secure, and low-cost transactions without the need for intermediaries.

Many experts believe that the idea of a decentralized monetary system is revolutionary, offering benefits such as settling transactions without counterparty risk, independence from political influence and central authority, and a public ledger of all transactions that is transparent, tamper-proof, and free to access. However, the concept of digital assets can be difficult to understand for those who have limited technical knowledge and interest in finance. In the early days, the lack of regulation and the high volatility in the cryptocurrency market, combined with negative media coverage, deterred many potential investors.

Despite the rapid growth of the cryptocurrency market, there is still a significant amount of criticism and skepticism. Critics often argue that virtual currencies are too complex and lack intrinsic value, making it difficult to predict their performance. Warren Buffett, Nobel Prize–winning Paul Krugman, and Microsoft founder Bill Gates all have their own reasons for not investing in Bitcoin.[17] It is important to note that while cryptocurrencies do not have intrinsic value, like fiat currencies, they offer the advantage of being decentralized, making them less dependent on central authorities such as central banks. This can be seen as a benefit for individuals who value self-determination and increased security over personal finances and data.

The truth about cryptocurrencies, like Bitcoin, lies in the middle ground between over-enthusiastic fans and staunch opponents. While it is important to consider both the potential benefits and risks, it is also crucial to understand that the perception of these benefits and risks varies depending on the individual's goals and perspectives. For example, some may view a decentralized financial system as a means of increasing self-determination and asset security, while others may prefer a central authority for greater control.

Professional market participants can be distinguished by their ability to provide well-founded statements and make rational decisions despite market fluctuations. It is important to consider all factors, including the current economic and political climate, when evaluating the potential benefits and risks of investing in cryptocurrencies.

In conclusion, while cryptocurrencies like Bitcoin may seem confusing and uncertain, they have the potential to revolutionize the financial system by offering faster, cheaper, and more secure transactions without intermediaries. As the technology and market continue to mature, it should not come as a surprise when cryptocurrencies become increasingly accessible and widely adopted in the future.

---

17 See Newbery (2021).

2.6 Interview with Fred Thiel

In this chapter, we present a transcription of an insightful interview with Fred Thiel, CEO of Marathon Digital, a leading company in the field of Bitcoin mining. The discussion addresses the widely misunderstood topic of Bitcoin mining, specifically focusing on its energy consumption and the myths surrounding this issue.

Bitcoin mining, the process of validating transactions and generating new Bitcoins through the resolution of complex mathematical problems, has raised concerns due to the vast amount of energy it requires. Several misconceptions circulate about Bitcoin's energy consumption, including that it is entirely coal-based and contributes to air pollution. In this conversation, Mr. Thiel gives a more nuanced view of the situation.

Additionally, Mr. Thiel elaborates on the argument that the energy consumption associated with Bitcoin mining is not inherently wasteful, as it plays a critical role in securing the network and preventing fraudulent activities. He also discusses the role of Bitcoin mining in the advancement of renewable energy sources, as mining companies, such as Marathon Digital, actively seek the most cost-effective electricity sources.

Through this informative and comprehensive conversation with Fred Thiel, readers will gain a deeper understanding of the complexities of Bitcoin mining and its energy consumption, challenging widespread misconceptions and providing valuable insights into this frequently misinterpreted aspect of the cryptocurrency domain.

Fred Thiel, born in 1960, is an American business executive and the current CEO of Thiel Advisors and Marathon Digital Holdings. His rich career has seen him serve as CEO of GameSpy, Local Corporation, and Lantronix, with the latter experiencing significant revenue growth and an initial public offering under his leadership. Thiel has also served on the boards of various technology companies and was the managing partner of the software group at Triton Pacific Capital Partners from 2007 to 2012. Since 2013, he has headed Thiel Advisors, advising organizations on value creation strategies. Additionally, Thiel is multilingual and a frequent speaker on digital trends and the transformation of industries by the "Internet of Things."

Q: **Fred, many of our readers are interested in understanding the core process of Bitcoin mining. Could you give us a quick rundown of how it works and explain how this process plays a crucial role in ensuring the security and stability of the Bitcoin Network?**

A: Sure. Mining is a bit of a misnomer in that we're not digging holes in the ground or looking for Bitcoin buried in places. What mining really is, is essentially a type of transaction processing. As a miner, we operate large data centers with specialized equipment that we call mining rigs. Unlike normal computers, they're specifically built to do one thing, which is to calculate an encryption algorithm called SHA-256. This encryption algorithm is essentially used as a way to ensure that transactions on the blockchain aren't able to be changed.

So, essentially what we do is assemble transactions that are in the mempool. Think of the mempool as a big funnel: all bitcoin trades and transfers between wallets flow through it. As a miner and as a pool operator, we take a set of transactions, typically using a first-in-first-out method and assemble them into a block. We then take the hash for the prior block, which is the output of an algorithm that is used when you calculate all the contents of a block together with the hash for the former block, and you get a new hash as an output. That hash is stored in the blockchain, and you can ensure that the transactions haven't been changed or modified in any way by simply going back and looking at the hash.

At its simplest level, Bitcoin mining is assembling transactions into a block and then using the hash of the prior block together with the data that's in the block and something called a nonce, which is essentially a number that you pick, to calculate the new hash. If the output of that is within the degree of difficulty that the blockchain requires, then you, as a miner, will get to propose that block to the validators. You will then receive payment from the blockchain for having mined a block, which today is about 6.25 Bitcoin, and you also receive any relevant transaction fees that were part of the transactions in the block that you won.

Q: **How does this ensure the security of the blockchain?**

A: The more people that are doing this, the harder it is for anybody to try and change transactions because this is a consensus mechanism. Everybody has to agree when a miner proposes a block, and then it's validated and becomes consensus. Typically, after there have been six validations, a block is considered to be final. The more miners you have doing this, the harder it is for somebody to try and cheat the system. Today, there are millions of mining rigs out there that are operating, and there's a concept called a 51% attack where if somebody could control 51% of all of the miners or the hash rate generated by those miners, they could, in theory, propose transactions that only they wanted. They could essentially do things like not approve a certain transaction but approve others, which is called the double-spend problem in Bitcoin.

By having lots of miners, it's very hard for any one person or party to aggregate 51%, and the more miners there are, the harder it gets. What makes it hard is the sheer amount of capital you have to apply. You have to spend billions of dollars to acquire these miners, build sites, and pay for the energy that these miners use. This is the determining factor in what makes Proof of Work the most superior method for consensus because, at scale, it is the most secure method. Proof of Stake, unfortunately, is a much more concentrated methodology where it's much easier for a group of people to get together and change things.

Q: **You mentioned Proof of Stake, and there's a hot debate in the cryptocurrency community about which is better: Proof of Stake or Proof of Work. Additionally, there's often talk of mining pools being very centralized. In your opinion, what can be done to address further decentralization in the Bitcoin protocol? Is it already perfectly decentralized, or are there also decentralization issues on a regional level?**

A: From the perspective of concentration in the Bitcoin world, mining pools are aggregations of hash rate. The mining pool doesn't decide what transactions are being validated; that's the miners' responsibility. Miners assemble blocks and propose them. Mining pools exist to aggregate hash rate, allowing for more even payouts, especially for smaller miners. Mining pools don't control transaction selection, so that's a fallacy.

Anytime someone has tried to change the Bitcoin blockchain, like during the SegWit wars in 2017, it did not pass even though more than 90% of the miners wanted the change. The concentration risk in Bitcoin requires a single party controlling a group of miners equal to or greater than 51% and maintaining that control. In the Bitcoin world, there's much less risk of concentration, especially as long as mining is done by pools.

Miners can switch pools based on factors like payout preferences. For example, Foundry didn't charge fees for miners to join and had the largest number of miners in their pool, but now that they charge fees, miners are going elsewhere. In Marathon's case, we operate our own pool because we're focused on the technology of mining. Like Apple, we want a fully integrated technology stack that we control, which includes our own pool, firmware, and even ASIC level in the miner.

When looking at other systems like Proof of Stake, there are different issues with concentration. For instance, in Ethereum, the Ethereum Foundation is a significant concentration risk. They propose forks and carry a considerable amount of weight in deciding what happens with Ethereum. While this allows Ethereum to innovate rapidly, it can also lead to forking.

In the world of Ethereum, it's the foundation and some core holders who make decisions, which extends to the staking area. When you stake your Ethereum, you're giving somebody else control of your Ether, and they're the ones validating the blocks. There's a greater risk of concentration in Ethereum, especially with large staking pool operators like Lido, who could effectively fork the Ethereum blockchain if they wanted to.

There are pros and cons to both mechanisms, but I firmly believe that Proof of Work remains the better method. With mining pools operating in Proof of Work, control lies with the nodes. This control is further decentralized through the use of Stratum V2, a protocol that allows miners to communicate with the pool. We're actively involved in rolling out Stratum V2, which gives miners more control over decisions previously made by the pool. In my opinion, Proof of Work is a better solution for having an absolutely secure blockchain versus a merely "secure enough" one.

Q: **You mentioned the technical process of Bitcoin mining being straightforward but challenging due to the need to stay ahead of the curve technologically. Besides the technical aspects, what are**

the main challenges of a Bitcoin mining company, such as cash flow management and staying competitive in an attractive market with not-so-easy payouts?

A: The Bitcoin mining market is maturing and operates in four-year cycles, with two years being profitable and the other two being borderline break-even. During unprofitable periods, or "winters," companies with poor business models struggle and may leave the industry. As the market recovers, new entrants are drawn in, often without considering the next winter's challenges.

To stay competitive, mining companies must have low energy costs, sufficient cash flow, low operating expenses, and energy-efficient mining rigs. The last winter saw a drop in Bitcoin prices and increased energy costs, forcing many miners to sell their Bitcoin to stay afloat. The industry is now consolidating around larger players and niche miners with unique advantages, such as access to low-cost power.

Adding capacity to a mining operation can take between 6 and 18 months, making the timing of expansion crucial. The best time to grow is during the darkest winter when mining rigs are cheapest and hosting is available. However, many miners invest heavily in expansion during peak periods, resulting in difficulties when the market declines.

One unique aspect of the industry is that it's a zero-sum game, with a fixed number of Bitcoin awarded daily. As more miners enter the market, the potential for each miner to win the block reward decreases due to increased competition. The network operates fairly, distributing rewards on a pro-rata basis, but luck can cause fluctuations in earnings over short periods.

Miners constantly face the challenge of predicting and responding to changes in global hash rate, energy costs, and Bitcoin prices. This capital-intensive process makes the industry secure, but it's also stressful for miners who have limited control over these factors. This dynamic is also present in proof-of-stake networks, such as Ethereum, where the more people stake, the fewer transaction fees are available, and eventually, staking becomes less attractive. The same balancing mechanism applies to Bitcoin mining, with miners shutting down operations when profitability drops and resuming when it becomes profitable again.

Q: **Regarding the time it takes to get hardware for mining, like the 18 months you mentioned, how do you project which chips or components are the best? Is it a kind of guessing, or do you have to really look into the details of how companies produce their products?**

A: The decision-making process varies depending on the scale of the mining operation. For small miners with, say, a hundred mining rigs, cost efficiency and energy efficiency are the primary concerns. They seek miners that use the least amount of energy for the same amount of computing power, or hash rate, and those that are more reliable.

For large-scale miners like Marathon Digital, vendor capacity and quality become exceptionally important. We work with the biggest vendors that can deliver the capacity we need and constantly invest in R&D to produce the most energy-efficient and high-performing miners. Our mining fleet's average energy efficiency is 24 joules per terahash, significantly better than the industry average of around 43 or 44.

Over time, as Bitcoin miners add capacity and become more energy-efficient, the total amount of energy used by the industry should eventually hit a point where it starts trending downward. This is aided by miners increasingly using stranded energy—energy that can't be used by other consumers because it's not connected to them. Examples include hydroelectric dams in Paraguay and wind farms in Texas.

In Texas, where Marathon operates, our miners are situated at wind farms that face grid congestion. By consuming electricity directly from these farms, we help keep energy rates low for consumers and ensure the profitability of these marginal wind and solar operators. Additionally, we balance the grid by being able to shut off our systems within 10 minutes and shed load to the grid when necessary. This has led to improved experiences for consumers during extreme weather events, such as the most recent winter storm in Texas. However, Bitcoin miners often don't receive credit for the positive impact they have on the energy grid.

Q: **ESG is a significant global concern. Do Bitcoin miners have a dedicated ESG [environmental, social, and corporate governance] strategy, or is it unnecessary since they tend to use cheap, stranded, or renewable energy sources?**

A: The energy markets are complex, and understanding them can be challenging for some institutional investors. Electricity cannot be traced back to its specific source, as it is a mix of electrons. The grid functions like a reservoir, with generating companies putting electricity in and consumers drawing it out. The grid cannot store energy; it can only transport it. Transmission lines are also inefficient at transporting electricity, losing 40–50% of the generated electricity.

Energy consumption follows a pattern called the "duck curve," with peaks in the morning and afternoon/evening. The grid has to constantly balance energy consumption and generation. Energy sources such as nuclear and coal are at the bottom, as they maintain a constant output. Natural gas is cleaner and more responsive to demand, while solar and wind energy are the last to be used and the first to be shut down.

In terms of ESG, most renewable energy sources tend to be stranded. About two years ago, a large number of Bitcoin miners formed the Bitcoin Mining Council (BMC) to publish data on energy use. Before China banned Bitcoin mining, over 50% of mining was done using coal energy. When mining shifted to the US, the energy grid had a higher percentage of clean energy sources. According to BMC data, over 50% of the energy used for Bitcoin mining is sustainable (wind, solar, nuclear, hydro, geothermal, etc.).

For miners on the grid, they have to assume a pro-rata mix of energy sources based on the input energies. Some Bitcoin miners contract to buy only sustainable or renewable energy, though the actual electrons they use may not come directly from those sources. It is a misconception that Bitcoin miners take away energy from consumers; more energy is generated than consumed worldwide, and miners seek the cheapest, stranded energy.

Q: **How does the push for energy-saving technology in Bitcoin mining impact the broader economy?**

A: The push for energy-saving chips in Bitcoin mining positively affects the broader economy. In the future, these chips could be used in various gaming hardware and other industries. The Bitcoin mining industry's focus on energy efficiency could also contribute to making the AI industry more energy-efficient, which is crucial as AI becomes increasingly important in the world.

Q: **In our book, we discuss investments and the next steps for institutional investors. What should one consider when evaluating a Bitcoin mining company? We see Bitcoin and cryptocurrencies as an asset class and Bitcoin equities as a proxy or something to add to a portfolio. What would you look for?**

A: Warren Buffett famously said that he doesn't want to hold gold, but he will invest in a gold miner because he gets the leverage of that company's profitability in addition to the gold. The same applies to Bitcoin miners. If you look at how Bitcoin mining company stocks move in the market, the price of Bitcoin may move up or down two or three percent, while the miners' stock may move up 5–10%. There's great leverage in investing in miners versus just buying spot Bitcoin. The reason is the inherent profitability of the miner; their cost to buy a Bitcoin is essentially lower than the market spot price. Many miners also hold a lot of Bitcoin on their balance sheets. For example, in our case, we hold over 11,000 Bitcoin on our balance sheet today. If the price of Bitcoin goes up 10%, the value of our balance sheet goes up by 10%. To raise the value of a company's balance sheet by 10%, you have to manufacture goods, sell them, and make a profit, increasing your net asset value by 10%, which is much harder. So, there's a double leverage if you hold a lot of Bitcoin on your balance sheet and have good cost of production, meaning low energy costs and efficient operations. There's a huge benefit to investing in miners versus just holding spot Bitcoin. Most importantly for institutions, they can buy equities but can't buy Bitcoin due to regulatory issues in Europe and the US, which is why many people use these stocks as a proxy.

Volatility in an asset class attracts people who want to trade because that's where you can make a lot of money. If there's no volatility, traders don't make any money, but that also brings risk.

Q: **Thank you very much for your insights, Fred. We appreciate your time.**

A: Absolutely, I appreciate the opportunity to share my thoughts. It's been my pleasure.

Enjoy the full conversation with Fred Thiel on our website by scanning the QR Code below.

2.7 References

Bashir, Imran. (2020). *Mastering Blockchain: A Deep Dive into Distributed Ledgers, Consensus Protocols, Smart Contracts, DApps, Cryptocurrencies, Ethereum, and More*, 3rd Edition. Packt Publishing.

Booth, Jeff. (2020). *The Price of Tomorrow: Why Deflation Is the Key to an Abundant Future*. Stanley Press.

Champagne, Phil. (2014). *The Book of Satoshi: The Collected Writings of Bitcoin Creator Satoshi Nakamoto*. e53 Publishing LLC.

Chaum, David. (1983). "Blind Signatures for Untraceable Payments." In *Advances in Cryptology*, edited by David Chaum, Ronald L. Rivest, and Alan T. Sherman, 199–203. Boston, MA: Springer US. https://doi.org/10.1007/978-1-4757-0602-4_18.

Frisby, Dominic. (2014). Bitcoin: The Future of Money?

Goldfeder, Steven, Harry A. Kalodner, Dillon Reisman, and Arvind Narayanan. (2017). "When the Cookie Meets the Blockchain: Privacy Risks of Web Payments via Cryptocurrencies." CoRR abs/1708.04748. http://arxiv.org/abs/1708.04748.

Mallo, Carlos. (2019, September). "Triennial Central Bank Survey of Foreign Exchange and Over-the-Counter (OTC) Derivatives Markets in 2019." *BIS Quarterly Review*. https://www.bis.org/statistics/rpfx19.htm.

Manager Magazin. (2021). "Ransomware-Angriff Auf Colonial Pipeline: FBI Greift Auf Digitale Wallet Zu Und Stellt Bitcoin Sicher." https://www.manager-magazin.de/finanzen/ransomware-angriff-auf-colonial-pipeline-fbi-greift-auf-digitale-wallet-zu-und-stellt-bitcoin-sicher-a-35f4d7cc-10ed-4854-97b7-c493ef8df902.

McDonald, Lawrence G., and Patrick Robinson. (2009). *A Colossal Failure of Common Sense: The Inside Story of the Collapse of Lehman Brothers*. Crown Business.

Newbery, Emma. (2021, June 9). "Here Are 4 of Bitcoin's Biggest Critics." The Motley Fool. https://www.fool.com/the-ascent/cryptocurrency/articles/here-are-4-of-bitcoins-biggest-critics/.

Schär, Fabian. (2021). "Decentralized Finance: On Blockchain- and Smart Contract-Based Financial Markets | St. Louis Fed." https://research.stlouisfed.org/publications/review/2021/02/05/decentralized-finance-on-blockchain-and-smart-contract-based-financial-markets.

Schrimpf, Andreas, and Vladyslav Sushko. (2019, December). "Sizing up Global Foreign Exchange Markets." https://www.bis.org/publ/qtrpdf/r_qt1912f.htm.

Szabo, Nick. (2021). "Bit Gold | Satoshi Nakamoto Institute." https://nakamotoinstitute.org/bit-gold/.

Voshmgir, Shermin. (2019). *Token Economy: How Blockchains and Smart Contracts Revolutionize the Economy*. Edition ed. S.l.: BlockchainHub Berlin.

3 The Taxonomy of Crypto Assets

"For every minute spent in organizing, an hour is earned."
Benjamin Franklin

The cryptocurrency realm has seen exponential growth, with thousands of unique digital assets now available. This plethora of tokens presents a double-edged sword for investors. On the bright side, investors have a multitude of options serving various functions at their disposal—from streamlining payments to granting access to specific products or services. However, the vast selection of tokens can overwhelm investors when it comes to evaluating and deciding on the best fit for their portfolio.

Interestingly, the token count does not seem to be slowing down, regardless of the market cycle's position. As is depicted in Figure 3.1, new protocols continue to emerge daily, even during bear markets. This constant evolution introduces further complexity for investors when allocating resources for token analysis. How should investors navigate this overwhelming sea of tokens? Is it beneficial to consider the entire token universe, or is it more pragmatic to streamline the focus to a selected few? These are key questions that investors must grapple with in the rapidly evolving world of cryptocurrencies.

3.1 Navigating the Crypto Categorization

"If crypto succeeds, it's not because it empowers better people, it's because it empowers better institutions."
Vitalik Buterin

To simplify the decision-making process in the expansive realm of cryptocurrencies, investors often analyze key factors such as the actual usage of a token, its underlying economics, and trading activities related to its unique growth drivers. An essential part of making sound investment decisions lies in the grouping and categorization of tokens. For this chapter, we rely on the methodology used by MarketVector, an index provider that applies a top-down approach to digital assets. This strategy is instrumental in condensing the intricate and diverse crypto space, offering investors a broader view of market trends beyond the myopic focus on individual tokens.

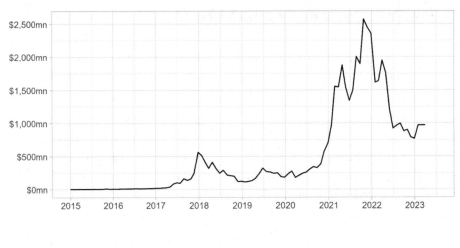

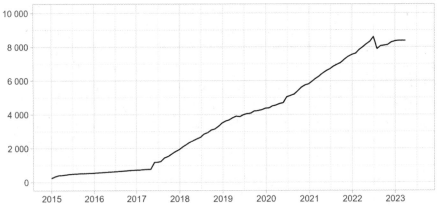

Figure 3.1: Total market capitalization (upper panel) and token count (lower panel) of the crypto market.
Source: MarketVector, CCData, data as of March 31, 2023. Figures are based on the universe of CCData. Other data providers may show different numbers.

The categorization process starts off with a framework resembling the Global Industry Classification Standard (GICS, developed by MSCI and Standard and Poor's) used by equity investors. Here, the classification is based on the business description of the digital asset, usually found on the digital asset's official website, its whitepaper, Discord channels, or third-party research. The applied categories are exclusionary, meaning each coin can only belong to a single category. Tokens are grouped based on their end-users' demand, simplifying the understanding of actual usage and the underlying economics that drive a token's growth. It is worth noting that the primary use case determines the category, as some protocols may serve different sectors. Also, investors should keep in mind that due to the rapidly evolving crypto landscape, a protocol's use case and consequently its category can change, even though the aim of a classification scheme is to maintain stability.

Establishing a well-defined crypto asset taxonomy is crucial for several reasons. First, it aids in managing risks as proper classification allows investors to assess risks linked with each category and distribute resources judiciously. Second, a standardized taxonomy enables investors to make well-informed decisions and evaluate the developments of various categories. Finally, a clear taxonomy simplifies regulatory compliance, as it provides regulators with tools to identify and monitor digital assets based on their traits, usage, and potential risks.

Both regulators and private entities, such as the Blockchain Research Institute (BRI), play significant roles in the classification of tokens. Don and Alex Tapscott, authors of the popular book *Blockchain Revolution*, are the masterminds behind the BRI. Chris Burniske, author of *Cryptoassets*, presents an alternative view on the available classification options.[1]

3.2 The Difference between Token and Coin

The terms *token* and *coin* are often used interchangeably in the world of cryptocurrency. However, there is a technical difference between the two. Coins are generated by Layer 1 networks and are typically awarded for mining (in the case of proof-of-work) or validating (in the case of proof-of-stake).

Tokens, on the other hand, are created using smart contracts—which are essentially applications built on top of Layer 1 smart contract networks. By leveraging these smart contracts, developers can create their own unique tokens that serve specific functions, such as providing access to a particular product or service, or representing ownership in a particular asset. A well-known example of a coin is bitcoin (BTC), which is generated by the Bitcoin blockchain through the mining process. BTC is primarily used as a store of value and a medium of exchange. An example of a token is the Basic Attention Token (BAT), which was created through the Ethereum blockchain and is used within the Brave ecosystem[2] to reward users for viewing ads and to pay publishers for their content.

---

1   See Burniske and Tatar (2017).

2   For more information about this browser visit the website brave.com.

Category	Definition	Examples
DeFi	Financial services built on top of distributed networks with no central intermediaries	Uniswap, Aave
Exchange	Tokens owned and operated by a centralized cryptocurrency exchange	Binance, OKX
Infrastructure Applications	A decentralized computer program designed to perform specific tasks	Chainlink, Filecoin, Render
Media and Entertainment (Metaverse)	Used to reward users for content, games, gambling, or social media	Axie Infinity, Decentraland, Basic Attention Token
Payments	Digital, nonstable money for use in distributed network	Bitcoin Cash, Litecoin, Dogecoin, XRP
Smart Contract Platforms	Blockchain protocols designed to host a variety of self-developed and third-party applications	Ethereum, Polkadot, Solana
Stablecoins	Designed to minimize volatility by, e.g., pegging to a more stable asset	Tether, USDC
Store of Value	Designed to hold or increase purchasing power over time	Bitcoin

Table 3.1: MarketVector digital asset categories.
Source: MarketVector

We focus on the eight token categories shown in Table 3.1.

Each of these categories serves a unique purpose, and it is important for investors to understand the differences. The only constituent of the "store of value" category, BTC, has been treated already in the previous chapter.

3.3 Payments

A payment token, also referred to as a digital currency or cryptocurrency, is a digital asset that can be used to purchase goods and services. This type of token leverages decentralized systems to record transactions in a secure and transparent manner.

With the growing popularity of payment tokens, there are now thousands of different options to choose from, each with its own set of unique features and capabilities. Some well-known examples in this category include Litecoin and XRP.

One of the key advantages of using payment tokens is the elimination of the need for a central authority or intermediaries to facilitate transactions. This not only grants individuals more autonomy and control over their funds but also results in lower transaction fees. Furthermore, payment tokens can be utilized for cross-border transactions without the need for currency conversion. Merchants and businesses are also beginning to adopt payment tokens, recognizing the benefits of faster and more cost-effective transactions. This trend is expected to continue as the use of payment tokens becomes more widespread. In recent years, two new sub-categories of payment tokens have emerged in the market: meme tokens and privacy coins.

Meme Tokens

The Binance Academy provides an overview of meme token.[3] Meme tokens are a type of cryptocurrency inspired by internet memes and jokes, and they have become increasingly popular in recent years. One of the most well-known meme tokens is Dogecoin (DOGE), which was created in 2013 as a parody of the popular Doge meme featuring a Shiba Inu dog. The price of meme tokens is often heavily influenced by the online community and social media, which can make them highly volatile and subject to rapid price fluctuations.

One of the reasons meme tokens have become so popular is the hype surrounding them. The trend began after the "meme stock" craze of GameStop (GME) and AMC Entertainment (AMC) in the stock market in late 2020, where the Reddit community pumped up the prices of these shares. This led to a similar joke about pumping up the price of Dogecoin on Reddit, which gained momentum with the help of tweets from Tesla CEO Elon Musk. Another reason meme tokens are appealing to retail investors is that their prices are often low. This makes them appear more accessible even to those with limited funds. For example, with just a few dollars, you can buy thousands or even millions of certain tokens. The misconception of looking at the number of assets acquired rather than the absolute amount of money invested is also evident among retail investors in the stock market. Additionally, many investors find it emotionally positive because they feel they are supporting a project when they buy the related token.

---

3   See https://academy.binance.com/en/articles/what-are-meme-coins.

However, it is important to note that investing in meme tokens is a very risky endeavor, even in crypto terms, due to their highly volatile nature and the lack of established tokenomics and often complete opaqueness regarding use cases and development.

Privacy Coins

"It used to be expensive to make things public and cheap to make them private. Now it's expensive to make things private and cheap to make them public."

Clay Shirky

Privacy coins are cryptocurrencies that focus on preserving the anonymity of the transactions made on their network. These coins use advanced privacy techniques to make it difficult for anyone to track the flow of money and determine the identities of the parties involved in a transaction. The two largest privacy coins by market capitalization are Zcash and Monero. See the corresponding feature box for explanations of the core concepts used for implementing privacy coins.

Privacy Coin Features Explained

Decoy Transactions

When a transaction is created by a user, along with this actual transaction, several other "decoy" transactions are also included in a transaction list. These decoy transactions are randomly selected from previous transactions in the Monero blockchain, and are mixed in with the new, real transaction. This makes it extremely difficult to trace the source of funds, as an observer cannot tell which inputs are real and which ones are decoys. Decoy transactions are a fundamental part of the use of ring signatures.

Ring Signatures

A ring signature is created by mixing the spender's transaction with the public keys of other unrelated transactions in the network. These other transactions act as decoys or "fake" inputs, making it difficult to determine which specific input was the true source of funds. This blending of inputs ensures that the true origin of the funds remains hidden.

Ring Confidential Transactions (RingCT)

Additionally to disguising the participants of transactions, RingCT ensures the confidentiality of transaction amounts. It obscures the actual amount being transferred by encrypting it with the recipient's public key and adding range proofs, which prove that the value falls within a valid range without revealing the exact amount. This feature prevents observers from deducing transaction amounts and enhances the privacy of the Monero network.

Zero-Knowledge Proofs

A zero-knowledge proof is a cryptographic protocol that allows one party, known as the prover, to prove to another party, known as the verifier, that a statement is true without revealing any additional information beyond the validity of the statement itself. In other words, it enables someone to prove knowledge of certain information without disclosing that information.

Stealth Addresses

A stealth address is a one-time destination address generated on behalf of the recipient for each transaction. It is derived from the recipient's public key, but it does not directly reveal the recipient's actual public address. When a sender wants to send funds to the recipient, they generate a unique stealth address specific to that transaction. Stealth addresses provide a significant privacy advantage as they make it challenging to track the flow of funds and identify the parties involved in transactions.

Mixers and Tumblers: "Shaken, Not Stirred"

Mixers and tumblers are not built into the crypto protocol but represent a service that can be used for transactions. They work by taking input from multiple users and mixing their funds together in a way that makes it difficult to trace the origin and destination of individual coins. The basic principle is to break the transaction linkages between the sender and the recipient.

Here is a simplified explanation of how mixers and tumblers typically work:

- User Inputs: Users who wish to enhance their privacy send their funds to the mixer or tumbler service.
- Mixing Process: The mixer or tumbler service combines the funds received from multiple users into a single pool. It then randomly splits and recombines these funds across different addresses.

- Shuffling Transactions: The mixer or tumbler service generates a succession of transactions within the pool, shuffling the funds between multiple addresses. This method makes it difficult to trace the origin and destination of the funds.
- Output to Users: After the mixing process, the mixer or tumbler service distributes the funds back to the users, typically to new addresses specified by the users. This step helps to further obscure the transaction trail.

By utilizing mixers or tumblers, users can add an additional layer of privacy to their transactions. These services make it difficult for external parties to trace the flow of funds and associate specific inputs with specific outputs.

Monero is one of the few privacy coins that is private by default, meaning that it uses one-time-use stealth addresses for each transaction, ring signatures to group genuine transactions with decoy transactions, and ringCT to hide the amount of Monero sent in a transaction.[4] Zcash, on the other hand, also allows for transparent transactions and provides users with the option of using zero-knowledge proofs for private transactions.[5]

The legality of privacy coins has been a topic of much debate, as regulators around the world seek to clamp down on illicit activities facilitated by these coins. Some countries have banned exchanges from offering privacy coins, while others have banned them altogether. This has been largely due to the tightening of "know your customer" (KYC) laws imposed by anti-money laundering (AML) regulators, such as the FATF Travel Rule and the AMLD-5 directive set by the European Union.

Bitcoin is often perceived as a privacy coin, but it is a pseudonymous cryptocurrency as it does not preserve anonymity, but instead preserves pseudonymity. This means that unless an address has claimed ownership, it is difficult to determine who owns it. While there are blockchain analytics companies that are developing tools to trace transactions, a recent

---

4   See https://www.getmonero.org/get-started/what-is-monero/.
5   See https://z.cash/technology/.

upgrade on Bitcoin's protocol called Taproot[6] offers the potential for enhanced privacy in certain transactions. Additionally, using a mixer or tumbler can also help to enhance the privacy of Bitcoin transactions.

It is important to note that privacy coins are not completely private, as there is always the potential for new analytical tools to be developed that can crack modern encryption methods. Nevertheless, under current encryption methods, privacy coins have proven to be resilient. For example, in September 2020, the IRS offered a $625,000 reward for anyone who could crack the Monero network, but despite these efforts, the network remains uncracked.

3.4 Stablecoins

> "The process by which banks create money is so simple
> that the mind is repelled."
> John Kenneth Galbraith

Stablecoins were created to offer the much-needed stability in the volatile crypto landscape. They have been designed to maintain a consistent exchange rate, mainly against the U.S. dollar, but they can also be pegged to other assets like commodities. The idea, though, is to make them as steady as traditional currencies.

The journey of stablecoins began in 2014 with the birth of "bitUSD" launched by the BitShares blockchain. Designed to mimic the value of the U.S. dollar, bitUSD used BitShares tokens as a safety net. Fast forward to 2015, the stablecoin universe welcomed Tether (USDT), and the concept of the fiat-pegged stablecoin really took off. Now, we have a bunch of stablecoins in the market, each offering unique features. However, this growth has not been without its hiccups. These digital assets have faced regulatory hitches and controversies, pushing the industry to bring about more transparent and decentralized solutions.

There are a few ways to keep a stablecoin's value steady against a traditional currency. The two most distinguishing factors are how centralized the system is and what kind of collateral is used. And that is what sets each one of them apart (Figure 3.2).

---

6   For detailed information regarding the Taproot soft fork, see https://bitcoin.org/en/releases/0.21.1/.

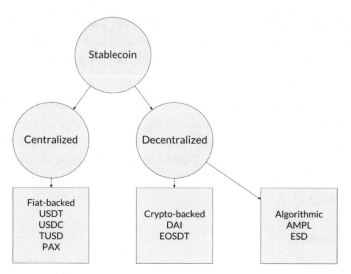

Figure 3.2: Categorization of stablecoins.

Users need to consider several factors before settling on a stablecoin:

- Purpose: What are you planning to use the stablecoin for? Will it be used for day-to-day transactions or do you just need a store of value?
- Centralization: How much control are you comfortable with third parties having over the coin? If a stablecoin is decentralized, it usually means it is less prone to censorship and more resilient to single points of failure.
- Regulation: What does the regulatory landscape look like for your stablecoin of choice? Some stablecoins are more closely regulated than others, and this could affect how you can use them and how much risk you are willing to take.
- Scalability: How well does the stablecoin cope with increasing numbers of transactions? If it cannot handle a high volume, it might not be the best choice for widespread use.
- Transaction Costs: The transaction costs of stablecoins are deeply influenced by the underlying blockchain. While Ethereum's widespread adoption offers robustness, it can suffer from high fees during periods of network congestion, impacting stablecoins like USDC or DAI. On the other hand, TRON, with its high throughput and delegated proof of stake mechanism, often ensures lower transaction fees, making stablecoins like USDT-TRON more cost-effective for users. The choice of the

base chain, therefore, plays a pivotal role in determining the economic efficiency of using a particular stablecoin.

Each stablecoin is created using a unique mechanism that brings with it a different kind of risk.

3.4.1 Off-chain Collateralized Stablecoins

Stablecoins tied to traditional assets like stocks, commodities, and cash are often called "asset-backed" or "off-chain collateralized" stablecoins. These digital currencies maintain their value thanks to these backing assets, which are managed by the stablecoin issuer. The primary advantage of these off-chain stablecoins is their capital efficiency. They do not require excessive backing like other stablecoin types. There are two main variations of these coins: fiat-collateralized and commodity-collateralized.

Fiat-collateralized stablecoins are the most common in the crypto world. They are backed by national currencies, like the U.S. dollar or the Euro. Tether (USDT), one of the earliest stablecoins and currently the one with the highest market cap, is an example. Other fiat-collateralized stablecoins include USD Coin (USDC), True USD, and PAX.

Alternatively, stablecoins collateralized by commodities derive their value from tangible assets such as gold, precious metals, oil, or real estate. This type of stablecoin allows investors to virtually trade these physical assets, which possess the potential to appreciate over time. However, such stablecoins are not without their complexities. The logistics involved in the transportation and storage of the underlying assets can pose significant challenges, especially in the case of commodities like gold. Additionally, the value of these stablecoins is intrinsically linked to the market performance of their collateral. Should the asset backing the stablecoin diminish in value, the stablecoin will similarly devalue. Regulatory factors also come into play. Stablecoins collateralized off-chain are centralized in nature, rendering them prone to governmental scrutiny and regulation. This vulnerability was exemplified when Basis, a noncollateralized stablecoin, was deemed a security under U.S. law, prompting its discontinuation and return of funds to investors.

Last, off-chain stablecoins carry counterparty risk. If the issuer does not hold enough reserves, the stablecoin's value may plummet. To mitigate this risk, users should look for stablecoins that provide transparency reports and regular audits of their assets. Preferably, these stablecoins should also be regulated.

3.4.2 Crypto-collateralized Stablecoins

Crypto-collateralized stablecoins are a type of stablecoin that is backed by on-chain crypto assets like Ethereum (ETH), other stablecoins like USDT and USDC, or other tokens that pay out interest. Users create these stablecoins by putting their crypto-collateral into a decentralized finance (DeFi) smart contract.

DAI is a prime example of a crypto-collateralized stablecoin, created through the Maker protocol. Users deposit assets, like ETH or USDC, as collateral and essentially take a loan in DAI. Since cryptocurrencies can be highly volatile, these types of stablecoins require over-collateralization to maintain their value, which is typically tied to the U.S. dollar. For instance, to generate $100 worth of DAI, a user might have to put down over $150 worth of ETH as collateral.[7] This supports the stability of the stablecoin even if the price of ETH fluctuates.

There are several benefits to using crypto-backed stablecoins. They are trustless, meaning there is no counterparty risk. The collateralization process is governed by a smart contract's code, which can be audited on platforms like Etherscan, ensuring transparency and trust. Moreover, these stablecoins are permissionless and resistant to censorship or control by governments. Their decentralized nature aligns with the ethos of the broader cryptocurrency ecosystem, making them an attractive option for those seeking stability in a volatile crypto market. Because the DAI stablecoins in circulation are overcollateralized, this approach effectively maintains price stability.

On the other hand, this allows users to leverage their position by minting DAI against an asset and then using that DAI buy more of the assets. As there is ample demand for leverage in crypto, Collateralized Debt Positions (CDPs) provide a useful service. One factor restricting this process is that stablecoin applications do not support every token as collateral.

---

7 It is important to note that the collateralization ratio and other parameters within the MakerDAO system change over time.

For good reasons the collateral chosen must be highly liquid and of relatively low volatility. Furthermore, the necessity to over-collateralize limits the capital efficiency of DAI. Finally, to attract users, the interest rates offered on the minted DAI must be higher than the alternative returns from using the asset used as collateral otherwise in Decentralized Finance.

3.4.3 Algorithmic Stablecoins

Algorithmic stablecoins are a complex type of stablecoin that utilize algorithms to maintain a price peg. These algorithms modulate the supply of stablecoins through various mechanisms, the most common being seigniorage.

Seigniorage Algorithmic Stablecoins

Seigniorage refers to the difference between the face value of a currency and the cost of producing it. For example, the seigniorage for a $10 bill would be the difference between $10 and the material and printing costs associated with producing the bill.

In the case of algorithmic stablecoins, seigniorage is utilized as a mechanism for maintaining the price peg. The process allows people to mint or burn stablecoins at a cost of $1. When the stablecoin's price deviates from $1, the seigniorage creates an arbitrage opportunity, which in turn, pushes the price back to $1. A popular example of seigniorage algorithmic stablecoin is seen in the Terra ecosystem, where two main tokens are related to each other: LUNA (the native coin of the Terra blockchain) and UST (the native stablecoin of the Terra blockchain). UST can be minted by burning $1 worth of LUNA, and conversely, $1 worth of LUNA can be minted by burning 1 UST.

When UST is priced above $1, individuals holding LUNA are incentivized to burn it to mint UST and then sell it in the open market to profit from the seigniorage, pushing the price of UST back down to $1. On the other hand, when UST is priced below $1, individuals are incentivized to burn UST and reduce its supply, profiting from the seigniorage of LUNA. This supply contraction pushes the price of UST back up to $1. Algorithmic stablecoins have several strengths, including being trustless, as the seigniorage mechanism is defined by open-source, audited smart contract code. They are also capital efficient, as there is no need to lock up any collateral. So much for the theory. Reality often looks different. The most significant, and sometimes terminal, drawback of algorithmic stablecoins is that because there is no collateral, the peg is much less secure. This was exemplified by the recent Terra Luna collapse.

Terra Luna Collapse

On May 9, the Terra Luna ecosystem suffered a large sell-off, pushing the price of UST to $0.70. This caused stakeholders to lose confidence in the system and led to a negative feedback loop comparable to a bank run, resulting in the collapse of the Terra ecosystem. The price of UST dropped to below $0.04 and LUNA's price to less than a penny (Figure 3.3).

The reason for the collapse was the loss of confidence in UST's ability to regain its peg, as the necessary amount of seigniorage would have resulted in hyperinflating LUNA's supply. This event, known as the "Death Spiral," highlighted the potential risks associated with algorithmic stablecoins.

Despite the recent collapse, algorithmic stablecoins have faced criticism about their similarities with fiat money and whether they are a suitable

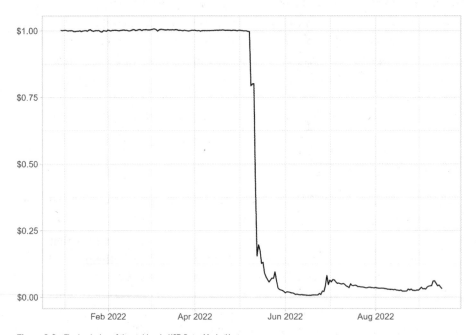

Figure 3.3: The implosion of the stablecoin UST. Data: MarketVector.

alternative to traditional financial systems. Nevertheless, they remain an area of active research and development, with many projects looking to improve the stability and security of algorithmic stablecoins.

3.5 Smart Contract Platforms

> "If a machine is expected to be infallible, it cannot also be intelligent."
>
> Alan Turing

The first smart contract platform, Ethereum, burst onto the scene in 2015, revolutionizing the way we think about blockchains beyond just transferring cryptocurrency. It introduced easy-to-use and versatile programmable smart contracts that execute when certain conditions are met, creating new possibilities for decentralized applications. Today, there are numerous smart contract platforms, each offering unique features and capabilities.

3.5.1 What Are Smart Contracts?

Smart contracts are the defining feature of smart contract platforms. These are essentially code modules that can be controlled externally or run autonomously. The term *smart contract* was first used by the well-known cryptographer, Nick Szabo, in the early 1990s.[8] Smart contracts run on networks like Ethereum or Solana and can be programmed using a corresponding programming language.[9] They can be simple or complex and can process inputs, generate outputs, and run automatically according to a pre-defined schedule.

One of the key benefits of smart contracts is that they can be made unstoppable, as they are protected from external interference. Moreover, they strictly adhere to a pre-defined rule set, which makes them ideal for applications like digital asset management. Another advantage is that smart contracts can control digital assets and send or receive them.

---

8   See Szabo (1994).

9   To be called Turing complete, a programming language must be capable of simulating any Turing machine, which means it can represent any algorithmic computation, given enough time and resources.

Smart Contracts: A Simple Example

There are various programming languages for smart contracts, including Solidity[10] for the Ethereum blockchain and Vyper.[11] To give a simple example of a smart contract program, the following code uses Solidity to store an integer that can be modified and retrieved via methods:

```
contract SimpleStorage {
uint storedData;
function set(uint x) public {
storedData = x;
}
function get() public view returns (uint) {
return storedData;
}
}
```

Smart contract programs can be combined to create more complex applications. For example, the following code provides a minimal version of a smart contract for generating a cryptocurrency:

```
contract Coin {
address public minter;
mapping (address => uint) public balances;
event Sent(address from, address to, uint amount);
constructor() {
minter = msg.sender;
}
function mint(address receiver, uint amount) public {
require(msg.sender == minter);
require(amount < 1e60);
balances[receiver] += amount;
}
function send(address receiver, uint amount) public {
require(amount <= balances[msg.sender], "Insufficient
balance.");
balances[msg.sender] -= amount;
balances[receiver] += amount;
emit Sent(msg.sender, receiver, amount);
}
}
```

10 See https://ethereum.org/en/developers/docs/.
11 See https://docs.vyperlang.org/en/stable/.

The preceding code shown can be used to create a smart contract that includes functions for sending and receiving tokens. The central control instance is eliminated in this case, making the smart contract autonomous. The mapping of a guaranteed payment stream can also be implemented using a smart contract. For example, a smart contract could be created to hold a certain amount of digital assets and protect them from external access. The program would then send specified amounts to an external address at pre-defined times, without the need for further interaction. This process is unstoppable and ends only if the entire network is destroyed.

The main benefits of smart contracts are:

- Speed and accuracy: It is not necessary to rely on a mediator or other third parties; instructions automatically executed with code.
- Trust: Blockchain transparency and transaction irreversibility ensure that there is only one definitive contract shared with all involved parties, which decreases the risk of fraud and manipulation.
- Cost reduction: The effects of automation and the removal of intermediaries are compelling economic arguments.

By appropriately parameterizing the contract, using external data, and implementing deposit and withdrawal options, a smart contract can quickly be transformed into a smart account.

While enterprises and governments can build closed blockchains to exploit smart contract functionality, it is often more practical to use existing open permissionless blockchain platforms that support smart contracts. Otherwise, users would have to rely on the good intentions of the owners of the permissioned blockchains.

3.5.2 What Are Smart Contracts Platforms?

Smart contract platforms function as blockchain software protocols that allow global transfer of value without requiring permission. They are essentially operating systems for smart contracts, much like iOS or

Android serve as operating systems for apps. Ethereum is currently the most recognized platform in this space.

These typically open-source platforms form the basis for decentralized applications (DApps) that operate on a distributed network rather than a centralized server. They facilitate the running of programmable code known as smart contracts, which can drive other decentralized apps and even generate their own tokens.

Every smart contract platform is distinct, with different strengths and trade-offs, including speed, security, cost, degree of centralization, and the hardware needed to run a node. Additionally, each platform comes with its own execution environment, programming language, fee structure, and governance system. The fees associated with using the platform are contingent upon the computational power necessary to deploy and execute the smart contract.

3.5.3 Categorizing Smart Contract Platforms

The key decision while implementing a Web3 protocol is the one between interoperability and modularity. Interoperability describes the ability of diverse blockchains to interact and collaborate, while modularity involves assigning specific tasks to distinct chains.

In the monolithic-and-interoperable model of Web3, one blockchain protocol performs all four main blockchain functions: execution, settlement, consensus, and data availability. The chains connect via communication hubs, and scalability is accomplished through sophisticated communication protocols or a process known as sharding (see the corresponding feature box).

Sharding
Think about a giant puzzle that represents a blockchain. Now, imagine if instead of one person trying to put this massive puzzle together, it was divided into smaller sections, or "shards," and several people worked on these smaller parts simultaneously. This is essentially the idea behind sharding in the crypto world. Sharding is a way to spread out the computational and storage demands of hosting transactions and smart contracts by splitting the

blockchain network into smaller pieces, known as "shards." Each shard contains its own independent piece of state and transaction history, which means that a node can process transactions only for the shard it belongs to, instead of processing all transactions in the network. This allows for high levels of parallel processing, significantly increasing the network's capacity and speed.

Rollups

Imagine you are in a packed sports stadium, and each person is trying to shout out their message at the same time. It would be total chaos, wouldn't it? Now, what if we elected one person to gather everyone's messages and then, using a megaphone, announce them one after the other. That is the core idea of rollups. In the crypto world, instead of each transaction shouting out its data on the blockchain, a rollup will bundle or "roll up" many transactions into one. This significantly reduces the amount of data we need to store on the blockchain, speeding up processing times and reducing costs.

State Channels

Continuing with the sports stadium analogy, imagine if two people in the crowd wanted to have a conversation without shouting over everyone else. They could step out into a hallway, have their discussion, and then return to their seats and announce only the result. This is essentially what state channels do in the blockchain world. They allow participants to conduct numerous transactions among themselves off-chain, and then post only the final state to the blockchain. It is like having a private conversation, and then only announcing the conclusion. This approach frees up resources on the blockchain, increasing speed and reducing transaction fees.

Side Chains

Let us go back to our sports stadium analogy. The main game is happening in the stadium (this is our main blockchain). But imagine if we could have smaller games or events in fields around the stadium (these are our side chains). These smaller games operate independently, but they follow similar rules, and occasionally, results from these smaller games (transactions or data) might make their way back into the main game.

In blockchain terms, a side chain is a separate blockchain that runs in parallel to the main blockchain. Assets can be transferred between the main blockchain and the side chains via a two-way peg, allowing the side chains to operate independently and relieve congestion on the main blockchain. This structure allows for more flexibility, scalability, and opens possibilities for innovative uses of blockchain technology.

On the flip side, the modular-and-stacked blockchain approach sees different protocols managing individual components and blockchain operations. One blockchain could handle settlement and consensus, while another takes care of data availability and execution. This ongoing debate between the monolithic-and-interoperable model versus the modular-and-stacked model is crucial for infrastructure providers, impacting the demand for access to and use of various blockchains.

Another method for understanding smart contract protocols, particularly from an investor's perspective, is to classify them into layers like internet protocols. These projects can generally be categorized as Layer 0, Layer 1, or Layer 2 blockchains. Each layer provides different functions and capabilities within the overall blockchain structure, contributing to the complexity and functionality of the cryptocurrency ecosystem.

Layer 0 (Cosmos, Polkadot): Layer 0 blockchains are a relatively new concept in the blockchain world, and aim to solve the problem of fragmentation in the ecosystem. Layer 0 blockchains are not built on top of other chains. They represent the underlying infrastructure for multiple blockchains to work together. The idea behind Layer 0 is to create a decentralized infrastructure that all blockchains can use, eliminating the need for each blockchain to have its own infrastructure. Thus, blockchains can share resources and infrastructure, resulting in a more efficient and cost-effective ecosystem.

Layer 1 (Ethereum, Solana, Cardano, Avalanche): Layer 1 blockchains are often referred to as public chains and are the most well-known among blockchain enthusiasts. The characteristics of Layer 1 blockchains are: they are independent and can work without relying on other chains; and they have their own structure and mechanisms, such as consensus mechanisms, ledgers, nodes, encryption algorithms, and tokens. Layer 1 blockchains can also support higher-level blockchains, protocols, and applications, and build their own ecosystems.

Layer 2 (Polygon, Optimism, Metis): Layer 2 blockchains are built on top of Layer 1 chains, and are designed to solve the scaling problem of Layer 1. Most of these projects are focused on solving the scaling issues of Ethereum. Layer 2 blockchains perform most tasks off-chain and only push the results back to Layer 1 for simple processing and recording. This mechanism reduces the burden on Layer 1, resulting in faster transaction verification speeds and lower transaction fees. Rollups and State channels are the most used solutions in Layer 2 projects (see corresponding feature box).

3.5.4 The Smart Contract Landscape

Ethereum is by far the largest smart contract platform. But other competitors are catching up. Layer 1 blockchains saw a dramatic increase in quantifiable user activity, largely driven by the emergence of DeFi ecosystems across the various platforms. Average transaction fees on Ethereum rose to record-high levels, at times leaving users paralyzed with exorbitant gas fees[12] and long confirmation times during times of extreme network demand. In this environment of significant network demand and rapidly increasing costs, non-Ethereum Layer 1 blockchains with comparatively lower fees began to take catch up as users sought cheaper and faster alternatives to Ethereum.

Total Value Locked as a Key Metric

A popular ratio for quantifying the success of a smart contract platform is the total value locked (TVL). TVL is the overall value of crypto assets deposited in a smart contract platform. Aggregated this number is a key metric for gauging the overall interest in this crypto sector. Figure 3.4 shows the development of the TVL over time in U.S.-dollar terms.

---

12 Gas Fees: *Gas* refers to the fee, or pricing value, required to successfully conduct a transaction or execute a contract on the Ethereum blockchain platform (see https://www.investopedia.com/terms/g/gas-ethereum.asp).

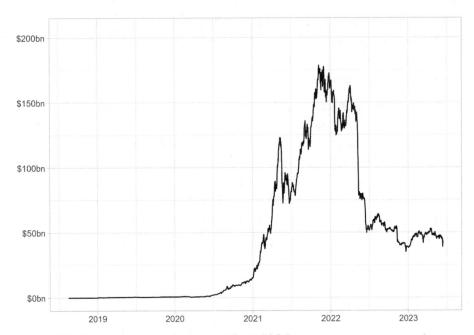

Figure 3.4: DeFi total value locked (TVL) on smart contract platforms in U.S. Dollar.
Source: MarketVector, DeFi Llama.

All Layer 1 chains aim to solve the so called blockchain trilemma. This expression was coined first by Ethereum founder Vitali Butlerin and describes the problem of finding the right balance among security, decentralization, and scalability.

> *"We will either solve the scalability and consensus problems or die trying."*
> *Vitalik Buterin, co-founder of Ethereum*

Optimizing the three goals of scalability, security, and decentralization presents a significant challenge for blockchain protocols. These goals are interconnected, and achieving high levels of all three simultaneously is a complex task.

Scalability refers to the ability of a blockchain network to handle a large volume of transactions efficiently. As more participants join the network and the transaction load increases, scalability becomes crucial. However, achieving high scalability often requires compromises in terms of security and decentralization. To enhance scalability, blockchain protocols may introduce mechanisms like larger block sizes, faster block confirmation times, or off-chain solutions. These solutions can improve transaction throughput and reduce congestion. However, increasing scalability can lead to potential trade-offs in security and decentralization. Security is vital for maintaining the integrity and trustworthiness of a blockchain. It involves protecting against attacks, ensuring data immutability, and preventing unauthorized access. Robust security measures often involve resource-intensive processes, such as cryptographic algorithms and consensus mechanisms that validate and confirm transactions. Balancing security while addressing scalability can be challenging, as adding more participants and increasing transaction throughput can introduce vulnerabilities and potential attack vectors.

Decentralization is a fundamental principle of blockchain technology, aiming to distribute power and decision-making across a network of participants. It ensures that no single entity or group has excessive control over the network, promoting censorship resistance and resilience against attacks. However, achieving a high degree of decentralization can hinder scalability and security. As more nodes participate in the network, reaching consensus becomes more time-consuming and resource-intensive, potentially slowing down the system.

Blockchain protocols must carefully navigate this trilemma, considering the specific requirements and trade-offs that align with their intended use cases. Different protocols may prioritize one or two of the goals over the others, depending on their objectives and target audience. Researchers and developers continuously explore innovative solutions to address the trilemma. Advancements in scalability, such as Layer 2 solutions like Lightning Network or Rollups, aim to improve transaction throughput without compromising security or decentralization. Similarly, new consensus algorithms, like proof-of-stake (PoS), aim to reduce the energy consumption associated with traditional proof-of-work (PoW) protocols while maintaining security and decentralization.

However, it is important to recognize that optimizing the blockchain trilemma is an ongoing process. Achieving a perfect balance among scalability, security, and decentralization remains a significant challenge.

Ethereum is moving toward a new system that incorporates sharding and Layer 2 solutions. Meanwhile, Polkadot, a Layer 0 protocol, aims to collaborate with other blockchains. Solana is investing in a costly infrastructure in order to enhance scalability. Avalanche, a proof-of-stake blockchain, utilizes a complex consensus method that offers both security and high transaction throughput. Like Binance Smart Chain, Avalanche is compatible with the Ethereum Virtual Machine (EVM), making it easy for Ethereum developers to transfer their applications. Cosmos calls itself the "Internet of Blockchains" and enables the creation of individual Layer 1 blockchains that can easily transact and transfer value between one another. Table 3.2 illustrates the different attributes of prominent smart contract blockchains:

	Ethereum	Cosmos	Solana
Architecture	Single-Chain (synchronous)	Multi-chain (IBC compatible)	Single-chain (synchronous)
Consensus	Proof-of-Stake	Tendermint Proof-of-Stake	Proof-of-History
TPS	15	10.000	50.000
Finality Time	5 min	1–3 sec	0.4 sec
CPU Cores	4	4	12
RAM (GB)	16	32	128

Table 3.2: Characteristics of different smart contract protocols.
Source: Coin98 Analytics, the Block Research. TPS is the number of transactions a blockchain network can process each second or the number of transactions executed per second. Finality Time is an accurate gauge of speed for blockchain networks and indicates how long it takes, until a transaction is confirmed. The values for CPU and RAM indicate how large the requirements are to run a node in the network.

When it comes to proof-of-stake algorithms, each blockchain focuses on a different approach, with varying hardware requirements. The Ethereum competitors excel in terms of transaction throughput, but the level of decentralization can be more challenging to evaluate. Oftentimes, a faster transaction speed may compromise security and result in centralization. If you are considering investing in Layer 1 blockchain coins, it is important to weigh the strengths and weaknesses, including scalability and composability, which determine the network's ability to process transactions and integrate components for specific products and services, such as DeFi or NFTs. Last, it is crucial for investors to consider the adoption rate of these smart contract chains and gauge the engagement of the user and developer community to assess the value of the network.

3.6 Infrastructure Applications

Centralizing hardware can make decentralized software vulnerable to censorship. Therefore decentralized software is only truly decentralized if the hardware that supports it is decentralized as well. Decentralized file storage, wireless internet, and cloud computing are examples of infrastructure projects that are necessary for the growth of the new decentralized internet, also known as Web3.[13] Scaling such hardware-intensive network profitably is difficult due to the significant capital investment.

While infrastructure protocols may have minimal utility on their own, when combined, they function similarly to LEGO blocks, allowing a developer to construct a variety of potentially new and beneficial user-facing Web3 applications. For example, the development of Chainlink oracles enabled the development of lending and borrowing platforms such as AAVE and Compound, which rely on high-quality, real-world data. Decentralized file storage protocols like Filecoin, IPFS, and Arweave are critical components in establishing a censorship-resistant, free internet.

3.6.1 Why Do We Need Web3 Infrastructure?

There are various attack vectors when it comes to crypto protocols. Centralization is a serious risk factor that affects various dimensions, including the community, the developer team, stakeholders, and infrastructure. The infrastructure aspect is often overlooked and not given much attention.

Ethereum and Solana are base layer protocols that perfectly demonstrate the paradox of centralization within decentralized blockchain infrastructure. Most of the backbone of these blockchain networks, which includes nodes and validators, are predominantly housed on the cloud servers of a handful of large technology companies. Interestingly, it is not just the base infrastructure that these tech giants host, but also the front ends and middleware of these protocols. This situation inadvertently places a significant amount of influence and control in the hands of a few

---

13 *Web3* has evolved into a catch-all word for the notion of a new and improved internet. At its heart, Web3 employs blockchains, cryptocurrencies, and NFTs to return power to users in the form of ownership. Web1 was read-only, Web2 was write-only, and Web3 will be read-write-own.

centralized entities, highlighting a key concern within the decentralized promise of blockchain technology.[14, 15]

Currently, the Ethereum network has more than 4,650 active nodes. Crypto analytics firm Messari states that about two-thirds of these nodes are located on centralized servers, with over half of them being controlled by Amazon Web Services (AWS). This centralization poses a risk to Ethereum, as it could lead to various failure scenarios. According to Messari, the Solana blockchain shows a similar vulnerability (Figure 3.5).

As more of the Web3 infrastructure is controlled by a few large tech companies and governments, these entities gain the power to censor and

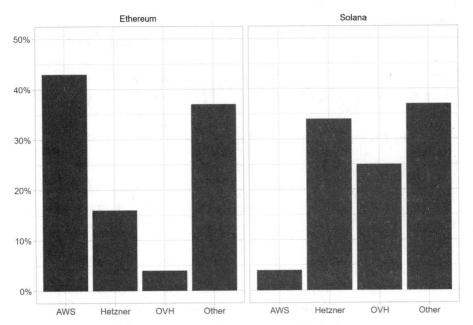

Figure 3.5: Hosting of Ethereum and Solana nodes. Three cloud providers represent 66% of hosted nodes. Source: messari.io, Akash: Solving Web3's Centralization Problems. Data as of June 2, 2022.

14 See Kassab (2022a).

15 In a blockchain network, a node is a computer or other device that participates in the network by maintaining a copy of the blockchain and validating transactions. These nodes work together to ensure the integrity and security of the blockchain by following a consensus protocol, which is a set of rules that govern how new transactions are added to the blockchain. A Validator, on the other hand, is a specific type of node that plays a key role in the consensus process. The Validators are responsible for verifying that new transactions are valid and then adding them to the blockchain. In order to do this, validators in the proof-of-stake world must have a certain amount of a cryptocurrency, often called a "staking token," as collateral. This is to ensure that validators have a financial incentive to act honestly and to deter them from attempting to cheat the system.

shut down protocols. Additionally, this concentration also makes it more likely for regulators to try to exert control over the sector. This is why a lot of Web3 front ends act as the primary attack vector.

There are various solutions available addressing the issue of centralization in decentralized infrastructure. One example is Akash Network, which aims to provide a decentralized infrastructure for cloud computing. Akash Network allows for a more distributed approach by enabling the use of a wider range of cloud service providers. Compared to working directly with a single, traditional cloud service provider, this arrangement is typically less expensive, more flexible, and more secure. Some of its key features include a permissionless structure and resistance to censorship. It is worth noting that there are other solutions that address the same problem.

Real-World Infrastructure

Through the coordinating powers of blockchain technology, crypto protocols can promote the construction of real-world infrastructure and hardware networks. Instead of a centralized institution, millions of sovereign individuals can work together to install and operate infrastructure in a trustless, permissionless, and programmatic manner.

This industry has been dubbed "proof-of-physical-work" by Multicoin Capital (PoPW).[16] PoPW compensates users for doing verifiable physical effort, such as setting up a 5G hotspot. Based on a predetermined set of rules, the protocol algorithm verifies the device's state and pays the owner. Many PoPW protocols are already coordinating hundreds of thousands of participants worldwide, encompassing industries such as wireless networks, mobility, the environment, computation, and storage.

Key Advantages of Using Web3 in Infrastructure

The use of decentralized protocols for infrastructure networks has two key advantages: the ability to quickly expand networks on a global scale, and the system being jointly owned by its participants rather than a limited number of stockholders, eliminating the need for a centralized market.

Web3 protocols enable people all around the world to create permissionless networks simultaneously. Participants with specific expertise of their

---

16 See Jain and Sengupta (2022).

jurisdiction can concentrate on deploying infrastructure that suits the needs of their local market. In exchange for expanding out the supply side of a network, participants gain ownership stakes in the network, which motivates them to see it flourish. It is feasible to collectively bootstrap a network without requiring permission or trust. This is also a more cost-effective technique for bootstrapping a network by dispersing the costs associated with developing and sustaining it to supply-side participants.

3.6.2 The Infrastructure Application Ecosystem

The MarketVector Infrastructure Application architecture names seven layers of decentralizing the infrastructure of Decentralized Apps (DApps) and Web3 services:

- **Blockchain-as-a-Service** (Stratis, Unibright): Includes B2B infrastructure application platforms which are marketed to blockchain developers but do not fit neatly into any of the preceding categories.
- **Computing Platform** (Ankr Network, Keep Network, Render Network): A network of computers operating together to accomplish a particular task. Decentralized compute networks connect individuals looking for compute resources to systems with idle computing power.
- **Data Management** (Arweave, The Graph, Filecoin): Tokens native to applications that use blockchain data's public nature to query, collect, process, encrypt, monetize, or broadcast data for various use cases. The category also contains a new generation of cooperative storage clouds to meet the storage requirements of new Web3 applications.
- **Digitization** (Civic, Ethereum Name Service): Protocols, taking care of real-world documents, contracts, public names and other data. With the help of the blockchain, transparency, publicly verifiable ownership, and immutability are guaranteed.
- **Interoperability** (Ren, Synapse): With the growth of L1, L2, and side-chain networks, there is an increased demand for cross-chain communication and interoperability to bridge value across the composite network space. Cross-chain bridges strive to serve this goal by allowing users to transfer value from one chain to another.
- **Internet of Things** (IoT): The *Internet of Things (IoT)* is a term used to describe devices that directly exchange data with each other via a network. Interoperability between IoT networks and Decentralized Apps is enabled through IoT platforms. IoT infrastructure applications

include those that collect and send information (sensors), receive information and act on it (3D printers), and those that do both (robots).

- **Decentralized Wireless Networks** (Helium): Incentivizing operators to deploy and maintain telecom hardware in exchange for token rewards.

3.6.3 What Is the Value Proposition of Web3 Infrastructure Protocols?

There has been a proliferation of infrastructure protocols. They are all faced with the difficulty of matching network usage to token pricing. Because Web3 protocols are still in their infancy, they require agreement on the best tokenomics standard.[17] The disparity between value generation and value accrual is seen in Uniswap.[18] Uniswap is a decentralized exchange (DEX) built on Ethereum, which allows users to trade tokens without the need for a central authority. Its token has struggled to gain value despite being the most popular DEX with the highest volume because its main benefit is protocol governance.

The basic idea of Web 3 infrastructure involves rewarding users for completing a verifiable physical activity.[19]

- The token payout encourages supply-side participants to build infrastructure.
- More supply-side participants are attracted by network fees produced by end customers.
- The network utility increases and so does the token price.

The **Burn-and-Mint Equilibrium (BME)** model and the **Stake-for-Access (SFA)** model are two popular token models used to construct a relationship between network consumption and token pricing.

The BME model operates by converting protocol usage into token buying pressure. In this model, users are required to burn (destroy) a certain number of tokens in order to access the network or perform a certain action. This creates scarcity in the token supply, which in turn,

---

17 Tokenomics: Token economics is the study of how tokens are used in blockchain networks, and how their value is determined. Tokenomics is the set of rules and incentives that govern the issuance, distribution, and circulation of tokens within a network.

18 Value accrual techniques: these are methods used to ensure that the value generated by a network is captured by its token.

19 See Kassab (2022b).

drives up the token's price. The token is then minted (created) back into the system in order to reward the network's validators or to be sold back to users. This creates a self-regulating mechanism to balance the token's supply and demand, and thus, its price.

On the other hand, the SFA model converts network involvement into token buying pressure. In this model, users are required to stake (lock up) a certain number of tokens in order to access the network or perform a certain action. The staked tokens are used as collateral to ensure that users act in the network's best interest. The longer the tokens are staked, the more access and benefits the user has on the network, and the more the token price increases. In summary, the BME model operates by converting protocol usage into token buying pressure through a burn-and-mint mechanism, while the SFA model operates by converting network involvement into token buying pressure through a stake-for-access mechanism.

The Chainlink protocol, for example, is a decentralized oracle network that enables smart contracts to securely access off-chain data feeds, web APIs, and traditional bank payments. It employs LINK as both a payments token and a work token. LINK is a payment token used to compensate Chainlink node operators for providing Oracle services. As a work token, LINK can be staked as collateral by node operators to perform oracle services, with node operators' staking incentives being decreased ("slashed") as a penalty in the event of errors or downtime. Filecoin, a data storage protocol, operates similarly.

3.6.4 Web3 Infrastructure Token Incentives

As the landscape of Web3 infrastructure progresses, it is crucial to recognize the instrumental role token incentives play in fostering network engagement and capturing value. For an effective design of a token incentive system, maintaining an equilibrium between propelling network expansion and ensuring that token holders receive due rewards for their participation is key. However, a significant hurdle arises when tokens are used to stimulate network adoption; they can inadvertently spur less beneficial activities if they are dispensed for inappropriate reasons. Moreover, early adopters may have an undue edge over subsequent participants, potentially leading to a value dilution for other stakeholders. Nonetheless, despite these impediments, token incentives continue to be a potent mechanism to bolster network growth and adoption.

3.7 Centralized Exchanges

As cryptocurrencies have become a popular investment and trading option, centralized crypto exchanges (CEXs) emerged as the go-to platform for individuals and institutions to buy, sell, and trade cryptocurrencies. These exchanges act as intermediaries, matching orders and facilitating transactions. They are controlled and maintained by a central authority or organization. In the next paragraphs we explore the value proposition of CEXs, including their convenience, liquidity, and support, as well as the risks associated with using these platforms.

The most significant event impacting this sector recently was, without a doubt, the collapse of FTX. This event has led to concerns about the safety of the industry and has dramatically influenced exchange flows, volumes, and liquidity on almost all centralized exchanges.[20]

3.7.1 The Value Proposition of Centralized Exchanges

A large chunk of the trading volume in the crypto market is generated on centralized exchanges.

Specifically, the following factors encourage investors to utilize these entities:

- Convenience: CEXs provide an easy-to-use platform for buying, selling, and trading cryptocurrencies. They also typically offer a wide range of trading pairs and advanced trading tools, such as margin trading and sophisticated order types.
- Liquidity: CEXs represent some of the most liquid crypto markets, meaning that they display high levels of trading activity. Turnover and relatively tight bid-ask spreads.
- Support: CEXs often have dedicated customer support teams that can assist users with technical and account-related issues. For example, Bitfinex, a centralized exchange, offers 24/7 customer support through live chat and email, making it easy for users to get help when they need it.

Centralized exchanges have become a popular way for individuals to transact cryptocurrencies, but there are also several risks associated with

---

20 See "What Happened to Crypto Giant FTX? A Detailed Summary of What We Actually Know So Far" (2022).

using these platforms. The following are some of the most significant risks and potential solutions for mitigating them:

- Security: Centralized exchanges are a prime target for hackers and other malicious actors. These attacks can result in the loss of user funds, as well as an interruption of the exchange's trading activities. Examples of high-profile security breaches include the Mt. Gox hack in 2014, where 850,000 bitcoin were stolen, and the Binance hack in 2019, where 7,000 bitcoin were stolen.[21] To mitigate this risk, users should only store funds used for trading on an exchange. Otherwise, the use of a hardware wallet to store funds offline is the way to go. Additionally, exchanges should implement robust security measures such as multi-factor authentication and cold storage.
- Censorship: CEXs are subject to the laws and regulations of the countries in which they operate. This means that they can be forced to censor certain trading pairs or activities, or even shut down altogether. For example, in 2017, China's government banned all cryptocurrency exchanges, leading many exchanges to relocate to more crypto-friendly jurisdictions.[22] To mitigate this risk, exchanges should choose to domicile in countries with sound laws and regulations. Additionally, users should be aware of the regulatory environment in their own country and consider using decentralized exchanges or peer-to-peer trading platforms if censorship is a concern.
- Counterparty Risk: They are a single point of failure. If the exchange were to become insolvent or go out of business, users' funds would be at risk. Examples of this include the Bitfinex hack in 2016, where 120,000 bitcoin were stolen and the QuadrigaCX exchange collapse in 2019, where users lost access to $190 million in funds. The latest debacle on the collapse of FTX shows, that outright fraud can lead to bankruptcy and huge losses of customer assets. To mitigate these risks, users should diversify their investments across multiple exchanges and consider using decentralized exchanges or peer-to-peer trading platforms.

3.7.2 What Is an Exchange Token?

The cryptocurrency exchange industry is highly competitive. Crypto exchanges realized they needed to stand out from the crowd, so they

---

21 Mt. Gox was once the world's largest bitcoin exchange.

22 See Shinh (2022).

turned to what they knew best—cryptocurrencies—and began to create their own tokens. These are referred to as exchange tokens. Exchange tokens, such as those issued by Binance and OKX, entitle holders to certain benefits on centralized exchanges.

Economic Benefit: Buyback and Burn

Some Exchanges promise to buy back their native tokens using revenue or profits generated from the exchange's operations. This is the primary way for exchanges to tie the value of their native token to the performance of the exchange (see Figure 3.6).

For example, Binance, one of the world's largest crypto exchanges, has pledged to use 20% of its profits each quarter to buy back and burn its native token, the Binance Coin (BNB) (Figure 3.6). This creates a direct positive relationship between the exchange's performance and the value of BNB.[23] While the token does not grant holders ownership or voting

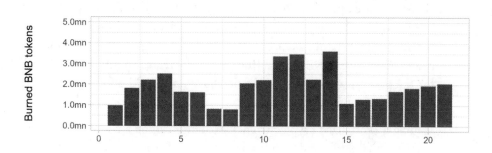

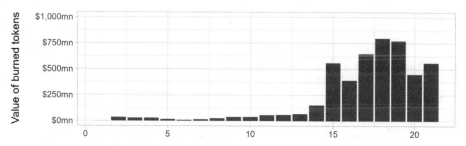

Figure 3.6: BNB burns: Quarterly amount of BNB tokens burned and corresponding value in U.S. dollars. Source: The Block, data as of January 15, 2023.

---

23 *Token burning* means removing coins from the overall supply of a cryptocurrency. This typically involves sending the coins or tokens to a wallet with no known private keys. This wallet can only receive assets, thus effectively making them inaccessible.

rights, the buyback and burn mechanism creates a direct positive relationship between the exchange's performance and the value of the token. Binance recently modified its burn process. The number of blocks generated on the BNB chain and the price of BNB are now used to determine the burn. This demonstrates how quickly the rules can change. The rights of token holders are unprotected, and even though they are frequently equated to stocks, token holders have no entitlement to any of the underlying exchange's residual cash flows.

Utility Benefits

Holding or staking exchange tokens can give discounts on trading and other fees. For example, holding BNB on Binance exchange can give you a 25% discount on trading fees. It may also give priority access to token sales on the platform. For example, holders of BNB are given priority access to exclusive token sales on Binance Launchpad.

Some exchange tokens are used for staking and governance on their associated smart contract chains (i.e., CRO). Additionally, crypto exchanges have also been closely associated with blockchains that use their native tokens as blockchain gas (see Table 3.3). An example of this is Binance chain, which uses BNB as gas. This approach creates an inherent demand for the token it otherwise would not have and could allow it to accrue some sort of monetary premium.

Valuing a centralized cryptocurrency exchange can be a complex task, but market capitalization and trading volume are two key metrics that can be used

Exchange	Ticker	Buyback and burn	Native Token	Fee Discounts	Access to IEO/ Launchpad
Binance	BNB	✓	✓	✓	✓
Crypto.com	CRO	✗	✓	✓	✓
Kucoin	KCS	✓	✓	✓	✓
Huobi	HAT	✓	✗	✓	✓
OKX	OKB	✓	✗	✓	✓
Bitfinex	LEO	✓	✗	✓	✗

Table 3.3: Exchange token incentives.
Source: MarketVector.

to gain insight into the value of an exchange. Additionally, price to trading volume can be an important factor to consider when evaluating an exchange.

3.7.3 Regulatory Challenges

Additionally, trust is an issue for CEXs, with the recent collapse of FTX leading to a greater push for self-custody of crypto assets and the use of crypto tools. CEXs are attempting to regain this trust through greater transparency and proof-of-reserves (PoR) statements, the latter one being a controversial figure.[24] The research provider "The Block" provides a valuable overview about proof-of-reserves. According to the analysts of the company PoR is only half of the picture when it comes to an exchange's financial health, as it does not consider the exchange's liabilities. Therefore, reliable external audits are still needed.[25]

Regulation is another factor to consider when analyzing crypto currency exchanges. Post the FTX fiasco, there is likely going to be more regulation. Depending on the regulator, this can play out differently in different regions, but in the long run, greater regulatory clarity should overall be seen as a positive. The likelihood of new regulatory initiatives aimed at increasing transparency in the crypto space, such as mandates for regular reporting and auditing of reserves, assets, and liabilities will lead to a convergence of the crypto ecosystem with the traditional financial system.

3.8 Decentralized Finance

> "The 2.5 billion adults [around the world] without access to financial services are disproportionately women and young people. There are at least 44 million unbanked or underbanked people in the United States, so clearly financial inclusion is needed in all markets."
> Ajaypal Singh Banga

Decentralized finance, or *DeFi* for short, refers to initiatives that seek to democratize financial access and eliminate centralized intermediaries like banks and other financial service providers. The idea is that of a cooperative: a business that is owned and run by its members. The core

---

24 Proof of reserves (PoR) is a method for cryptocurrency exchanges to publicly account for their digital assets, ensuring that user deposits are secure and withdrawable. PoR is a technique for cryptographically auditing a cryptocurrency exchange.

25 See Toh (2022).

idea behind Decentralized Finance is that, at least in theory, no one person or group should own or run a project by themselves.

But typically, projects start as projects with centralized teams. These initiatives are frequently funded and supported by Venture Capital (VC) investors, through an ICO (Initial Coin Offering) or an IDO (Initial DEX Offering).[26] The founding teams in this case distribute governance tokens to engaged community members once the initiative gets going. Communities of supporters can be found on platforms like Twitter (now X), Discord, or Telegram.

3.8.1 Types of Protocols

Decentralized Finance protocols provide the rules, infrastructure, and environment for the creation of computer programs (smart contracts) that run on top of another protocol such as Ethereum, Solana, or Avalanche and use that other protocol's assets, along with their own and others, to automate financial services. DeFi protocols link buyers and sellers, as well as lenders and borrowers, without the need for a centralized institution (see Table 3.4).

DeFi protocols can be further broken down into several subcategories that focus on specialized applications:[27]

- **Decentralized exchanges**, or DEXs (Uniswap, SushiSwap), enable peer-to-peer trading of digital assets. Even when the trading volume of the underlying asset is too low and therefore not appealing to larger centralized exchanges, DEXs nonetheless offer access to trading pairs. Either a decentralized order book or an algorithm for matching orders and determining prices can be used for transactions.
- **Platforms for lending and borrowing** (Compound, Aave): These include linking lenders and borrowers to issue interest-bearing instruments that must be repaid at maturity.
- **Derivatives** (Synthetix): Users can generate "shares," which symbolize entitlement to a payout, contingent on the results of occurrences such as elections, games, or fluctuations in the market. This utility extends

---

26 An Initial DEX Offering (IDO) is a way for projects to sell their freshly created crypto tokens to the community through a decentralized exchange (DEX). A typical IDO lets investors lock their money into a smart contract right before a project's native token is released. When a project launches its token, at the token generation event, investors get these new tokens in exchange for the locked funds, which are sent to the project.

27 See Sigel (2021).

	Traditional Finance	DeFi
Custody of Assets	Held by regulated service provider or custodian.	Held directly by users in noncustodial wallet or via smart contract-based escrow.
Units of Account	Fiat.	Denominated in digital assets or stablecoins.
Execution	Intermediaries process transactions between parties.	Via smart contracts operating on the users' assets.
Clearing and Settlement	Processed by service providers or clearinghouses, may take days.	Writing transactions to the underlying blockchain completes the settlement process instantly.
Governance	Specified by the rules of the service provider, marketplace, regulator, and/or self-regulatory organization.	Managed by protocol developers or determined by users holding tokens granting voting rights.
Auditability	Authorized third-party audits of proprietary code or potential for open-source code that is publicly verified.	Open-source code and public ledger allow auditors to verify protocols and activity.
Collateral Requirements	Transactions may involve no collateral, or collateral less than or equal to the funds provided.	Overcollateralization generally required, due to digital asset volatility and absence of credit scoring.

Table 3.4: Key differences between TradFi and DeFi.
Source: MarketVector.

beyond the realm of prediction markets, enabling the trade of tangible assets like stocks, foreign exchange, and commodities through crypto-denominated tokens.

- **Asset management** (Mirror, Numeraire): Enables users to build and optimize portfolios.
- **Insurance** (Nexus): Offers safety against risks by trading a premium for the right to receive a payout if a certain event happens.
- **Aggregators** (yearn.finance): Protocols that provide a variety of financial products and services.
- **Asset-backed reserves** (Olympus Dao): Protocols aiming to provide protocol-controlled liquidity through an integrated approach of rebasing, bonding, and the accrual of additional stable coins or digital assets.

The majority of DeFi apps do not request personal information during registration. Anyone can utilize DeFi products by accessing the website of an application and connecting using a wallet (i.e., MetaMask) or equivalent protocol. DeFi is a rapidly expanding field, but it is still in its infancy, with numerous unresolved economic, technical, operational, and public policy challenges that need to be addressed.

3.8.2 Project Valuation for DeFi

Like growth-stage startups, DeFi build products can generate cash flows for token holders in the future. While total value locked (TVL) is a valuable indicator for assessing the value deposited into a protocol's smart contracts, it does not always provide information for investors regarding the protocol's financial health.[28] For instance, in the case of Compound, TVL is the difference between assets deposited and assets borrowed. This is because a portion of these deposits are taken out of the markets when users borrow the assets of other users on Compound. Therefore, concentrating on borrowing volume (current debt) and interest paid would be a more accurate way to assess the success of a lending protocol.

Because DeFi protocols are usually open source, they can easily be cloned. This has resulted in a proliferation of imitators and a fee race to the bottom. In addition, numerous investors were alarmed by the statements of global regulators. Like smart contract platforms, DeFi protocols typically make money by collecting transaction fees. The fees are either paid out to token holders as payouts or through "burns,"[29] which lower the number of tokens in circulation. While burning tokens raises each user's relative share of the network similarly to a share repurchase, payouts provide a direct reward to market participants.

There are different ways to generate yields in DeFi:

- **DEXs**: DEXs charge a low fee, around 0.3% for exchanges like Uniswap.
- **Lending**: DeFi lending protocol helps lenders to earn interest on crypto assets.
- **Options**: Through earning premiums.
- **Staking derivatives**: Earning block rewards and transaction fees.
- **All protocols**: Governance token incentives.
- **Yield aggregators**: Combine the previously mentioned ways of generating yields.

---

28 See Fang (2021).

29 Burning tokens depletes a cryptocurrency's supply of coins overall. Usually, this entails transferring the money to a wallet whose private keys are unknown. Assets are inaccessible since this wallet can only accept them.

Alternatively put, yields in DeFi originate from the fees paid by demand-side users of these platforms and token inflation. It is important to consider how much of the fee revenue or usage is linked to token incentives that are paid to users.

Token incentives are supplementary rewards offered for the protocol's basic usage, often focusing on the protocol's supply-side users. Boosting growth with token incentives is a common way to get more users to sign up, but it is not clear if this method will work in the long run. One could think of this metric as the cost of customer acquisition.

3.8.3 Challenges and Risks

DeFi has a lot of benefits, but there are also drawbacks and trade-offs to consider. According to Fabian Schär, professor of distributed ledger technology and fintech at the University of Basel, there are several challenges and risks.[30]

One of these risks lies in the lack of transparency regarding the real degree of decentralization. What is commonly referred to as *Decentralized Finance* is frequently highly centralized. DeFi protocols are often influenced by centralized data feeds and are prone to highly concentrated governance token allocations held by individuals. It is crucial to distinguish between true decentralization and businesses that advertise themselves as DeFi but offer centralized infrastructure.

Even one of the core features of blockchains, the immutability of entries on the distributed ledger, is not always an advantage. Investor protection may be more difficult to enforce, and programming errors in smart contracts may have grave repercussions. Privacy concerns may be raised by the blockchain's openness and decentralized approach to block formation. As all transactions are documented on-chain. This permits the extraction of rents by widespread front-running as implemented by the maximum extractable value (MEV) mechanism. Sophisticated market participants who see a transaction with an instruction to trade assets on a decentralized exchange can attempt to foreclose (or sandwich) that action. Potential remedies exist, but they come with trade-offs and may only partially alleviate the issue.

---

30 See Schär (2022).

Another problem are transaction costs. It is difficult to scale public block-chains without sacrificing some of their distinctive characteristics. High frequency of transactions is often associated with high costs of transactions. So-called Layer 2 protocols are a potential fix. It is helping Ethereum run computations off-chain and only publish transaction data on-chain in order to increase speed and reduce gas fees. Although this is a good strategy, it frequently still needs trust and different kinds of centralized infrastructure as part of the process moves off-chain.

Despite its difficulties, DeFi can nevertheless significantly enhance the current financial system. The better efficiency due to the obsolescence of mutual trust and the lower cost of doing business could greatly enhance the processes in the financial sector.

3.9 Non-fungible Tokens

Non-fungible tokens (NFTs) have become a popular topic in recent years, particularly in the world of digital art and collectibles. While some may question the legitimacy of the hype surrounding NFTs, they represent an important development in the world of digital assets, with unique technological considerations that make them distinct from other types of digital assets.

When you hear the term NFT, you might think of a digital image or artwork being sold for an exorbitant sum of money, such as the famous *Everydays: The First 5000 Days* NFT by artist Beeple, which sold for $69 million at Christie's auction house. However, NFTs can also represent other types of assets, such as videos, music, or other forms of digital media. The concept of *fungibility* refers to the idea that an asset is interchangeable and identical. For example, a 10€ bill is interchangeable with any other 10€ bill, and there is no difference between two standard gold bars. On the other hand, non-fungible assets, such as real estate, wine, or works of art are unique and cannot be replaced by an equivalent asset.

In the digital world, NFTs are unique digital assets that are represented by a token on a blockchain. These tokens are used to transfer the proof-of-ownership of digital assets and have several key properties that make them different from other forms of digital assets.

Uniqueness: Each NFT has properties that are stored in the metadata file on the blockchain, such as an image, a video, a message, or music. This information is given a unique digital signature, making every NFT one-of-a-kind. It cannot be replicated or copied. The data stored on the blockchain is immutable and can be viewed by anyone.

Scarcity: The creators of an NFT can specify the number of tokens that will be created, ensuring that the asset is scarce and has limited availability. For example, an NFT can represent a limited edition of a digital video, with a fixed number of tokens representing the video. This scarcity is guaranteed by the blockchain and ensures that the NFT has value.

Indivisibility: NFTs cannot be divided into smaller units and must be transferred in their entirety. This indivisibility makes the transfer of the NFT more secure and ensures that the asset remains whole.

Ownership: The holder of an NFT has ownership and control over the asset. The entire history of the NFT, including all transactions, is stored on the blockchain, making it transparent and traceable to everyone.

For artists and investors, NFTs have the potential to revolutionize the way not only digital assets are bought and sold. For artists, the ability to programmatically store rules for royalties can ensure that they receive a share of the profits from their artwork without the need for a large contract or intermediaries. For investors, the low correlation between NFTs and other asset classes, combined with the ability to acquire unique digital goods in the form of easily transferable tokens, makes NFTs an attractive addition to any crypto portfolio. The use cases for NFTs extend far beyond just digital art, and include areas such as music and streaming, decentralized social media, digital identity, gaming, and tokenized real-world assets.

Decentralized Social Media: NFTs serve as the backbone for many decentralized social media platforms, representing digital profiles and identities, content, rewards for engagement, and gating content. A well-known example of a decentralized social media platform that uses NFTs is Lens, which has an average of 35,000 active users and supports front-end applications such as Lenster and Phaver.

Digital Identity: NFTs can be used for on-chain credentialing, where individuals' qualifications, skills, or other information can be verified through unique NFTs that contain data and metadata. Platforms that focus on proof-of-attendance, identity, and learn-to-earn, such as POAP and Galxe, are examples of platforms that are leveraging NFTs for digital identity purposes.

Tokenized Real-World Assets: Tokenizing real-world assets such as real estate, art, or collectibles using NFTs solves inefficiencies, reduces the cost of intermediaries, and provides a better way to verify and track assets. Projects that tokenize physical assets include RealT and Artory.

These are just a few examples of the many potential use cases for NFTs beyond digital art. NFTs are a rapidly evolving technology, and new use cases are likely to emerge as the technology continues to mature. The value of NFTs can be challenging to determine, but this is no different from the world of tangible goods. The general use of NFTs is often overshadowed by the more sensational examples of NFTs, such as digital art. However, NFTs have the potential to "tokenize" a wide variety of assets, including real estate, financial products, and private equity investments. By transferring ownership rights to a fixed number of digital tokens, NFTs can enable the easy distribution of large assets among many investors, improving transparency, liquidity and expanding portfolio diversification opportunities.

3.10 Media and Entertainment

> "The Internet is disrupting every media industry. People can complain about that, but complaining is not a strategy."
> Jeff Bezos

The media and entertainment industry is facing several challenges in the current digital landscape. From a lack of transparency in revenue split to high fees for content creators, the traditional industry models are struggling to adapt to the digital age.

However, the rise of blockchain technology offers new solutions to these problems, providing opportunities for the media and entertainment industry to create, distribute, and monetize content in new and innovative ways. By leveraging non-fungible tokens (NFTs) and decentralized platforms, the industry can establish more equitable economic conditions for creators and provide a more direct connection between creators and their audience.[31]

To better understand the potential of blockchain technology in the media and entertainment industry, it is important to first examine the current challenges facing the industry. In the following paragraphs, we delve into the problems facing the media and entertainment industry and explore how blockchain technology can be leveraged to overcome these challenges and create new opportunities.

3.10.1 The Problem of the Media and Entertainment Industry

The media and entertainment landscape is vast and diverse, encompassing many subcategories such as music, film, and gaming. Each subcategory has its own unique revenue model, challenges, and trends.

Music, for example, is a billion-dollar industry that has traditionally relied on album and concert ticket sales. However, the rise of streaming services has led to a decline in album sales and revenue for musicians. Additionally, the music industry has long struggled with copyright infringement and lack of transparency in royalty payments. Film, on the other hand, is a highly centralized industry, with large studios and theaters controlling distribution and exhibition. While there has been an accelerated shift toward streaming platforms in recent years, independent filmmakers still face challenges in distribution and monetization.

Blockchain Technology as a Solution

There are several advantages that blockchain technology can provide the media and entertainment sector with the opportunity to establish more equitable economic conditions for creators is one of the key benefits. In typical Web2 platforms, creators frequently have limited control over how their work is distributed or how much money they receive from the site. While offering substantially lower take-rates, Web3 platforms utilizing blockchain technology, such as NFT markets, give producers more control over their work and income. The stark contrast in take-rates between

31 Non-fungible tokens (NFTs) are digital assets that prove ownership or authenticity of a unique item or piece of content, like a digital artwork, song, or video. They are created with blockchain technology. NFTs can be bought, sold, and traded like traditional collectibles and are kept on a blockchain.

Meta (almost 100%) and the NFT marketplace OpenSea (2.5%) serves as an illustration of this (see Figure 3.7).

The capacity to appropriately compensate producers is another advantage of blockchain technology in the media and entertainment sector. In its 2022 state of crypto report, the venture capital firm Andreessen Horowitz talks in depth about how creators are paid.[32] According to data research, the main sales of Ethereum-based NFTs in 2021 generated $3.9 billion in revenue in addition to royalties on secondary sales (see Table 3.5). While Spotify and YouTube paid out more to creators in absolute terms, the "per capita" disparity is astonishing. When you consider that Web3 paid out $174,000 to each creator while Meta paid out $0.10 per user, you can see that Web3 platforms provide more equitable economic terms.

Defining the Web3 Media and Entertainment Category

Media and Entertainment is a category of blockchain projects that aim to decentralize traditional media and entertainment platforms, such as

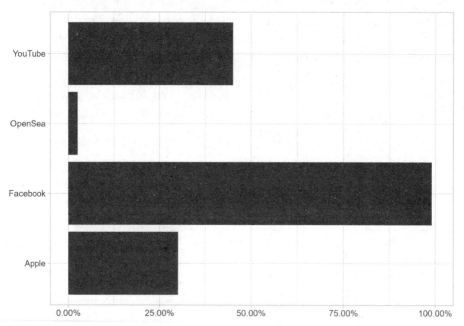

Figure 3.7: Take-rates of popular creator platforms.
Source: a16zcrypto, 2022 State of Crypto Report.

32 See Matsuoka et al. (2022).

Platform	Total Revenue distributed	Revenue per Creator
NFTs	$3,900,000,000	$174,000.00
Spotify	$7,000,000,000	$636.00
YouTube	$15,000,000,000	$405.00
Facebook	$300,000,000	$0.10

Table 3.5: Estimated creator revenues by source (2021).
Source: a16zcrypto, 2022 State of Crypto Report.

social media, gaming, and content creation. The goal is to increase direct peer-to-peer interaction between content creators and audiences, while also maintaining user privacy, security, and ownership of data and digital assets.

The Media and Entertainment category can be divided into the following industry groups:

- **Art** (Rarible, SuperRare): Platforms focused on non-fungible tokens (NFTs) and their use in the digital art space. This includes platforms that allow for the creation, buying, and selling of NFTs. These marketplaces are decentralized and noncustodial, meaning users have full control and access to their cryptocurrency wallets. They also allow for direct peer-to-peer interaction between buyers and sellers. The industry group also includes decentralized marketplaces for trading NFT artwork and native tokens for these marketplaces.
- **Social** (Chiliz): Social tokens are used to support social platforms and communities that do not have a central authority. They are used to make it easier for users, content creators, and sponsors to communicate to each other and do business. You can also use these tokens for other things, like decentralized government. The value of social tokens comes from how much the community and creators they represent grow and work together. By turning these communities into tokens, it creates ecosystems that are more interesting and rewarding than traditional advertising and subscription models.
- **Content and Advertising** (BAT, Theta): Projects that aim to decentralize social media platforms, such as broadcast streaming and video sharing, and enable it for content creators, consumers, and advertisers to connect directly with each other. This industry group also includes platforms for peer-to-peer sales and content distribution as well as royalty

payments and usage-based billing models. This means that advertisers, content creators, and audiences can connect directly with each other instead of using the traditional advertiser-to-consumer model.

- **Metaverse** (Decentraland, Sand): The Metaverse includes a network of virtual worlds that are based on blockchain technology. These virtual worlds are characterized by their social connections and interactions, and they include gaming realms and virtual land. The virtual worlds within the metaverse have a decentralized marketplace and allow for the tokenization and trading of digital assets. The open metaverse is a highly scaled, interoperable network of real-time, rendered 3D virtual worlds that may be experienced by many people simultaneously while maintaining data continuity such as identity, history, entitlements, items, conversations, and payments. It provides consumers with a unique experience of presence and has the potential to disrupt the gaming, advertising, payments, and lending industries.

3.10.2 Impact of Blockchain on the Economics of Media and Entertainment

Web3 protocols in the media and entertainment category provide new revenue streams for creators, increase transparency and ownership for consumers, and create more engaging and rewarding user experiences.

An example of this can be seen in the music industry, where Web3 protocols allow musicians to directly connect with and monetize their fanbase through tokenization of their music and merchandise. Musicians can tokenize their album releases and sell them as NFTs, giving fans ownership of a unique and scarce digital asset. Additionally, through smart contract-based platforms, musicians can receive royalties directly from streaming services, bypassing intermediaries, and increasing their revenues.

In the art industry, Web3 protocols enable creators to mint and trade unique digital artworks as NFTs, which can be bought, sold, and collected by art enthusiasts. This creates a new market for digital art and allows for a more efficient and secure way for creators to monetize their work.

The open metaverse has the potential to revolutionize industries such as advertising, gaming, conferences, payments, and the internet itself. The total addressable market for the metaverse is estimated to be $8 trillion of U.S. consumer spending that is increasingly moving to digital. PwC predicts that the metaverse market size will reach $783 billion by 2024, with a compound annual growth rate of 13%.[33]

The growth of the gaming market can be attributed to the rise of interest in video games and NFTs in recent years. The number of video gamers is projected to reach 3 billion with a projected 5–7% CAGR in the next few years. Additionally, NFT sales surpassed $15 billion in 2021, with secondary sales of NFTs in blockchain games accounting for 20% of total NFT sales. Virtual world games like Decentraland and The Sandbox have also generated nearly $500 million in cumulative NFT sales.

3.10.3 Challenges of Web3 Media and Entertainment: Product-Market-Fit and Valuation

Blockchain technology and digital assets are being used by Web3 metaverse developers to make more immersive and meaningful virtual worlds, but the industry is still in its early stages. The infrastructure is not quite ready yet, there is not enough interesting content, and it can be hard to get into these virtual worlds. Even among early adopters, this has made people less likely to adopt.

The lack of a clear product-market fit is one of the biggest problems facing the metaverse industry. Social and gaming are the two main types of Web3 metaverse. Social metaverses, like Decentraland and Voxels, are virtual worlds that should resemble the real world and are mostly used for socializing. These metaverses have soft benefits like better looks and status symbols that do not change the way a player plays. On the other hand, gaming metaverses like The Sandbox provides hard benefits such as in-game rewards that directly affect the player's abilities in the metaverse.

The problem is that land speculation is more likely to happen in social metaverses than in gaming metaverses. For example, many of Decentraland's lands have not been built on for years. This is why The Sandbox is curating its content experience by partnering with big brands. They want to get people to explore and take part in their virtual world by making it more interesting.

Valuation is another problem that the metaverse industry must deal with. In 2021 and the beginning of 2022, a lot of social and gaming-focused

33 See Kanterman (2021).

metaverse platforms popped up. These platforms were valued at between $230 million and $340 million. But these prices seem to be based on guesswork since these metaverses are still in the process of being built.

The metaverse is still very much a work in progress, and that is the bottom line. The industry is still trying to find its footing, and it will take time to work out the bugs and make a virtual experience that is truly immersive and meaningful. But like any worthwhile journey, the result is worth the trouble.

3.11 Conclusion

Bitcoin, as the first crypto asset, is often seen as the epitome of the entire crypto ecosystem. However, this perspective is rather limited, as there are numerous projects and distinct sectors within the space. At present, certain tokens hold dominant positions within their respective categories, but given the dynamic nature of the industry, it would be unwise to assume that the crypto landscape will look the same a decade from now. Many of the almost 20,000 existing tokens probably will not endure, as projects could disband or vanish, while new ones rise to prominence.

The crypto ecosystem is still in its early stages, with most projects being under development. Considering this, relying solely on market technical metrics for investment decisions can be a reasonable strategy to avoid major pitfalls. However, not all investors are content with a purely technical approach, and there are various fundamental methods for valuing crypto assets. We explore both the technical and the fundamental approaches in the subsequent chapter.

3.12 References

Burniske, Chris, and Jack Tatar. (2017). Cryptoassets: *The Innovative Investor's Guide to an Entirely New Asset Class*. McGraw-Hill.

Fang, Lucius. (2021). "How to DeFi: Advanced: Gecko, Coin, Fang, Lucius, Hor, Benjamin, Azmi, Erina, Khor, Win."

Kanterman, Matthew. (2021, December 1). "Metaverse May Be $800 Billion Market, Next Tech Platform | Insights." *Bloomberg Professional Services*, sec. Research and Analysis. https://www .bloomberg.com/professional/blog/metaverse-may-be-800-billion-market-next-tech-platform/.

Kassab, Sami. (2022a). "Akash: Solving Web3's Centralization Problems." https://messari.io/ report/akash-solving-web3-s-centralization-problems.

———. (2022b). "How Are Web3 Infrastructure Protocols Trying to Capture Value?" https://messari.io/report/how-are-web3-infrastructure-protocols-trying-to-capture-value.

Matsuoka, Daren, Eddy Lazzarin, Chris Dixon, and Robert Hackett. (2022, May 17). "Introducing the 2022 State of Crypto Report." A16z Crypto. https://a16zcrypto.com/posts/article/state-of-crypto-report-a16z-2022/.

Schär, Fabian. (2022). "DeFi Promise and Pitfalls Fabian Schar." IMF. https://www.imf.org/en/Publications/fandd/issues/2022/09/Defi-promise-and-pitfalls-Fabian-Schar.

Shinh, Francis. (2022, January 31). "What's behind China's Cryptocurrency Ban?" World *Economic Forum*. https://www.weforum.org/agenda/2022/01/what-s-behind-china-s-cryptocurrency-ban/.

Sigel, Matthew. (2021). "Crypto Categories: Defining DeFi | VanEck." Crypto Categories: Defining DeFi | VanEck. https://www.vaneck.com/us/en/blogs/digital-assets/matthew-sigel-crypto-categories-defining-defi/.

Szabo, Nick. (1994). "Smart Contracts." https://www.fon.hum.uva.nl/rob/Courses/Information InSpeech/CDROM/Literature/LOTwinterschool2006/szabo.best.vwh.net/smart.contracts.html.

Toh, Arnold. (2022). "Rapid Insights: Looking into Proof-of-Reserves of Major Exchanges." *The Block*. https://www.theblockresearch.com/rapid-insights-looking-into-proof-of-reserves-of-major-exchanges-188063.

"What Happened to Crypto Giant FTX? A detailed Summary of What We Actually Know So Far." (2022). Forbes. https://www.forbes.com/sites/qai/2022/12/13/what-happened-to-crypto-giant-ftx-a-detailed-summary-of-what-we-actually-know-here/.

"What Is a Vampire Attack in Crypto? (SushiSwap Stole Uniswap's Money?)." (2021, June 18). *WhiteboardCrypto* (blog). https://whiteboardcrypto.com/what-is-a-vampire-attack-in-crypto/.

4 Valuation of Crypto Assets

"Price is a liar"
John Burbank, CIO of Passport Capital

John Burbank's quote "Price is a liar" challenges the notion that market prices are always "right" and reflect all available information, as suggested by the efficient market hypothesis (EMH). Instead, Burbank believes that prices simply represent the equilibrium of liquidity, which is the point where buyers and sellers agree on a given price for a security or asset. His quote also highlights the importance of critical thinking and independent analysis in investment decision-making, rather than solely relying on market prices as a reflection of an asset's true value.

Assessing the fair pricing of Bitcoin and other crypto assets is no easy task. This chapter presents a range of valuation methods, from Metcalfe's Law to statistical models, providing the foundation for crypto asset valuation. No single model is flawless as each comes with its strengths and limitations. Before diving into valuation techniques, it is critical to comprehend what a token represents within a blockchain ecosystem and how it differs from established instruments like equities. As institutional participants venture into the digital asset realm, a rigorous vetting process becomes imperative, assessing everything from token use cases to regulatory compliance. The prerequisite for understanding the valuation of crypto assets is an awareness of their structure, which differs significantly from conventional asset classes. We therefore start with a look at the differences between equities and crypto assets.

4.1 Tokens Explained: What They Are and Why They Matter

By Matthew Sigel

As Head of Digital Assets Research and Portfolio Manager for the VanEck Smart Contract Leaders Fund, Matthew Sigel helps guide VanEck's digital assets strategy and sits on the investment committee of several of the firm's private funds. He produces frequent research on Bitcoin, smart contract platforms, and emerging markets adoption of digital assets, and is a regular guest on Coindesk, Bloomberg, and other media outlets. Prior to VanEck, Sigel worked as a research analyst and portfolio strategist at CLSA;

an analyst and portfolio manager at AllianceBernstein; and a journalist at Bloomberg, CNBC, and NHK Japan Broadcasting, where he covered finance. Sigel is a CFA Charterholder and has a B.A. from Harvard University.

Crypto tokens are a new asset class whose total value approached more than $3 trillion during the peak of the bull run in 2021. Because they represent a novel asset class whose value relates to intangible qualities like network effect, monetary premium, franchise value, digital utility and trust, crypto tokens have sparked lively debates about appropriate valuation techniques. Also called digital assets or cryptocurrencies, these emergent assets have seen great price volatility with some tokens even losing the entirety of their value. This has prompted more than a few analysts to contend that the sole determinant of digital asset is speculation.

However, while the space has been polluted by pseudonymous bad actors, and speculative frenzy, crypto currencies represent the outcome of combining cutting-edge economics, cryptography, and computer science. The nexus of these important academic disciplines has created the ability to send, hold, and trade value without trusted intermediaries while remaining semi-anonymous. As a result, cryptocurrencies enable the creation of a financial system that minimizes counterparty risk and enables true self-custody. Simultaneously, they combine internet-first functionality (peer-to-peer instant settlement) with predictable monetary policy, two features that enhance the competitive edge of digital asset ecosystems versus traditional financial systems. In this chapter, we explore how tokens can complement equity or debt instruments, how to define a profitable blockchain, and how to use a traditional discounted cash flow (DCF) to model the long-term income stream.

4.1.1 How Tokens Can Be a Complement to Equity or Debt

Crypto tokens have emerged as an innovative way for companies to raise capital and to distribute portions of value among many types of stakeholders, not just equity owners. Unlike traditional equities where businesses remit profits only to shareholders, tokens allow businesses to direct financial benefits to both investors and the company's customers. This can be accomplished through price appreciation of the token, token buybacks, airdrops of new value, and even dividends from the business. The net effect is that tokens empower businesses with a unique mechanism to direct and incentivize desirable user behaviors.

Another benefit is that tokens effectively tie the user base to the success of the project, adding an element of stickiness and as well as a marketing vector to the project's business. Token holders, understanding that the value of their tokens relates to the success of the business, are motivated to get others to patronize the business. However, unlike equities whose value accrual to shareholders can become contentious and is subject to the fickleness of litigation, tokens often rely on a verifiable and immutable code that enshrines value to the token. In the world of tokenization, code is law (as long as it's legal).

However, while many crypto firms rely solely on the token to represent ownership stake in the endeavor, some crypto entities operate dual token/legal equity ownership structures which cloud this picture. While a coded token commitment is often immutable, crypto project code is often open source and little legal protection exists to prevent a company from abandoning code and redeploying similar code to create a new business. Though abandoning a token would destroy a customer base and alienate investors, tokens still rely on an entity honoring its commitment to token holders. Arguably, tokens lie one echelon below common stock in the capital table, but this low status is offset by the importance to the crypto project's business model. Tokens, because of their unique properties which enable revolutionary value creation, have risks and benefits not seen with traditional equities. Therefore, they should be viewed as a compliment to equity rather than a replacement.

Digital assets further extend their value proposition because they can provide investors with unique benefits that are not available from investing traditional equity or exchanging services for fiat. For example, tokens derive their name, tokens, from their ability to be used as an exchange mechanism to receive services or products. They can be understood to be bearer assets that provide users with an efficient and seamless experience analogous to a credit or debit card without having to absorb transaction fees. Likewise, different types of users can be more easily identified by their interactions with the crypto business and rewarded using the same medium of exchange—the tokens. For example, early token holders and product users may be given additional rewards for continual loyalty. This kind of dynamic is analogous to airline points or membership tiers, but represents more tangible value because tokens are priced and traded on the open market. The net effect is the creation of a priming engine to attract new users who can be selectively targeted with rewards that may become very valuable. This can lead to faster adoption of the entity's products and services while potentially translating into higher revenue and profits.

Another interesting feature of tokens relates to the governance rights conferred by their ownership. These governance rights can be more powerful than those conferred to shareholders. Where equity investors appoint delegates to influence business direction via board of director elections, token holders often have substantially greater say in the direction of crypto projects. In practice, and depending on the crypto business, token holders not only directly appoint business leadership, but also have unrestricted say in business direction, marketing efforts, budget spend, and even the economics of the token themselves. Investors can choose to dilute tokens, incentivize participation in governance, direct revenue toward new projects, and even vote themselves a portion of the business's stream of income or the firm's treasury funds. Though this feature may transform digital assets into securities or lead to lengthy ownership disputes, token voting opportunities constitute a revolution in corporate governance that places power into the hands of both the investor and the customer.

As an additional feature, tokens can provide investors with liquidity that is not available through traditional equity investments. It also allows business customers the ability to buy services or products in advance, using the token, or quickly liquidate those tokens, essentially "accounts receivable," on liquid markets. Most tokens can be traded on crypto exchanges, both centralized and decentralized, providing investors and crypto project customers with the ability to buy and sell their assets quickly and easily. The many-sided nature of these coins, as investments, governance rights vessels, and as utility items, further encourages liquidity because there are many diverse avenues of demand. This liquidity can help investors to manage their risk and optimize their investment portfolios, which can lead to higher returns over time.

4.1.2 How to Define a Profitable Blockchain

A blockchain can be thought of as a business that generates revenue through transactions that occur on the blockchain and incurs costs by paying to secure the blockchain. This profit and loss can be simplified into an understanding of demand for that chain's native tokens versus supply. Demand for the token stems from the need to pay for transaction using that blockchain's native cryptocurrency, whereas supply comes in the form of token inflation, newly generated tokens, that is transmitted to nodes or miners who secure the network. Therefore, a profitable blockchain is one where the fees generated from transactions exceed the cost of issuing new tokens. Over the long run, transactions must cover the costs of maintaining the network or the value of the tokens will continue to decline due to sell pressure from nodes and miners who receive inflationary tokens.

The cost of issuing new tokens can vary depending on the blockchain's consensus mechanism, how new it is, and the amount of computing power required to maintain the network. Generally, newer blockchains must give away larger shares of its ownership, in the form of inflationary tokens, to secure the network. Regardless, to be profitable, the cost of issuing new tokens should be less than the fees generated from transactions. Perhaps the most important factor to consider when evaluating the profitability of a blockchain is its user adoption. A blockchain with a large, more active user base is more likely to generate higher transaction fees, which can help to offset the cost of issuing new tokens. Conversely, a blockchain with a small user base may struggle to generate enough transaction fees to cover its costs, making it less profitable in the long run.

The simple model of transaction revenue versus security issuance costs is a good first-order understanding of blockchain profitability. However, the picture is clouded by the fact that blockchains can derive revenue from other sources besides transactions. One of the most important sources of revenue is MEV, or maximal extractable value, which allows blockchain users the ability to pay to receive a higher priority in the transaction execution queue. This is analogous to highways that allow drivers to pay for a less congested fast lane or stock exchanges that charge high-frequency traders for the right to locate their server's closest to the exchange trade execution engine. Being first is valuable, and blockchains can extract more profit by putting certain transactions in front and charging users for that privilege. Likewise, on the cost side, blockchains also issue tokens to foundations who maintain the chain. Also, others argue that the costs of a blockchain should extend to the profit and loss statements of the business entities behind the miners or nodes who provide blockchain security.

4.1.3 Using Discounted Cash Flows

To value a token, it is possible to use a traditional DCF model to estimate the long-term income stream generated by the token. This involves estimating the future cash flows generated by the token, and discounting them back to their present value to account for the time value of money.

The first step in this process is to estimate the future cash flows generated by the token. This can be done by analyzing the underlying blockchain's economics as well as the entity or group of individuals that issues the token. Factors to consider may include the growth rate of the blockchain, the level of user adoption, the types of applications most suitable to run on each blockchain, and the eventual fees generated from such transactions. Cash flows can come from transaction fees, staking rewards, MEV, and token buybacks.

Once the future cash flows have been estimated, they can be discounted back to their present value using a discount rate. The discount rate should reflect the opportunity cost of investing in the token, and may be influenced by factors such as the volatility of the token price, regulatory risk, and the risks of technical failures or hacking.

4.2 Value Capturing in Crypto: Market Dynamics

Building a great technological solution is not enough to win in the market. To succeed, a business or a protocol must understand and navigate the complex market dynamics. A product is the combination of technology, product, user acquisition, distribution channels, and target market. Recognizing high-value capture points in the market is crucial, such as owning the end-user relationship, which enables businesses to capture more value and have more leverage. The interplay among different players in the market is an essential consideration when building the right product or deciding to start a company. Understanding where the users are coming from, how the market has evolved, and what other market participants will do is vital. Product building requires bottom-up thinking, which involves understanding who the users are and the problems they face. However, it is equally crucial to consider all other players in the market, how they are trying to solve problems for users, and how they interplay with each other. The subsequent analysis is derived from a lecture by Avichal Garg of Electric Capital, which was presented at the University of Berkeley's Web 3 MOOC on Entrepreneurship in Web3.

4.2.1 Things to Be Learned from Web2

Market dynamics play out in every industry, and different players in the market are trying to solve problems for users. This supply chain or value chain exists in every market, and the relationship between the participants in the chain determines who captures the value, and ultimately, the profits. The businesses that own the end-user relationship are at one end, while high-capital expense technology businesses or platforms, such as AWS, are at the other end. The u-shape relationship in the market determines who captures all the value. High-value capture businesses, such as Netflix, Tesla, and AWS, capture most of the value, while people in the middle get squeezed (Figure 4.1).

Market structures are not fair, and different parts of the market have varying amounts of leverage over others. The people at the high-value capture points use their advantages to retain their business's pricing power, margin, and profit. The severe dynamic market requires businesses to move to the high-value capture points to succeed. Disney's launch of Disney Plus

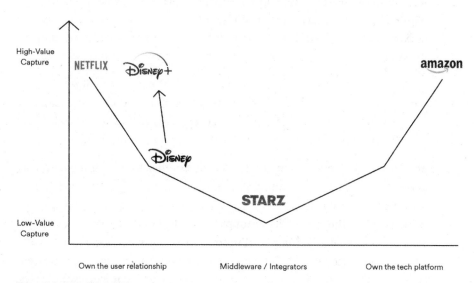

Figure 4.1: Value chain in Web2.
Source: MarketVector.

is a perfect example of this. To compete with Netflix, it needs to have leverage over the rest of the supply chain and own the end-user relationship, which is where all the value capture and high-margin business is. Netflix is going to try to commoditize everybody that comes below it in the market. The company squeezes people in the middle, and this is where the unfair market structures start to come into play. Even if you have the world's best content, if you ultimately must go through Netflix to distribute it, you are not in a great position. The same thing happens if you are building some sort of open-source software that will ultimately run on AWS. AWS has all the pricing power as many open-source products have gone through this unfortunate realization.

4.2.2 High-Value Capture Points in Web3

The world of crypto is dynamic, and many protocols are trying to move up the value chain to capture high-value points. The same methodology of a value chain that exists in any market can be applied in the crypto industry. At one end of the curve are high-value capture businesses such as Coinbase and Binance, while at the other end are Bitcoin and Ethereum. Between them lies a full supply chain. For example, companies such as CoinGecko and CoinMarketCap must start building liquidity and owning the end-user relationship to capture more value. To be clear, while being a data provider is not an unfavorable business, in order to achieve maximum value capture, the provider must shift towards the left-hand side of the curve (Figure 4.2).

To be successful in the crypto industry, a company must move up the curve and capture higher-value points. For instance, Polkadot, Near, and Cosmos must start competing with Ethereum and become the de facto Layer 1 that everyone wants to build their products on top of.

Similarly, Uniswap is moving up the left side of the curve, building end-user applications because the protocol is not allowing it to capture enough value. To have a defensible basis, the company needs to capture the high strategic value point in the curve. For example, it could build an end-user application and a mobile app. Many DeFi protocols struggle to capture high token value because they lack a direct relationship with users. This is unlike centralized exchanges, which benefit from better user interfaces, experiences, and support. Furthermore, open-source protocols are easily replicated.

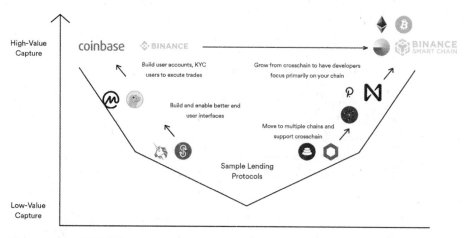

Figure 4.2: Value chain in Web3.
Source: MarketVector.

Without the ability to maintain a direct relationship with users, it becomes challenging to preserve pricing power.

The curve also has some potential predictive power. Binance's launch of the smart contract platform BNB was a clever move because it gave them two high-value leverage points in the curve. The company also acquired CoinMarketCap to take out a competitor below it and gain even more leverage. Similarly, Coinbase has expanded its scope of services. With the launch of its Layer 2 network, Base, it has transitioned from merely being a cryptocurrency exchange to also managing a blockchain layer on top of Ethereum, tapping into another high-value segment. Knowing who has leverage over whom is essential in the crypto industry, and understanding the positioning of a business in the curve is critical in building a successful product. Without leverage, a product that solves an important problem may still fail if it is at the bottom of the curve.

The Crucial Role of Metrics

By Token Terminal

Startups often thrive during technological platform shifts, like blockchains, that provide a new computing platform and modify the business model for Web2 companies by making data open. Blockchain technology enables the creation of global, open, and shared databases, which used to be the domain of traditional businesses. This allows entrepreneurs to build their businesses on blockchain without reliance on traditional companies.

Blockchain applications are expected to outperform their predecessors due to their auditability, cost-efficiency, and distribution. As internet-native services, they are globally accessible, competing worldwide from the onset. They are also fully auditable, with real-time activity tracking, and accessible to anyone with an internet connection.

The functioning of blockchains and decentralized applications resembles traditional marketplace businesses. With supply-side participants (like Ethereum validators) offering services to the demand side, and token holders owning and operating the blockchain or decentralized application, earning revenue from user fees.

Crypto projects generally fall into three categories. (1) Blockchains like Ethereum and Solana, which are open, global application platforms available to anyone who pays transaction fees. (2) Decentralized applications like Aave and Uniswap, which are separate applications comprising smart contracts running on an underlying blockchain. (3) Application-specific blockchains like Osmosis and dYdX, which only run one decentralized application, typically employed by mature projects that want to control the platform their application runs on.

For the first five years, at a time when the crypto market was mostly comprised of Bitcoin, the metrics that investors used to assess the market were often related to price, supply, miner decentralization, and so on. With the launch of Ethereum, a general-purpose application platform, and the subsequent rise of DeFi and NFTs, the metric that many investors came to rely on was total value locked or TVL. TVL represents the value of assets locked in a project's smart contracts, but a high TVL does not by default mean that a project is performing well from a business perspective.

More recently, as both the DeFi and NFT projects have gained more use, we have started to see fundamental metrics emerge onchain. Metrics such as trading volume, active loans, assets

How do crypto protocols make money?

	Uber	Uniswap	Aave	Lido	OP
Build	Build a platform that seamlessly connects drivers to riders	Build a platform that seamlessly connects LPs to traders	Build a platform that seamlessly connects lenders to borrowers	Build a platform that seamlessly connects stakers to PoS blockchains	Build a platform that seamlessly connects L1 validators to L2 users
Charge	Convince riders to pay a fee for the great service that they get	Convince traders to pay a fee for the great service that they get	Convince borrowers to pay a fee for the great service that they get	Convince PoS blockchains to pay a fee for the great service that they get	Convince L2 users to pay a fee for the great service that they get
Capture	Capture a % of those fees for Uber Inc.	Capture a % of those fees for Uniswap DAO	Capture a % of those fees for Aave DAO	Capture a % of those fees for Lido DAO	Capture a % of those fees for OP DAO
Pass on	Pass on the rest of the fees to the drivers	Pass on the rest of the fees to the LPs	Pass on the rest of the fees to the lenders	Pass on the rest of the fees to the stakers	Pass on the rest of the fees to the L1 validators

Table 4.1: Web2 versus Web3 Business Models.
Source: TokenTerminal. Business models for Uber, Uniswap (exchange protocol), Aave (lending protocol), Lido (staking protocol) & Optimism (L2 scaling solution built on Ethereum).

staked, fees, revenue, earnings, and so on represent data that directly speaks about the financial performance of a blockchain or decentralized application. As a result, we have now seen the first iteration of income statements based on onchain data get built on Token Terminal.* As a result of their strong financial performance, these projects have also been at the forefront of designing open-source governance and value distribution mechanisms. Over time, we expect the open-source nature of these organizations to result in high governance and operating standards, and provide unique participation opportunities for a diverse set of stakeholders.

Token Terminal is a platform that aggregates financial and alternative data on blockchains and decentralized applications that run on blockchains.

4.3 Due Diligence: The Importance of Digital Asset Vetting

From early 2020 to 2023, the total market capitalization of digital assets went from approximately $200 billion to a peak of about $3 trillion in late 2021, before retracing back to the $1 trillion range. This move raised mainstream awareness and increased institutional investors' interest. However, as the volatility shows, digital assets are not without their own unique risks. The overwhelming and ever-expanding number of digital assets, their open-source nature, and regulatory ambiguity all contribute to the need for a comprehensive diligence process.

A robust digital asset vetting process allows institutional market participants to understand an asset's unique risks, potential value, and regulatory standing. In the subsequent section, we detail key factors institutional investors should assess to understand a digital asset's risks and potential value.

4.3.1 Key Digital Asset Vetting Factors

By Marco Manoppo

Marco Manoppo is the Research Director of Digital Asset Research (DAR), a specialized provider of "clean" digital asset data, insights, and research for institutional clients. Prior to DAR, Manoppo was an analyst at Digital Capital

Management, a San-Diego–based crypto hedge fund. Manoppo also has prior experience as an angel investor and consultant for crypto token projects.

Token Use Cases, Economics, and Supply-Demand Dynamics

One unique attribute of digital assets is their ability to have multiple use cases. Unlike traditional equities that represent ownership and voting rights in a company, digital asset use cases are defined in their code and can vary to include functionality like securing a blockchain network, owning a certain percentage of a protocol's revenue, holding protocol governance rights, or more. Gaining an understanding of how and why a digital asset is used is an important step in vetting the asset. Relatedly, understanding a digital asset token's economics or "tokenomics," including how the token was initially launched and distributed, is crucial for assessing the asset's long-term sustainability. A digital asset's supply-demand mechanism will also affect its circulating supply and inflation rate, which are factors that can potentially impact its price.

For example, Ethereum completed its "Merge" upgrade in September 2022 (see Figure 4.3), which fully transitioned the network's consensus mechanism from proof-of-work to proof-of-stake. The upgrade changed

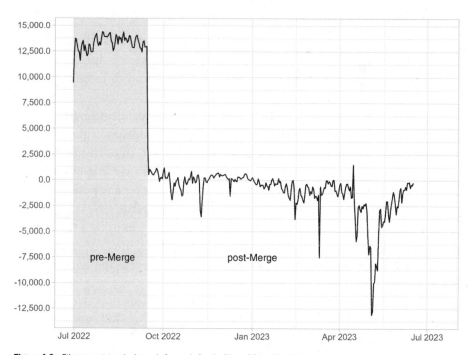

Figure 4.3: Ethereum net supply change before and after the "Merge." Data: MarketVector.

the way new ETH is issued, and as a result, the supply rate for ETH decreased, which resulted in a lower inflation rate.[1]

Technology and Cryptographic Standards

Digital assets rely on their underlying technology and cryptographic standards to ensure security, scalability, and performance. To vet an asset, it is critical to understand how its underlying blockchain or distributed ledger technology (DLT) works. Factors such as permission requirements, transaction speed, energy efficiency, and interoperability with other blockchain networks are important considerations when assessing an asset's potential longevity, safety, or possible investment growth.

Additionally, assessing the cryptographic standards used to secure an asset's network to determine if they meet current best practices set by organizations such as the National Institute of Standards and Technology (NIST) is a key step in identifying potential vulnerabilities. For example, Ethereum utilizes the Elliptic Curve Digital Signature Algorithm (ECDSA), which is a NIST-approved signature algorithm; whereas Solana, a newer asset than Ethereum, utilizes an EdDSA signature algorithm, which is based on a newer elliptic curve[2] that the NIST only adopted as of February 2023.

Codebase Assessment

A secure and well-maintained codebase is important for the success of a digital asset. Unlike traditional software, the smart contracts used by digital assets have unique properties that make it much more difficult to change their underlying code after it is published. To assess a digital asset's codebase, check that the asset has undergone independent smart contract audits from reputable firms and addressed any codebase vulnerabilities. The asset should also be taking active measures to further ensure its safety, possibly including incentivizing white hat hackers via bug bounties, or engaging third-party intelligence firms to monitor for any potential loopholes in the codebase. For example, a proposal to update Aave's risk parameters was submitted to the protocol's governance forum by a third-party risk management firm. As a DeFi lending protocol, it is critical for Aave to have monitoring for its risk parameters to prevent the accumulation

---

1 The reduction in supply is, of course, not related to the move from proof-of-work to proof-of-stake. It is the result of another protocol change that took place with the merge.

2 In the context of cryptology, an *elliptic curve* refers to the application of elliptic curve mathematics to create a robust public key cryptography system, which provides strong security with relatively small keys, making transactions more efficient and faster.

of bad debt. A bad debt can occur if a malicious actor tries to game the lending-borrowing system; such an event happened in November 2022.

Validation and Consensus Mechanism

The consensus mechanism and validation process are core to the security of a digital asset's network, as well as the network's capability to scale and resist attacks. Evaluating the consensus mechanism (such as proof-of-work or proof-of-stake) that an asset's network uses and considering related tradeoffs among security, decentralization, scalability, and energy efficiency are important when vetting a digital asset. Often, founders and original investors have a high level of control over newer assets, which adds an element of centralization and counterparty risk. When vetting a digital asset, it is important to evaluate if there is enough validator (or miner) diversity to ensure that the blockchain network is not susceptible to bad actors or collusion among participants. For example, Solana is a newer blockchain network than Ethereum. As of March 2023, the top 54 Solana validators control more than 50% of the network (see Figure 4.4).

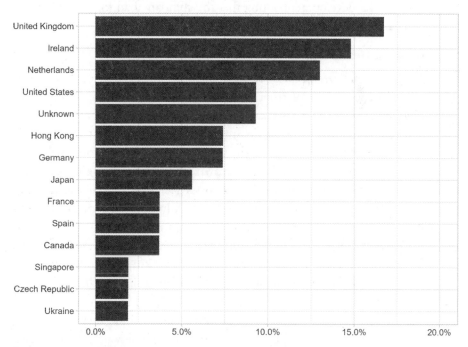

Figure 4.4: Geographic breakdown of Solana's top 54 validators that, in sum, control more than 50% of the network. Source: https://solanabeach.io/validators.

By contrast, Ethereum hit over 500,000 validators as of January 2023. As a best practice, the number of validators should increase as a network decentralizes.

Regulatory Compliance

As a new and digital-first asset class, digital assets must navigate a complex and evolving cross-jurisdictional regulatory landscape. Market participants from all over the world can interact in on-chain digital asset markets, which means that digital assets are exposed to regulatory requirements globally. Issuers of digital assets need to understand the legal landscape extremely well and ensure compliance with regulations. As part of asset vetting, evaluating a project's legal strategy and its approach to addressing potential regulatory issues is crucial. In addition, it is important to consider whether an asset's use cases might draw scrutiny from regulators, with revenue sharing and stablecoin mechanisms drawing the most attention from regulators historically. For example, the U.S. Securities and Exchange Commission (SEC) charged LBRY for conducting an unregistered sale of "crypto asset securities." The SEC won the case, and LBRY was unable to continue its development, citing that the company had to pay millions of dollars in legal fees.

Network Health and Decentralization

The goal of any permissionless blockchain network is to decentralize. For instance, the founder of Ethereum, Vitalik Buterin, no longer has controlling power over the network. Although Buterin has a strong reputation and following, at this point his influence and impact over Ethereum is dependent on his work. A healthy and decentralized network is vital for the long-term sustainability and growth potential of a digital asset. As part of asset vetting, evaluate the network's decentralization by examining factors such as the distribution of token holdings, node distribution, and its governance structure. Often, a blockchain network might look like it has been decentralizing, but the ultimate owners of the underlying tokens might only be a small number of groups; this is akin to an individual who obfuscates corporate ownership via shell companies. Additionally, it is critical to assess the network's robustness by looking at metrics such as transaction density, cliques, and network paths. These metrics provide insight into how value is being transferred in the network. A decentralized blockchain network should have decentralized network metrics.

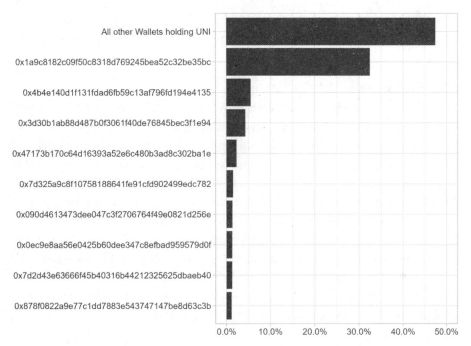

Figure 4.5: Top 10 wallets holding UNI tokens (share of total supply).
Source: Digital Asset Research.

For example, the top 10 richest wallets for Ethereum hold ~28.94% of ETH's total supply, while the top 10 richest wallets for Uniswap hold ~52.61% of UNI's total supply as of 17 May 2023 (see Figure 4.5).

Asset Vetting Takeaways

As institutional market participants increasingly explore digital assets, a rigorous vetting process is essential to assess the strength and legitimacy of an asset. By carefully evaluating factors related to token use cases, tokenomics, technology, cryptography, codebase construction, regulatory compliance, and decentralization, institutional participants can make informed decisions and minimize their risks when interacting with this emerging asset class.

4.3.2 Case Study: Terra LUNA

Terra, a popular blockchain platform, experienced a catastrophic setback when its UST stablecoin destabilized and lost its peg in 2022. UST was designed to maintain a 1:1 peg to the U.S. dollar, but lost its peg due to a death spiral caused by its stability mechanism, resulting in billions of dollars in losses for investors.

Background

Terra is a blockchain network with a dual native token system. LUNA, the network's native token, serves as the governance and gas token powering the underlying blockchain network. UST, the network's native stablecoin, is algorithmically pegged to LUNA via an arbitrage mechanism. The relationship between LUNA and UST was that 1 UST could always be redeemed for $1 worth of LUNA, regardless of the current market price of LUNA. When the price of UST went below $1, investors could buy UST for less than $1, exchange it for $1 worth of LUNA, and sell LUNA in the open market for profit. Additionally, the supply of LUNA was elastic. As a result, when the price of UST decreased, new LUNA was issued and sold on the open market by arbitrageurs. This loop caused the price of LUNA to further drop, leading to a death spiral.

The UST Stablecoin Failure

UST's algorithmic design was the primary factor that caused its failure. The mechanism relied on LUNA as collateral to support UST's value, but the value of LUNA was highly volatile. This volatility undermined the stability of UST, and eventually led to a rush to exit that turned into a death spiral. What happened to LUNA was a combination of a traditional bank run combined with a circular looping mechanism that led to a loss of value for both LUNA and UST.

How Digital Asset Vetting Could Have Helped

A comprehensive digital asset vetting process would have included a thorough examination of the supply-demand dynamics of the LUNA token. Through asset vetting, market participants would have learned about:

- Potential risks associated with the nature of the LUNA asset's issuance. A deep evaluation of the digital asset space would have also shown that similar concepts had not been successful previously.
- A lack of transparency in Terra's governance structure. The capital that was raised to defend the 1:1 peg might have not been utilized appropriately.
- Demand for UST being artificially inflated via Anchor protocol, an entity that was associated with the team behind Terra, which promised a 20% annual yield on a stablecoin that was supposedly pegged to the U.S. dollar.

Conclusion

The failure of Terra's UST stablecoin serves as a reminder of the importance of thorough due diligence and digital asset vetting for institutional market participants. By carefully examining a digital asset's supply-demand dynamics and governance structure, market participants can better understand potential pitfalls and make informed decisions about whether to interact with a particular digital asset. In the case of Terra LUNA's UST stablecoin, a rigorous vetting process could have helped investors identify the red flags in its algorithmic design, the lack of transparency surrounding its governance, and potential liquidity challenges.

4.3.3 Case Study: XRP

A lawsuit between Ripple Labs Inc. (Ripple), the company behind the XRP (XRP) digital asset, and the SEC is one of the most important ongoing events in the digital asset regulatory space. In December 2020, the SEC filed a complaint against Ripple, alleging that the company had conducted a $1.3 billion unregistered securities offering.

Background

The XRP digital asset was created in 2012 by Ripple Labs to facilitate cross-border transactions. Proceeds from XRP's sale were used to fund Ripple's operational activities as the firm developed its Ripple payment network. Over time, XRP became one of the top digital assets, often ranking in the top 10 largest digital assets by market capitalization. The SEC alleged that the sales of XRP met the four prongs of the framework for an investment contract laid out in 1946 case *SEC v. W.J. Howey Co.*, 328 U.S. 293. In that case, the U.S. Supreme Court found that an investment contract means a contract whereby "[1] a person invests his money [2] in a common enterprise and is led to [3] expect profit [4] solely from the efforts of" others. Here, the SEC has argued that Ripple conducted an unregistered securities offering because purchasers of XRP relied on Ripple's efforts to increase the value of XRP.

The XRP Case and Its Implications

The legal case between Ripple and the SEC is ongoing, but its outcome will have significant consequences for both the company and the broader digital asset space.

Following the SEC's complaint, many exchanges delisted XRP from their platforms, causing its price to plummet. A decision that is unfavorable to

Ripple could cause XRP's price to fall again as well as create consequences for other digital assets with similar mechanisms and issuance models to XRP. A decision against Ripple might also mean that notable crypto exchanges have been facilitating the transaction of unregistered securities.

Whatever the outcome of the *Ripple* case is, it will set a precedent that will likely impact digital assets and how they are viewed by regulators globally.

How Digital Asset Vetting Could Have Helped

The definition of what makes a digital asset a security from a legal and regulatory perspective is the most important unanswered question in the crypto industry. However, a comprehensive digital asset vetting process would have included a thorough examination of the XRP token's issuance mechanism, which is one of the factors critical to that analysis. Through digital asset vetting, market participants would have been aware of:

- Potential risks related to how XRP conducted its initial token sale and allocation. Unlike some assets where new supply issuance is controlled by validators, foundations, or strict decentralized governance processes, the entire supply of 100 billion XRP tokens were initially pre-mined. The founders retained around 20 billion XRP while the remaining 80 billion have been continuously sold throughout the years, with Ripple having control over sales.
- Potential risks associated with how new XRP tokens are released into circulation. Unlike Layer 1 blockchain networks such as Ethereum, Ripple has continuously sold XRP, even after the SEC lawsuit. Both ETH and XRP conducted an initial coin offering (ICO), but new ETH can only be received by validators who actively participate in the network; the team behind Ethereum cannot sell additional ETH tokens to the open market. Whereas in Q1 2023, Ripple sold $361 million worth of XRP tokens.

Conclusion

The XRP lawsuit serves as a reminder of the importance of rigorous digital asset vetting for investors in the digital asset space. The nascent nature of the asset class often means that there is currently uncertainty surrounding token security classification and regulatory compliance. By carefully examining how an asset was issued, its ongoing supply-demand mechanisms, and its level of decentralization, investors can better understand potential pitfalls and make more informed decisions about their investments. In the case of XRP, a rigorous vetting process could have helped investors identify red flags surrounding its pre-mining and the issuance mechanisms of new XRP tokens. This information could have helped market participants assess the risk of the token being considered a security and allowed them to weigh the potential consequences of an SEC lawsuit.

As the regulatory environment surrounding digital assets matures, institutional investors must prioritize thorough digital asset vetting processes to adapt to changes, minimize risks, and make well-informed decisions.

4.4 The Network Effect and Metcalfe's Law

As global communication becomes more simplified and affordable, large economic networks have emerged whose importance and market value depend not only on the number of participants, but also on their interconnectedness. The best-known example of such networks is social media. In this section, we explore the concept of network effects and how Robert Metcalfe's Law applies to the value of crypto networks.

Network effects are the phenomenon in which the value and utility of a network increase proportionally as more participants join. A larger network offers more opportunities for interaction and sharing of resources, leading to an overall increase in the network's usefulness. This can be observed in many products and services such as social media platforms. Similarly, in the case of messaging apps or video conferencing software, the more people using the platform, the more communication and collaboration opportunities are available to users. So overall, the value of a network does not just depend on the quantity of its users, but also on the degree of interconnection among them, which enhances the usefulness, and consequently, the worth of the network.

4.4.1 The History of Metcalfe's Law

Robert Metcalfe, one of the co-inventors of Ethernet and co-founder of network equipment manufacturer 3Com Corporation, was the first to popularize the concept of network effects. The Ethernet provided the technological basis for networking computers in a local area network. For the first time, computers could share resources such as memory or peripheral devices and exchange data without additional media via a cable. The company 3Com developed and manufactured the network cards required for this.

Metcalfe's Law describes how the utility and potential value of a network change as the number of subscribers increases. According to Metcalfe, the cost of building a network increases proportionally to the number of users, while the benefit and thus the value of the network increases proportionally to the square of the number of participants. This measure of the maximum connectivity of all network participants was the first version of Metcalfe's Law. The number of all possible connections in a network with N nodes is $N * (N - 1)$, and thus, for large numbers approximately N^2.[3] The impact of Metcalfe's Law can be seen in the example of Ethernet cards. In the beginning, potential customers were hesitant to invest in expensive Ethernet cards, as it was not clear why they should spend so much money on them. To address this issue, Metcalfe drew a diagram (see Figure 4.6) that showed the relationship between the cost of building a network and the benefit derived from it.

According to Metcalfe's Law, the benefit of a network with 10 participants (100) is four times higher than the benefit of a network with 5 participants (25).

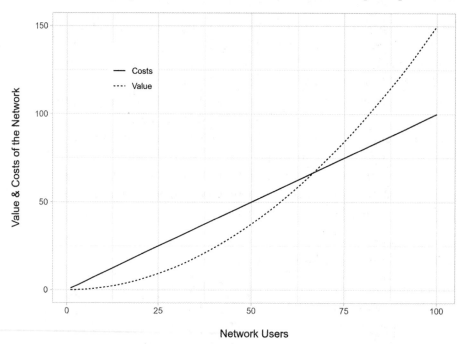

Figure 4.6: Development of costs and benefits of a network.

3   See Briscoe, Odlyzko, and Tilly (2006).

As the number of participants continues to increase, the benefit of the network exceeds the costs, and the value of the network rises sharply. As it was only possible to use Ethernet with the appropriate equipment, 3Com's sales staff, and eventually its customers, followed this reasoning, and sales of Ethernet cards rose from a few hundred to several million. This strategy helped 3Com gain popularity. The company was eventually listed on Nasdaq and later acquired by Hewlett-Packard.

Network effects and Metcalfe's Law are essential concepts for understanding the value of interconnected networks. As networks continue to grow and become more complex, their value will continue to increase exponentially. As professional investors, it is important to recognize the potential value of these networks and invest accordingly.

4.4.2 Metcalfe's Law and Facebook: Modeling the Value of Social Networks

A revised version of Metcalfe's Law was presented in a 2013 paper by Metcalfe himself, coinciding with the anniversary of Ethernet. The original model, which assumed that all nodes in a network could communicate with each other, was criticized for its quadratic and nondecreasing growth of network utility. Metcalfe's modified approach incorporated a function that considers the number of participants in contact, solving the issue of unrealistic assumptions.

This function, which follows an S-shaped progression, is based on the sigmoid or Gompertz function commonly used in biological models of population growth (see Figure 4.7). In his evaluation of Facebook using this modified model, Metcalfe was able to provide a more accurate representation of the network's value. This approach offers a more nuanced understanding of network effects.

The modified version of Metcalfe's Law accounts for the diminishing returns of additional participants when a network is already extensively connected. This places a limit on the network effect, and ultimately, on the network's overall value. To accurately model this effect over time, Metcalfe chose to use the sigmoid function, which is well-suited to capturing the impact of increasing saturation. This is crucial, as even a network has its limits and the contribution of each individual user gradually diminishes until it becomes insignificant. Using a regression model, future values can

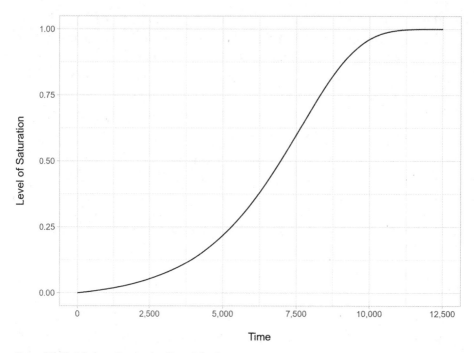

Figure 4.7: Modeling a growth process by a Gompertz function.

be forecasted based on just a few years of data, as shown in Figure 4.8. Such insights are particularly valuable for institutional investors that are seeking to make informed decisions in an early stage.

While impressive, evaluations of this nature must be approached with caution. There is a risk of adjusting model parameters to achieve an almost perfect fit with existing data, which can be tempting for some. While optimizing model parameters can be useful, overuse can result in unstable models that lack any predictive value. As such, it is important to strike a balance between optimizing models and ensuring that they are not overfitted to historical data.

4.4.3 Metcalfe's Law and Bitcoin

> "Apple is a mobile network, Google is a search network, Facebook is a social network, Bitcoin is a monetary network. All benefit from advances in software & hardware technology, as well as Metcalfe's law. Many understand the former, few understand the latter."
> Michael Saylor, CEO MicroStrategy

Metcalfe's Law can be used to predict the price of Bitcoin in the same way that sales on Facebook can be predicted. Unlike Facebook, where

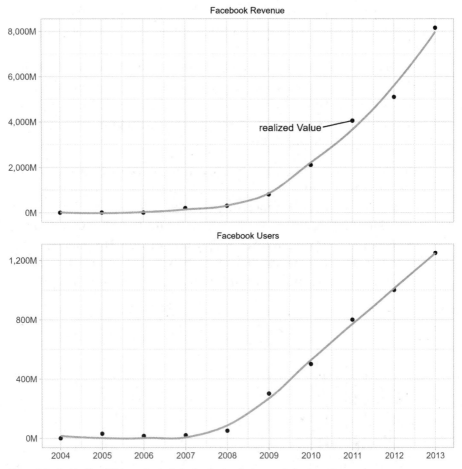

Figure 4.8: Applying Metcalfe's Law to Facebook. Predicted and realized revenue and user growth.

users have user accounts, Bitcoin users manage their Bitcoin addresses directly. This direct connection between the valuation of the network and the users through their ownership of tokens makes the network more susceptible to price fluctuations caused by speculation.

While the interest of token owners in the network's steady growth has a stabilizing effect, the direct connection also attracts users with a purely speculative interest who may not be concerned with the network's long-term development. This increases the likelihood of significant price changes, both upward and downward. Even a broad global acceptance of a crypto network may not fully mitigate this effect. This makes it challenging for alternative networks to attract new users, even if they offer technical improvements.

In terms of acceptance, and thus, also of attracting new users, the largest networks always have the best starting position.[4] The development of new technologies and improvements can require a great deal of patience, as evidenced by the various hard forks of the Bitcoin Blockchain, including Bitcoin Cash and Bitcoin SV. Despite technical advancements, the adoption of Bitcoin PoS, a low-energy version of Bitcoin utilizing proof-of-stake instead of the proof-of-work algorithm, has not gained significant user traction (see Figure 4.9).

The Bitcoin PoS white paper highlights the weaknesses of the original Bitcoin version and presents solutions. This new version boasts three times faster transaction processing and a 99% reduction in power consumption, making the network more resistant to 51% attacks. Similar to Bitcoin, the maximum token supply is limited to 21 million. Despite interesting features, the adoption of this new variant remains limited and it does not pose a significant threat to the largest network, like previous

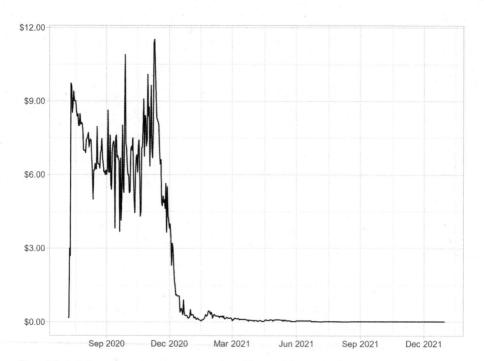

Figure 4.9: Lack of acceptance and resulting price development of Bitcoin PoS. Data: MarketVector.

4   See Arthur (2010).

hard forks. This highlights the dynamic and evolutionary nature of crypto assets, which can be modified within the technical restrictions of the protocol. Users are unlikely to switch to a newcomer network simply because it appears more attractive in some aspects, but instead prefer existing networks that adapt gradually through software adjustments.

The data basis for the application of the Metcalfe model to Bitcoin is available to everyone due to the transparency of the blockchain. The number of unique addresses are needed as an approximation for the number of users and the history of the Bitcoin price. The reference currency is the U.S. dollar (Figure 4.10). The number of addresses serves as an approximation for the number of users, but this is a very rough estimate, since each user can use any number of addresses. A detailed derivation of the model can be found in the publications of Timothy F. Peterson of Cane Island Alternative Advisors.[5]

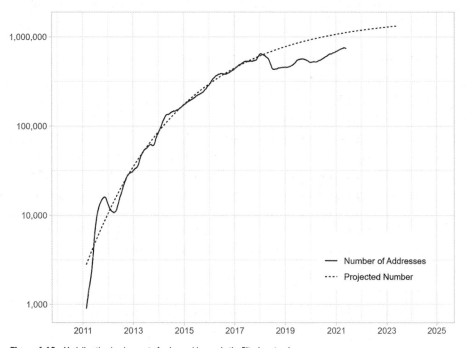

Figure 4.10: Modeling the development of unique addresses in the Bitcoin network.

---

5   See Peterson (2018).

While the theoretical background of the Metcalfe model is more solid than that of the stock-to-flow model,[6] there is well-founded criticisms of this approach as well.

4.4.4 Q&A with Timothy Peterson, Cane Island Research

Timothy Peterson is well known and respected as one of the industry's leading experts on alternative investments. He is a published expert on crypto-currency investment and valuation, having authored the first peer-reviewed article on valuing Bitcoin as a network: "Metcalfe's Law as a Model for Bitcoin's Value" (Alternative Investment Analyst Review, *2018), as well as the book* Performance Measurement for Alternative Investments *(London: Risk, 2015). Peterson speaks frequently at investment conferences and universities around the world on digital asset valuation and other investment topics.*

Peterson has over 25 years in global investment experience, and is a Chartered Financial Analyst, Chartered Alternative Investment Analyst, and holds an M.S. Finance (honors), and B.A. Economics from the University of Colorado.

Q. How Well Does Metcalfe's Law Explain the Value of the Bitcoin Network?

A. Network economics is an emerging field within the information society. Its premise is that products and services are created—and value is added—through networks operating on large or global scales. The tenet is that large networks have more value than small networks by offering greater access to trading partners (liquidity), error detection, and information sharing. This result is pricing power, and eventually, monopolistic dominance. We have seen this in telecommunications companies (Bell), software (Microsoft), social media (Facebook), and even transportation networks like the Roman Roads in Europe or the 19th-century British Fleet.

This value principle stands in sharp contrast to industrial-era economies, in which ownership of physical or intellectual property originates from a

---

6 The stock-to-flow (S2F) model is a method used to predict the price of assets like Bitcoin and other commodities such as gold and silver. It focuses on the ratio of the existing stock of an asset (stock) against its production rate (flow). The underlying principle is that the value of these assets increases as they become scarcer, which is often due to a lower production rate.

single enterprise. Metcalfe's Law, which is closely tied to Shannon Information Theory, quantifies value creation and sharing over networks of all types: the value of a network is proportional to the square of the number of users (or nodes).

For example, Google economist Hal Varian attributed the value and dominance of the U.S. dollar to network effects. Metcalfe's Law applies just as equally to telephone networks such as Bell Telephone in the 1920s as it does to Tesla's supercharging network in the 2020s.

Bitcoin's value is determined by network effects which can be measured using Metcalfe's Law (see Figure 4.11). Metcalfe's Law explains the long-term (periods of 1 year or more) value trend and price elasticity explains the short-term (periods of less than 12 months) value trend. Prior to 2016, there is no data for off-chain mempool transactions. That data set is an important indicator of short-term demand. Otherwise, since 2016, the model is an exceptional fit as well as a leading indicator.

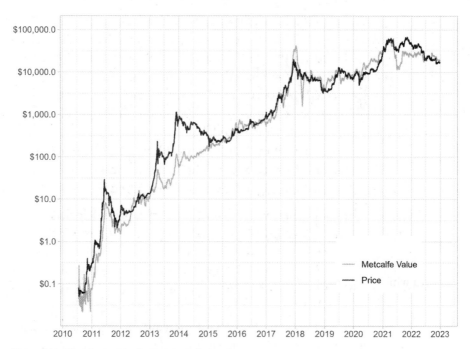

Figure 4.11: Bitcoin's value determined by network effects.
Source: Cane Island Research.

Q. Does Metcalfe's Law fully explain the relationship between the number of Bitcoin users and the value of the network, or are there other factors at play?

A. Models are simplified explanations of what has happened in the past. As such, no model fully captures every factor, let alone every possible outcome. Cane Island's model explicitly incorporates:

a. The size of the network (or more specifically, the growth rate in network size), which is based on an adoption curve.

b. Network use in terms of transaction activity. An unused network has little value; a clogged or impaired network also has a low value proposition.

c. Price elasticity of demand, in other words, the sensitivity of price to high demand periods.

d. Irretrievably lost coins. "Lost coins only make everyone else's coins worth slightly more. Think of it as a donation to everyone." (Satoshi Nakamoto).

e. The level of interest rates in the market. All assets are affected by interest rates and Bitcoin's adoption value is no different. The model value is based on the present value of the future adoption curve. Satoshi Nakamoto wrote: "A rational market price for something that is expected to increase in value will already reflect the present value of the expected future increases. In your head, you do a probability estimate balancing the odds that it keeps increasing" (Satoshi Nakamoto). Information theory states that a diffusion function can estimate that probability, and we find that statistical software works a little better than trying to figure it out in your head.

Of course, there are other things that affect market price. Shocks like the COVID scare in March 2020 affected the price of all assets globally. Humans are irrational and asset prices often reflect emotions. The perception of Bitcoin as a technological innovation creates correlation with technology stocks. And Bitcoin's price has also been subject to manipulation, with the most famous documented case being wash-trading bots operating on the Mt. Gox exchange in 2013. Most of these factors are not able to be modeled or predicted.

Q. What does Metcalfe's Law say about the growth of the network, for example, when the growth accelerates or if network growth slows to zero?

A. Dr. Metcalfe initially did not consider growth rates as part of his model. He only specified that there was a diminishing marginal return per user which he termed *affinity*. Later, he clarified that the number of users follows an *S* curve and reaches a saturation point.

No technology adoption follows a smooth curve. While the multi-year trend may resemble an *S* curve, the actual adoption zigzags along that curve, with periods of slow or zero growth and periods of above average growth.

We can look at the year-over-year growth rate in Bitcoin addresses and see this meandering along the trendline (see Figure 4.12). Also, that growth rate slows over time. This is diminishing marginal returns.

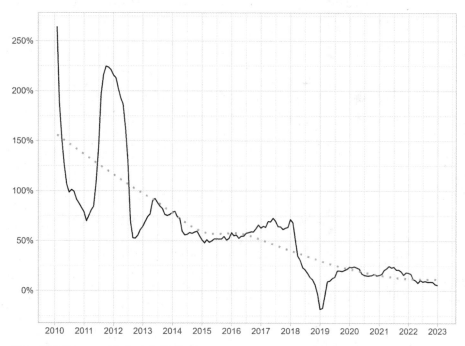

Figure 4.12: Year-over-year growth rate in Bitcoin addresses.
Source: Cane Island Research.

If growth in users slows to zero or falls, the value will do the same. This was evident in the disrupted adoption of the landline telephone in the United States during the Great Depression (see Figure 4.13). Bell Telephone revenues, and its stock price, declined during that time.

This happened again with Bitcoin after Elon Musk tweeted that Tesla would not accept Bitcoin for payment, reversing an earlier position of the company on that matter. Facebook's stock price and revenue reacted similarly when it began to lose users.

It is not a great revelation that value goes up (or down) when users go up (or down). What Metcalfe's Law does is quantify the nature of that relationship. As an estimate, the "Rule of 2" states that

$$\%change\ in\ Value = 2 \times \%change\ in\ Users$$

For those who are mathematically inclined, the "Rule of 2" is the second derivative (the rate of change) of Metcalfe's Law: $d/dx\ [x^2] = 2x$.

If Bitcoin or any other network lost 10% of its users, we would expect value to fall by 20%. But because value is unobservable, price takes time to correct to value.

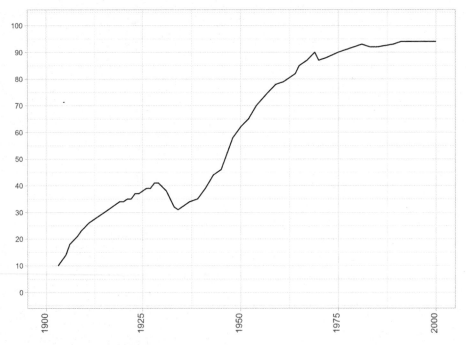

Figure 4.13: Telephone adoption in the United States.
Source: Cane Island Research.

Q. How does the concentration of Bitcoin ownership affect the value of the network under Metcalfe's Law?

A. One would think that large users would have more impact on the value of a network than small users. That is true, but there are more small users than large users. Which is more important: the impact of a few large users or the impact of many small users?

Distributions of wealth—whether ownership of Bitcoin, real estate, personal net worth, or the GDP of nations—are known to follow Zipf's Law. Zipf's Law is often expressed as the "80/20 Rule," for example, 80% of the wealth is held by 20% of the participants. This phenomenon occurs naturally and is found in the distribution of city sizes as well as animal herd sizes. It seems to be the way our universe is wired. Not coincidentally, Zipf's Law is an integral part of Shannon Information Theory (see Figure 4.14).

Because the distribution of Bitcoin ownership follows Zipf's Law, it is possible to calculate the impact of each user or node on network value. The math is very complex (matrix algebra, anyone?), but essentially the many small users have the same impact on network value as the few large users. This is not true in the short term, where "whales" can drive the price up or down. But recall that price is not value. And the price eventually corrects to Metcalfe value based on total number of users, regardless of user size.

Q. Do you apply your model also to Altcoins? Is it useful to distinguish between the valuation models for proof-of-work and proof-of-stake networks?

A. Cane Island has applied Metcalfe's Law to dozens of altcoins as well as traditional electronic payment systems like PayPal and Square. The result is always the same: the value of the network is a function of the square of the number of users, less diminishing marginal returns. It does not matter if the token uses a proof-of-work design or a proof-of-stake design. However, we conducted a statistical analysis of altcoin prices and found that many altcoins simply mimic Bitcoin's price movements, while others seem to exhibit fundamental network effects on their own. For example, the value of Ethereum and ChainLink tokens can be attributed primarily to network size and transaction activity independently, with little influence attributable to Bitcoin's price.

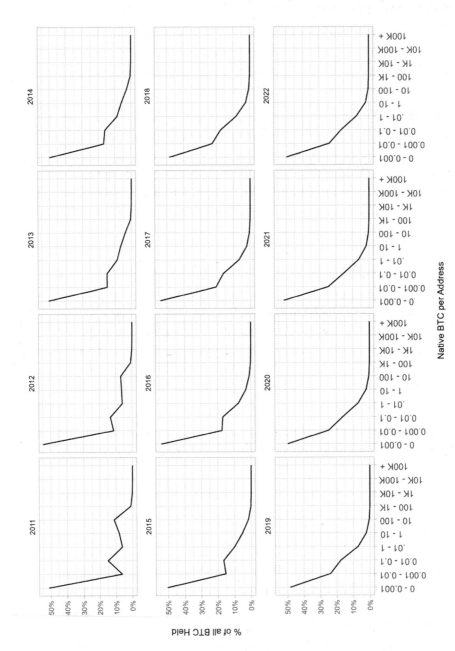

Figure 4.14: Zipf's Law: Distribution of Bitcoin addresses by size since 2011.
Source: Cane Island Research.

Litecoin and Doge, on the other hand, attract speculators based solely on price movements that correlate almost exclusively to Bitcoin's price movements.

4.5 Statistical Valuation Approach

> "It is a capital mistake to theorize before one has data."
> Sir Arthur Conan Doyle

Utilizing the distribution of historical returns is an alternative approach to developing a model that accurately represents the historical price developments and generates useful forecasts. This bootstrapping method uses past realized price changes and adjusts them for the influence of longer-lasting trends by considering the autocorrelation of returns. By concatenating a large set of randomly drawn values from this empirical distribution to form a new yield path, possible developments over the future periods can be determined. This step is repeated frequently to create a multitude of possible future developments, from which key figures such as the mean value of returns or drawdowns, the median, or any percentiles of return and risk key figures can be determined.

An example of this method applied to the daily returns of Bitcoin is shown in Figure 4.15, with the empirical data collection period being two full up and down cycles between January 2015 and November 2022. This approach provides institutional investors with an additional tool to evaluate the potential risks and returns of crypto assets. It is important to note that relying solely on this method or any other approach would be unwise, and further questions must be answered, such as how the best time period for data collection may be determined and which adjustments might be necessary.

Assessing the probability of certain future events, such as the likelihood of future drawdowns, exceeding a target return, or the risk of total loss, can provide valuable insights for institutional investors. These evaluations are particularly informative as they are based on realized returns and indicate the potential risks even without any structural changes in the market. However, the drawback of this approach is that it may not accurately account for the market's reaction to structural changes, which could result in significant market movements in either direction. Despite this limitation, assigning probabilities to potential future developments

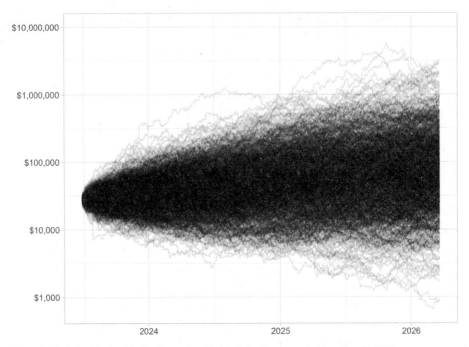

Figure 4.15: Paths of simulated Bitcoin prices produced through the bootstrapping method (as of June 27, 2023). Data: MarketVector.

is a practical and credible approach, as opposed to relying on point forecasts that are often adjusted and not particularly useful. For example, displaying the median path and other percentiles of the simulation results can be helpful (Figure 4.16).

For institutional investors, it is crucial to consider not only desirable scenarios, but also the possibility of undesirable outcomes. Rather than fixating on specific price targets, assessing potential risks is the top priority in a professional setting. This involves considering the path that an asset may take from its starting point to its end point. As important as the final total return may be, for investors it is quite interesting when an asset price rises from 100 to 110, whether it has fallen to 70 or only to 95 in the meantime.

While the median annual performance is 44.3%, looking at the 25th percentile and the 10th percentile with annual returns of 17.4% and 0.02%, respectively, helps ensure that risks are not overlooked. This is especially true considering that this simulation is heavily influenced by the enormous bull market of 2015.

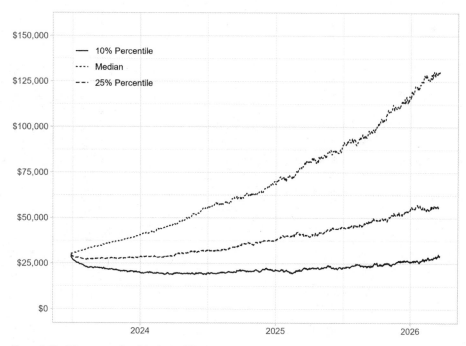

Figure 4.16: Different percentiles of the simulated Bitcoin price paths (as of June 27, 2023). Data: MarketVector.

Using the simulation, it is also possible to determine the probability of experiencing losses at a given point in time based on the data used (see Figure 4.17). As expected, this probability decreases with longer investment durations due to the historical data. This information provides institutional investors with a more complete and nuanced understanding of potential risks associated with crypto asset investments.

Optimizing Investment Risk with Simulations

The ability to accurately predict the extent of losses based on the values shown is limited. In addition to evaluating the probability of a loss, simulations can also be used to determine the probability of achieving a certain target return or range of returns. This is particularly relevant when designing investment guidelines, as it can help to determine the influence of allocation limits.

This simulation only serves to illustrate a possible process. For real risk requirements, the approach would be extended, for example, by integrating the decline in Bitcoin's total returns observed over time with continued high volatility risks. The same applies to the losses that are also

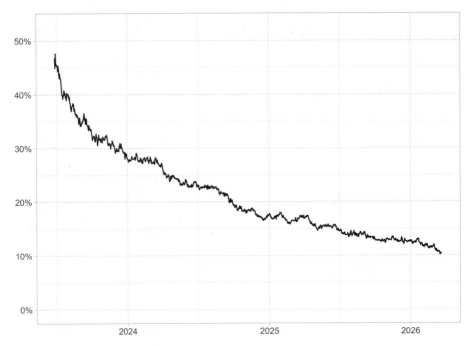

Figure 4.17: Simulation based probability to suffer a loss with (as of June 27, 2023). Data: MarketVector.

possible according to the simulation results, for which, especially in a new asset class, not only the probability of occurrence but also the impact is important.

While simulation methods are not perfect and have been criticized for being too simplistic, proposed alternatives often involve overoptimized models that only accurately represent a certain market for a specific period. Such models may look good in retrospect, but they are not always practical for real-world scenarios. Professional portfolio managers understand the limitations and advantages of simulated returns, and recognize that they are useful and flexible tools, but cannot be relied on as crystal balls.

4.5.1 Concluding Thoughts on Token Valuation

The valuation of financial instruments is often perceived as more of an art than a science, which does not give enough credit to various credible approaches. A hedge fund manager once stated that everything in financial markets could be expressed in terms of discounted cash flows and probabilities. The challenge, and what makes capital markets captivating, lies in the frequent disparity between an asset's perceived fair value and the price that others are willing to pay. This difference fuels the financial markets and offers an immense earnings potential.

Although established markets also experience fluctuations, new markets are especially susceptible to rapid and significant price shifts. Analysts can quickly establish a plausible valuation for stocks or bonds using existing methodologies, but this is more challenging for crypto assets. Valuing an asset is never a simple task, and often sophisticated forecasting methods hold little interest for the capital market. Temporary price developments depend largely on the number of investors following one of several competing models. In the case of crypto assets, the short history and ongoing transformations of existing projects compound the difficulties.

The most straightforward way to value assets is by discounting their cash flows. But as some of the existing crypto tokens totally lack cash flows, Investors simply acquire them with the expectation of reselling them at a higher price later, as is the case with nondividend-paying stocks. Therefore, alternative valuation approaches are needed, some of which have been discussed in this chapter.

4.6 References

Arthur, W. Brian. (2010). *The Nature of Technology: What It Is and How It Evolves*. Penguin.

Briscoe, Bob, Andrew Odlyzko, and Benjamin Tilly. (2006). "Metcalfe's Law Is Wrong—IEEE Spectrum." IEEE Spectrum: Technology, Engineering, and Science News. https://spectrum.ieee.org/computing/networks/metcalfes-law-is-wrong.

Glasner, Joanna. (2022, July 5). "The Case for Going Public Too Early." Crunchbase News. https://news.crunchbase.com/public/ipo-spac-going-public-timing/.

Harper, Colin. (2018). "The Anatomy of Anonymity: How Dandelion Could Make Bitcoin More Private." Bitcoin Magazine: Bitcoin News, Articles, Charts, and Guides. https://bitcoinmagazine.com/culture/anatomy-anonymity-how-dandelion-could-make-bitcoin-more-private.

Peterson, Timothy. (2018). "Metcalfe's Law as a Model for Bitcoin's Value." SSRN Scholarly Paper ID 3078248. Rochester, NY: Social Science Research Network. https://doi.org/10.2139/ssrn.3078248.

5 Cryptos as an Asset Class

> "Compound interest is the eighth wonder of the world. He who
> understands it, earns it, he who doesn't, pays it."
> Albert Einstein

Within just a few years, a new asset class has emerged, with Bitcoin lay-
ing its foundation. Around a multitude of digital tokens, a biotope of new
projects has sprung up, and the professionalization of global trading venues now allows even financial institutions to invest in digital assets.

5.1 Characteristics of an Asset Class

Every financial market participant knows the economist William F.
Sharpe and has already dealt with the results of his work. The economist
was honored in 1990 with the Sveriges Riksbank Prize in Economic Sciences in Memory of Alfred Nobel[1] for his work in developing models to
aid investment decisions. His name is synonymous with the Capital Asset
Pricing Model (CAPM) and one of the best-known risk indicators, the
Sharpe Ratio, is named after him.

Sharpe defined three characteristics that distinguish an asset class:

- Different asset classes must be mutually exclusive. An investment can
  only belong to one asset class.
- An asset class must be comprehensive and include many investments
  in order to enable diversification within the asset class.
- The correlation of returns from different asset classes should be low.

Like so much in economics, the rules sound clearer than their practical
application.

The boundaries between asset classes are often fluid and influenced,
among other things, by the prevailing market regime. For instance, during crisis situations, the character of a hybrid bond resembles that of a
stock, and the correlation of corporate bonds to stocks[2] also depends on

---

1 This prize for outstanding achievements in economics was first awarded in 1969. The Nobel Memorial
   Prize in Economic Sciences is officially known as the Sveriges Riksbank Prize in Economics and is
   administered by the Nobel Foundation.

2 Correlations always refer to the returns of the assets. For better readability, however, we simply refer to
   correlated assets.

the specific rating category and maturity of a bond. A degree of pragmatism is also called for when categorizing crypto assets.

While many digital assets resemble a stock or commodity investment, there are also constructs that differ entirely from conventional asset classes. Due to their structure and the extensive opportunities for diversification within crypto assets, they meet the requirements for a standalone asset class. This is also indicated by the wide range of correlations between individual crypto assets and the low correlations of digital assets with other asset classes. Cryptos are a different kind of animal.

In this chapter, we provide a brief overview of the established asset classes. Afterward, we consider crypto assets and finally examine stocks related to crypto assets as a possible alternative or complement.

5.2 Conventional Asset Classes

The most important and largest asset classes are stocks, bonds, and real estate. Alongside these, gold, which has been used as a store of value for thousands of years, and many alternative investments such as art are used by capital allocators.

When classifying an asset class, it is helpful to look at the global distribution of investment assets. In all discussions about the market value of individual assets, it is striking how many people underestimate the size of the global capital market and overestimate the share of crypto assets. Therefore, it is important to compare compilations of investable asset classes, such as the "Global Market Portfolio" of investable assets (see Figure 5.1).

The categories contained in the portfolio, which do not include many items from the area of alternative investments, amount to more than 250 trillion U.S. dollars.

However, such a view can only provide a rough orientation. On the one hand, different sources give considerably different values for the individual segments. On the other hand, the global real estate market is much larger than the portfolio of investable assets in this segment suggests. As markets fluctuate even in quiet times significantly different values for the global allocation occur merely from the choice of the reference date.

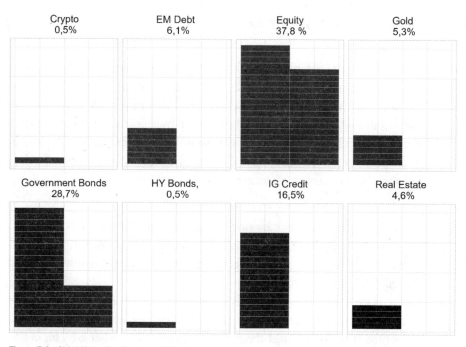

Figure 5.1: Global Market Portfolio. Data: SIFMA, BIS, MarketVektor.

Even after some strong price increases in the past, crypto assets play no significant role in terms of potential risks to the financial system. Currently, the total market value of crypto assets is only at the level of individual heavyweights of the U.S. stock market. Regardless of how one assesses the valuation of Bitcoin and other crypto assets, no systemic threat is imminent from a sector of this weight.

In order to better classify crypto assets into the existing investment world, we will not only consider the size of each asset class as previously shown, but also their historical returns and drawdowns. Furthermore, we will examine the importance of market timing. As can be easily understood, the success of an investor who invests at the peak of an asset class differs from that of one who starts investing after a crash. In addition to charts that encompass the entire time series, we therefore also show the development across many possible paths since the beginning of the time series.

For the long-term considerations, we will exclusively look at real total returns. When considering manageable time periods, nominal returns can be sufficient. However, they can lead to a considerably too positive assessment of investment success over long periods of time, the infamous "money illusion."[3]

The often-heard argument that inflation affects all asset classes is misleading. While it sounds intuitively correct, the loss of purchasing power of the currency hits different asset classes at different phases. For example, the real drawdowns in an asset class can be significantly stronger if inflation hits an existing downtrend. This is the case, for example, with bonds in an inflationary environment. Conversely, these securities benefit disproportionately strongly from a deflationary development and falling interest rates.

In our book, we mainly examine the development of the U.S. markets, which historically have performed best over the long term. While the U.S. markets have had their crashes from time to time, in many other regions there were significantly harsher breakdowns, up to a collapse of the financial system. These financially catastrophic events include unpleasant things like currency collapses, state bankruptcies, and hyperinflations. Therefore, investors should classify the results here as what is by far at the upper end of the range.

5.2.1 Inflation: The Enemy of Wealth

> "Inflation is when you pay fifteen dollars for the ten-dollar haircut you used to get for five dollars when you had hair."
> Sam Ewing

The longer investors look back on the time axis, the more important it is to consider the effect of inflation. The continuous loss of purchasing power, reversed only in the most extreme phases, already leads to noticeable effects on the investment horizons of ordinary small investors, as the compound interest effect also applies to the loss of purchasing power. Since some contemporaries still believe that declining inflation is synonymous with falling prices, it is worth pointing out once again the permanence of the damage of currency devaluation. The purchasing power that is once gone is permanently gone. Anyone who loses 10% of their purchasing power in the current year starts the following year from a lower base. Even a low inflation rate of 2.5% leads to a loss of purchasing power

---

3   See Shafir, Diamond, and Tversky (1997).

of more than 50% over 30 years. Not every asset class can always compensate for this. Often, negative effects even intensify during inflationary phases. This is the case, for example, when bond holders are confronted simultaneously with a high loss of purchasing power and falling prices due to rising yields.

The impact of inflation on the long-term real return of a capital investment is enormous. This is shown, for example, when looking at the nominal as well as the real total return of a broad investment in commodities since the beginning of the 20th century (Figure 5.2).

As impressive as the nominal development of commodities may have been in certain phases, in the long term, and this is quite plausible, commodity prices develop roughly in line with inflation.

For the reasons mentioned, in this chapter, when we take a very long-term look at conventional asset classes, we look at the development of real, that is, inflation-adjusted total returns. Therefore, if some price developments seem uncommon to you, it is because usually only the nominal values are reported. This applies particularly to advertising brochures. Ultimately,

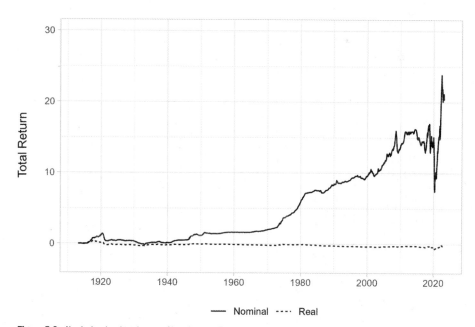

Figure 5.2: Nominal and real total return of broad commodity investments. Data: Ibbotson SSBI® dataset, NorgateData.com.

however, what matters is not only how much money is left after a life of investing, but what you can buy with it.

Neither the absolute development of inflation nor its range of fluctuation is constant (see Figure 5.3). Major economic upheavals, but especially permanent structural changes in the world currency system, have left their mark on the history of inflation. Looking at the 20th and 21st centuries, the gold standard, and its end, as well as the Bretton Woods currency regime and its collapse, are particularly worth mentioning.

In the late 19th and early 20th centuries, the world used a monetary system called the gold standard, in which each country's currency could be exchanged for a predetermined amount of gold. The system provided stability by tying currencies to a tangible asset, which helped limit inflation. However, the rigidity of the gold standard ultimately contributed to its collapse during the Great Depression as countries tried to devalue their currencies to boost exports and promote economic growth.

After World War II, the Bretton Woods system emerged as an international currency framework to again promote the stability of the global economy. Under this system, currencies were pegged to the U.S. dollar,

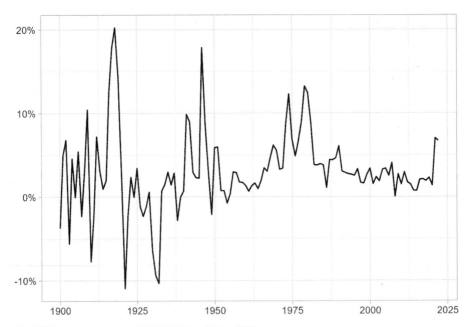

Figure 5.3: Annual rate of change of the U.S. CPI. Data: Ibbotson SBBI®.

which in turn, was convertible into gold at a fixed rate. Although the Bretton Woods system provided stable exchange rates and facilitated international trade, it was not without flaws. The USA, due to the Vietnam War and Social Security programs, faced increasing fiscal pressure, which led to a loss of confidence in the value of the dollar and an increased demand for gold.

The Bretton Woods system officially ended in 1971 when President Richard Nixon "temporarily" suspended the convertibility of the dollar into gold. This marked the beginning of the era of floating exchange rates and fiat currencies, where the value of a currency is determined by market forces and not tied to a commodity or another currency.

The end of the gold standard and the Bretton Woods system had significant impacts on the volatility of inflation. Before the 1970s, inflation volatility was higher, and there were both phases of inflation and deflation. However, the average inflation was relatively low. After these systems were abolished, the average inflation rate increased, as there were no more deflationary phases and as central banks pursued a policy of maintaining positive inflation rates.

Despite the higher average inflation rate, the volatility of inflation has decreased since the end of the Bretton Woods system. This is partly because central banks today have greater flexibility in managing monetary policy as they can better respond to economic shocks with fiat currencies and strive for price stability. The flexibility gains associated with this system come with the risk of a permanently lax monetary policy due to political pressure. This is manifested both in a reflexive expansion of the money supply at the first signs of an economic slowdown and in a generally too low level of interest rates.

5.2.2 Stock Indexes

Stocks represent a share in a company. For businesses, they are a way of raising equity capital, and for investors, they are a volatile asset class with historically relatively high returns. Logically, the success of such an entrepreneurial investment largely depends on the legal and political framework conditions. This, of course, applies in varying degrees to all types of investments.

The stock market has existed for centuries in various forms. The stock market, as we know it today, originated in the 17th century in Amsterdam, where the first exchange was founded in 1602. Over time, stock markets also emerged in other countries, including the London Stock Exchange in 1801 and the New York Stock Exchange in 1817. Some important historical milestones in the history of the stock market are the great crash of 1929 and the Great Depression, the "Black Monday 1987," and the bursting of the dot-com bubble. An extraordinarily good phase, on the other hand, is represented by the "Great Bull Market" from 1982 to 2000.[4] These events illustrate why it is important not to calculate with averages over 100 years, but to look at various possible earnings paths and the dispersion of their final values. Few things are more costly in the capital market than overly high expectations that tempt investors to take too much risk.

Historical Returns and Drawdowns

The upper panel of Figure 5.4 shows the developments of a one-time investment in U.S. stocks that started in 1900 in real terms. The lower panel shows the real drawdowns from the most recently reached high.

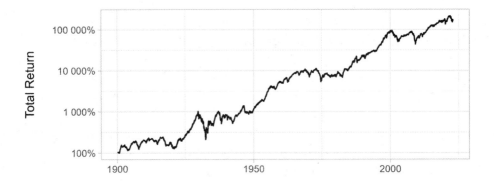

Figure 5.4: Real total return and real drawdowns of U.S. large cap stocks. Data: Ibbotson SSBI®, NorgateData.com.

4   See Mahar (2004).

Over the long term, stocks meet the expectations placed on them. We find it remarkable how negligible even the major price crashes seem in retrospect when you look at such a long investment horizon. This is of particular interest to investors such as family offices or foundations that are designed for eternity. However, even corrections of 30% are often emotionally difficult to bear for the average private and institutional investor. While the long-term development of stocks is impressive, investors do not get this for free. The price is the high fluctuation risks that have tempted generations of investors to make the wrong decision at the wrong time. Such a decision can quickly cloud the image of impressive total returns.

Many people are classical buy-and-hold investors that save and invest over periods of 30 years or even longer. To give an impression of the greatly varying developments of the opportunities and fluctuation risks of this market we look at all real total return paths spanning three decades since 1900 (see Figure 5.5). The graphic shows the spread of individual results in the respective month up to the 360th month, which represents the end of the investment horizon. Because of the logarithmic scaling, the values start at 100%.

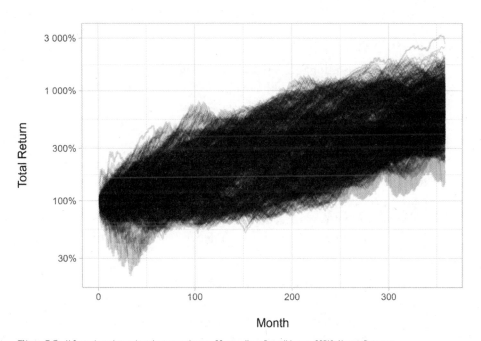

Figure 5.5: U.S. stock market real total return paths over 30-year slices. Data: Ibbotson SSBI®, NorgateData.com.

The greatly varying developments depending on the starting point high-light the significant importance of the time of investment. As this not only depends on the personal financial situation, investors can only moderately influence the result of their lifelong investment and are to a considerable extent also at the mercy of the luck factor.

When it comes to the best performance in the history of the developed stock markets, experienced investors directly think of the great bull market from 1982 to 2000. Above all, the steep rise of the Nasdaq remains in many people's memory. The same applies to the subsequent bear market, which caused the technology indexes to drop by 80%. Despite all intermittent collapses, the long-term development of the stock markets in many industrialized countries has been positive.

While the U.S. markets have dominated the scene not only in recent decades, the example of Japan not only illustrates the perpetual uncertainty of long-term stock returns in individual sectors or regions. From this uncertainty regarding the development of regional stock markets, the awareness for globally diversified stock investments emerged step by step. This reduces the risks, but naturally also leads to a reduction in the maximum achievable return.

5.2.3 Bonds

For many institutional investors, interest-bearing securities are required holdings for compliance with government regulations. The term *the bond market* is frequently used in everyday conversation. This term makes many people think the bond market is simpler than it is. This phrase is an almost grotesquely simplified representation of a market segment that is very diverse and offers professional investors an almost inexhaustible number of investment strategies. Compared to the stock market, interest-bearing securities have significantly more dimensions with immediate relevance for performance, including duration, convexity, rating and seniority, any integrated derivative path dependencies, and the colorful garden of potential covenants.

Bonds are debt securities through which companies and governments raise capital from investors with the promise of repaying the principal amount and making regular interest payments. These markets play a crucial role in the global economy as they offer governments and businesses opportunities to borrow and open investment opportunities for individuals and institutions.

The bond market has its roots in ancient civilizations, where loans were granted in the form of debt contracts. The modern bond market took shape in the 12th and 13th centuries with the emergence of government bonds issued by European city-states like Venice and Florence. The first corporate bond was issued in the 17th century by the Dutch East India Company. Other milestones in the development of the debt securities market were the founding of the Bank of England in 1694. The English central bank issued government bonds to finance its business and manage the country's debt. The groundwork for the U.S. Treasury market was laid in 1790. In this year, the U.S. government began issuing bonds to consolidate and finance debt that had grown during the Civil War.

A significant step for the standardization of bond investments was the introduction of the first benchmark index by the investment bank Salomon Brothers in 1981. The index bore the telling name "Salomon Brothers World Government Bond Index." It allowed investors and traders around the globe to judge the development of the global bond market quickly. The Eurobond market emerged in the 1960s. This segment has nothing to do with the Euro currency, but includes bonds that were issued in a different currency than that of the issuer. The 1970s also brought a long-term relevant innovation for interest-bearing securities traders—the market for securitizations. The issuance of mortgage-backed securities in the United States began, enabling the packaging and trading of various types of debt securities. Ultimately, like other segments, the global trading of bonds was accelerated by the introduction of electronic trading platforms, after which it grew to previously unimaginable proportions.

So, over time, the global bond market has significantly evolved in terms of both products and trading possibilities, adapting to the changing economic conditions, the needs of issuers and investors, as well as technological advances. The reference point of the global bond market, and an asset investable for all investors, has been represented by U.S. government bonds for several decades. Therefore, in the following presentations, we focus on U.S. Treasury Notes with a 10-year term (see Figure 5.6).

The completely different structure of the development compared to the stock market is immediately noticeable. The development is characterized

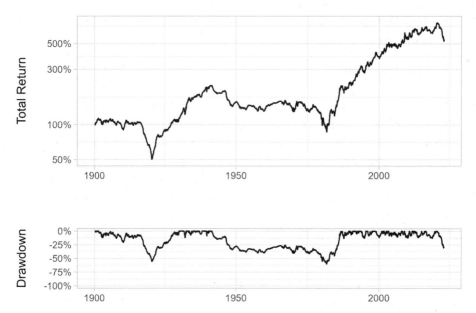

Figure 5.6: Real total return and real drawdowns of U.S. government bonds. Data: Ibbotson SSBI®, NorgateData.com.

by long-lasting cycles and the real drawdowns last significantly longer, but with declines of more than 50%, they are painful. Overall, the real total return is positive, but the dependence on the starting point of an investment in fixed-income securities is much higher than is the case with stock investments. This is due to the nature of the instruments. Apart from the case of a default by the debtor, bond investors, unlike stock investors, receive exactly the return at the maturity date that was stated when the securities were purchased.

The largest real drawdown of bonds in the USA since the beginning of the 20th century began in the 1940s. State finances had gotten out of control due to the Second World War. Within a few years, U.S. government debt rose from 30% of GDP to 110% of GDP. The U.S. Federal Reserve bought U.S. government bonds because the state's refinancing needs were so great that the private sector alone could not absorb the massive volume. In addition, a new control element called yield curve control was introduced, a nice name for fixing the entire yield curve. The highest interest rate at the long end of the yield curve was set at 2.5%; at the short end, it was 0.38%. As soon as the interest rates dared to go above the mentioned target marks, the Fed (Federal Reserve Bank) bought bonds until the interest rate reached the desired level again. At the same time, the massive government spending programs caused short and intense bouts of inflation. Although the development of the loss of purchasing power was erratic, the cumulative inflation rate in the 1940s was comparable to the values of the 1970s, when the OPEC oil embargo left deep traces among others.

The duration of the drawdown is also remarkable when one considers the intermittent interest rate increases and the thus successively rising interest income. Owners of bond portfolios had to wait for around 50 years until the real wealth had reached its original value again. Anyone who bought long-term U.S. government bonds in 1941 had to wait until 1991 to enter the profit zone. If one looks at rolling periods, the risks of bonds do not look much better.

Figure 5.7, similar to the plots in the section on stocks, shows all real paths of the development of an investment in U.S. government bonds with a 10-year term. The difference from stocks is obvious. There are numerous paths that led to a noticeable loss of purchasing power even after 30 years.

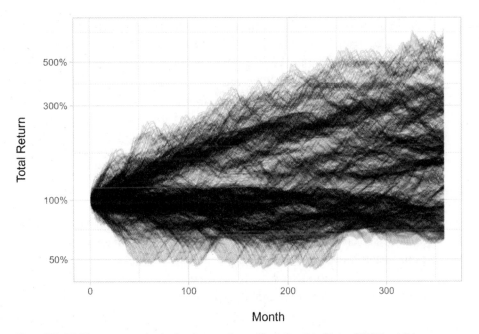

Figure 5.7: U.S. 10-year government bond real total return paths over 30-year slices. Data: Ibbotson SSBI®, NorgateData.com.

When considering a 10-year holding period, the worst stock performance was even better than the worst bond performance. Nevertheless, investors assign a high weight to bonds in the portfolio. Behavioral economists Benartzi and Thaler confirm this behavior in their paper "Myopic Loss Aversion and the Equity Premium Puzzle."[5] Investors would not hold more stocks compared to bonds because they focus too much on short-term performance and volatility instead of long-term performance goals. This loss aversion leads to reduced stock holdings, lower stock prices, and increased equity risk premiums. The focus on short-term volatility prevents one from staying invested in the markets longer term and earning a high equity risk premium. Of course, legal and regulatory restrictions additionally encourage this behavior. Thus, investors are somewhat forced to build a high exposure in bonds.

As early as 2012, Warren Buffett warned in his annual shareholder letter about having too much exposure in bonds, saying: "They are among the most dangerous of assets. Over the past century these instruments have destroyed the purchasing power of investors in many countries, even as these holders continued to receive timely payments of interest and principal. Right now, bonds should come with a warning label."

The long cycles should make bond investors think twice before deciding for an allocation. Since the 1970s, apart from a few temporary market distortions, bondholders have had little reason to complain. The cycle was upward and as inflation fell, so did interest rates. The end of this cycle was marked by the phase of very low interest rates, which gave government bonds a big boost on their way to the top. Those who were already invested benefited from both the low-interest-rate policy and the regularly topped-up purchase programs of the central banks. However, this low-interest-rate policy led to increasingly major problems with the reinvestment of freed-up funds.

The significant price losses due to the rapid increase in yields since 2022 illustrates the importance of market timing for bond investors. And another point is significant for bond investors. Notable real drawdowns have been rare in the past. However, when they do occur as a result of inflation and interest rate increases, they can last very long.

---

5 See Benartzi and Thaler (1995).

5.2.4 Commodities

Commodities represent one of the most interesting segments of the capital market. The trading of futures contracts has been the site of numerous historical price explosions and collapses. But commodities are a difficult asset class for purely passively oriented investors. For this reason, systematic trading approaches were developed early in the commodity market. To this day, trend-following approaches and strategies that exploit the structure of the term structure of certain contracts are used successfully (see corresponding feature box).

The term *structure of a commodity market* refers to the pattern of prices across contracts that are identical in every way except for their expiration date. The term *structure* is typically represented by a curve on a graph with the y-axis as the price of the commodity and the x-axis as the time to expiration of the contracts.

There are three main types of term structures:

- **Contango:** When the prices of futures contracts are higher than the spot price of the commodity, it is called contango. This is typically the normal state of most commodity markets, and it implies that the cost to carry the commodity (such as storage costs for physical commodities) is positive.
- **Backwardation:** When the prices of futures contracts are lower than the spot price, the market is said to be in backwardation. This situation can arise when the commodity is in high immediate demand, or when market participants expect the spot price to fall in the future.
- **Flat:** In this case, the prices of futures contracts are the same as the spot price.

Investors who invest in futures or in futures-based commodity ETFs should be aware of the term structure, as it impacts the total return. If the market is in contango, then each time the ETF rolls its futures contracts to avoid expiration, it is buying more expensive contracts, which could lead to a loss over time. This is known as "roll yield." Conversely, in backwardation, the roll yield could be positive, potentially enhancing returns.

The global commodity markets play a crucial role in the world economy as they facilitate trade in fundamental resources such as energy, metals, and agricultural products. The emergence of these markets goes back to the need to balance supply and demand for commodities and hedge price risks. The standardization of contracts is an essential aspect of commodity trading as it enables efficient and transparent price formation. Only through standardized contracts like forwards or futures can market participants easily trade with each other as the quality, quantity, and delivery conditions of the traded commodities are clearly defined and thus comparable.

Looking at developments since the 19th century, the establishment of the Chicago Board of Trade (CBOT) in 1848 was an essential step. The CBOT introduced standardized contracts for the trading of agricultural products. Twenty years later, the futures contract on wheat was launched, the foundation of modern commodity trading. In an environment of dynamically changing needs amid rapidly developing new industries, the New York Mercantile Exchange (NYMEX) was founded. In its founding year 1872, it was still called the "Butter and Cheese Exchange of New York," but later it became the world's largest trading venue for energy and metal futures. Half a decade later, the London Metal Exchange (LME), a European competitor specializing in global metal trading, followed.

In addition to the introduction of electronic trading in the 1980s and 1990s, which led to an acceleration of trading processes and enormous market growth, the establishment of exchange-traded funds (ETF) and exchange-traded notes (ETN) in the late 1990s was another significant event for the commodity market. More than for the commodity traders, these products changed the possibilities for investors to participate in developments in this segment.

Considering inflation adjusted returns, buy-and-hold commodity investments have reliably disappointed investors (see Figure 5.8). Not without reason the saying "nothing helps so well against high prices like high prices and nothing helps so well against low prices like low prices" was coined in this market. The classic cycles are at home in this segment. Long downward movements lead to falling investments and closures of production capacities. This results in a shortage of supply. Since an expansion of supply is not immediately possible due to the lack of capacities, prices rise again. Higher quotations make investments interesting again.

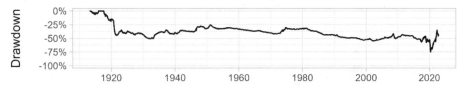

Figure 5.8: Real total return and real drawdowns of the broad commodity market. Data: Ibbotson SSBI®, NorgateData.com.

New capacities are created, supply increases, and prices fall again. What sounds like a calm cycle is indeed a cycle, but it is usually anything but calm. Both a shortage and an oversupply can lead to massive price changes in a short period. Whoever is on the right side at this point can profit massively, whoever misses the right point can lose a lot very quickly.

We show here, analogous to the approach in the section on stocks, the real development of all possible paths for investors buying and holding over three decades (see Figure 5.9). The displayed trends may be disappointing for some investors who had hoped for more return from an investment in commodities.

The occasional strong price increases in the commodity markets are impressive even at the index level. This applies even more to individual contracts. However, the subsequent crashes are no less clear. Since commodity investments are usually implemented with futures, there is also a dependency on the term structure. Investors in the commodity markets do not buy at the spot price but at the forward price. This differs significantly from the spot price in many markets. The prices at different maturities of the underlying futures contracts form the futures curve. If the forward price is higher than the spot price, an investor incurs losses

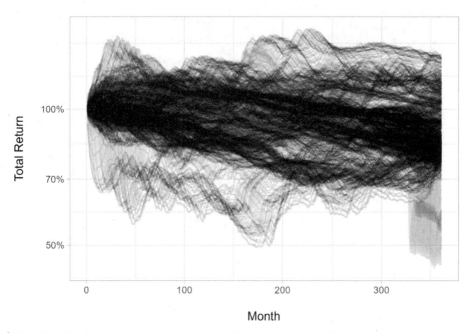

Figure 5.9: Broad commodity index real total return paths over 30-year slices. Data: Ibbotson SSBI®, NorgateData.com.

over time if the spot price remains unchanged. In the opposite case, profits can be collected simply from the fact that the futures price and the spot price converge. Their impact on the overall development of a commodity investment is enormous. Especially investors who want to hold commodities as a long-term investment should keep this in mind. An insightful evaluation on this topic can be found in the paper "Facts and Fantasies about Commodity Futures."[6]

Most institutional investors invest indirectly in this segment by buying shares of the commodity producers. For long-term oriented investors in the commodity area, active approaches such as a systematic trend follower can be a sensible alternative to a direct investment.

5.2.5 Real Estate

The global real estate market represents a significant part of the world economy. Over time, real estate investments have become a significant asset class for both private and institutional investors.

---

6   See Gorton and Rouwenhorst (2004).

A distinction is made between privately used real estate and investable real estate. *Privately used real estate* refers to the residential and commercial property inventory that is used by the owners themselves. *Investable real estate* are properties that are bought by investors to generate income or achieve an increase in value. Investable real estate can be acquired either through direct or indirect investments.

Direct investments involve the purchase of properties such as residential or commercial properties that the investors own and manage themselves. Indirect real estate investments are repackaged financial instruments that allow investors to participate in real estate assets without having to directly own or manage the properties (see Figure 5.10). Examples of indirect real estate investments are Real Estate Investment Trusts (REITs) and exchange-traded funds (ETFs) that invest in real estate stocks or projects.

One of the cornerstones of the development of this asset class from a lightly structured to an efficient market is the emergence of mortgage banks in the 18th and 19th centuries. These institutions allowed a broader layer of people to borrow money to acquire real estate. From an investor's perspective, the introduction of Real Estate Investment Trusts (REITs) in the USA in 1960 was an important milestone.

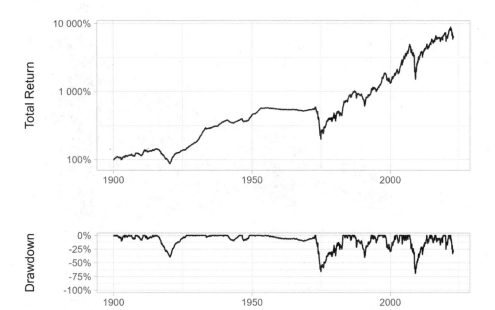

Figure 5.10: Real total return and real drawdowns of real estate investments based on real estate price indexes until the introduction of global REIT ETFs. Data: Ibbotson SSBI®, NorgateData.com.

For the first time these listed securities allowed small investors to easily invest broadly in real estate with small amounts, without having to directly own or manage these properties. In the 1980s and 1990s, the globalization of real estate markets picked up speed. As part of the economic globalization and increasing international capital flows, international investors expanded their real estate investments to markets outside their home countries. The emergence of REITs allowed investors to achieve notable diversification in the real estate sector. The investment opportunities now extend not only to office and residential properties, but also to more specific topics such as farmland, forest, and data centers. Recently, other vehicles for investing in real estate have emerged, including crowdfunding platforms and tokenization projects.

Over the long run, real estate investments show a positive development in inflation adjusted terms (Figure 5.11). The use of data from real estate indexes for the time before the creation of exchange-traded REITs results in lower volatility of the time series during this period. However, this does not change the basic statement. Even when looking at the 30-year paths (see Figure 5.11), the generally positive development becomes clear.

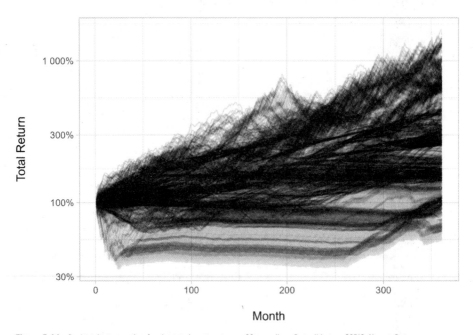

Figure 5.11: Real total return paths of real estate investments over 30-year slices. Data: Ibbotson SSBI®, NorgateData.com.

In the past, real estate investments have often performed well despite sometimes rising interest rates. This has several possible causes. Real estate has achieved steady value growth in many places over time, outweighing the negative impacts of rising interest rates. This is mainly due to the scarcity of land and the increasing demand for living space. Therefore, real estate has a reputation as an investment that provides protection against inflation, as both construction costs and rental income and property values generally rise with the general price level.

From the scarcity of real estate, it is only a short step to another scarce asset: gold.

5.2.6 Gold

The history of gold as an investment is millennia old. The precious metal has been used as a currency, jewelry, and store of value for thousands of years. It holds a special place in the world economy, as it serves as a hedge against inflation, a safeguard against political and economic uncertainty, and a diversification tool in investment portfolios.

There are two main approaches to investing in gold: direct investments and indirect investments. Direct investments involve the physical purchase of gold in the form of coins, bars, or jewelry. This method requires the secure storage of physical gold, which can be associated with costs and risks but also with the advantage of knowing that the metal is within reach. Many investors therefore keep at least a part of their gold allocation in bullion or coins.

Indirect investments in gold include the purchase of financial instruments linked to the price of gold without physically owning the precious metal. Examples include gold ETFs that invest in physical gold or gold stocks, gold futures, and shares of gold mining companies.

The developments of the past and the rising gold stocks of the global central banks impressively show the two faces of this asset class. On the one hand, it is a commodity, but at the same time, it acts as an important global reserve. This importance and the characteristic of gold as a natural opponent of fiat money bring financial opportunities but also latent regulatory risks for investors. This is also evidenced by a look at the financial market history.

Over the decades, there have sometimes been restrictions on the ownership of gold. The United States Gold Reserve Act of January 30, 1934, for example, required all gold and gold certificates in possession of the Federal Reserve to be returned and transferred into the sole ownership of the U.S. Treasury. The Treasury and financial institutions were forbidden from redeeming dollar bills for gold. To control the value of the dollar without the approval of the Federal Reserve, the Exchange Stabilization Fund was established under the control of the Treasury. The U.S. President was authorized to fix the gold value of the dollar by proclamation.

Immediately after the law was passed, President Franklin D. Roosevelt changed the statutory gold price from 20.67 USD to 35 USD per troy ounce. A year earlier, in 1933, Executive Order 6102 had criminalized the possession of or trade in gold for U.S. citizens anywhere in the world, except for certain pieces of jewelry and collector's coins. These prohibitions were relaxed beginning in the year 1964. On April 24, 1964, gold certificates were again permitted for private investors, and from 1975, Americans were again free to own and trade gold. A year earlier, gold futures were introduced at the COMEX. The first gold ETF did not come into existence until 2003 when the SPDR Gold Shares (GLD) was launched.

Since the representation of the price development before 1975 is not very enlightening due to the mentioned developments, Figure 5.12 shows the real development of the metal after this break.

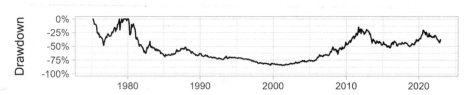

Figure 5.12: Real total return and real drawdowns of gold. Data: Ibbotson SSBI®, NorgateData.com.

Over the entire period, gold was able to fulfill the inherent promise to preserve purchasing power. However, the real drawdown since the price peak at the beginning of the 1980s shows that the precious metal is an investment that is subject to long and deep cycles.

The impact of the entry point on the long-term real return of an investor is enormous as the long price trends that began in 1980 and in 2002 show. On the other hand, it is important to note the property of the metal, which allows those owners who are worried about state bankruptcies or a meltdown of the financial system to sleep well despite interim real price losses. Since these problems are virulent in different countries at different times, gold has a varying level of importance depending on the region. People own gold "just in case."

Figure 5.13 shows the real development of an investment in gold over all 30-year periods since 1975, analogous to the previous shown asset classes.

In some parts of the Western world, the status of gold is often laughed at, but this is not justified. On the one hand, the metal has earned this positive status over the centuries, and who knows what the future holds? On the other hand, not all investors globally have the same means or

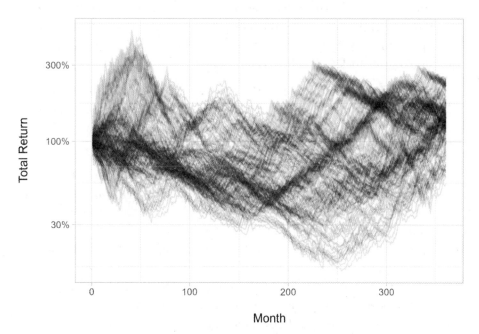

Figure 5.13: Real total return paths of Gold over 30-year slices. Data: Ibbotson SSBI®, NorgateData.com.

opportunities to engage in the global equity markets. In conclusion, it must be noted that gold cannot be as insignificant as it is often portrayed. After all, it continues to serve as a relevant reserve asset for central banks all over the planet. But as the long-term development shows, gold is more of an anchor in times of systemic crises than a direct hedge against rising inflation.

Following this succinct review of the principal liquid asset classes, which form the backbone of most investment portfolios, we now shift our focus to shed light on the nuances of digital assets.

5.3 Crypto Assets

The question of whether digital assets represent an independent asset class is more of a theoretical one. Of practical relevance, however, is whether the crypto biotope has the necessary size and liquidity to be suitable not only for private investors but also for institutional investors.

The following presentation of digital assets will be more extensive than the brief overview of conventional asset classes. In addition to presenting the performance and drawdowns of crypto assets, we also examine the correlations with other investments and within the crypto sectors. Subsequently, we consider the properties of cryptos as a store of value and medium of exchange and examine the relationship to gold before finally looking at stocks related to crypto assets.

Given the volatility of the most important digital assets, it is not surprising that the market capitalization of the entire crypto market fluctuates strongly. Enormous price increases in phases of euphoria and sobering price collapses are reflected in the overall development (see Figure 5.14).

In addition to the overarching picture, the distribution of market capitalizations within a segment is also interesting. When it comes to cryptos, people usually only talk about Bitcoin or Ether. Other tokens are mentioned less frequently. This can be intuitively justified with the different market capitalizations. But even the sectors of globally observed stock indexes are sometimes dominated by a few titles. Just as the American benchmark index, the S&P 500, contains a lot of other significant constituents besides Apple and Microsoft, the crypto universe is also not only made up of its two best-known members.

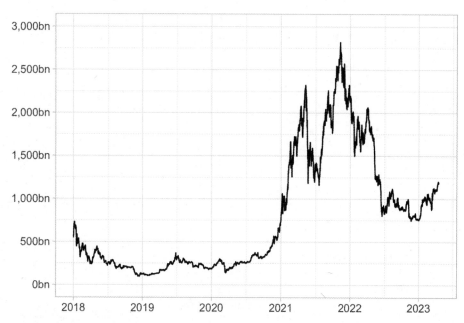

Figure 5.14: Total market capitalization of the crypto market. Data: MarketVector.

There are thousands of tokens, but currently fewer than 100 have a market capitalization of over 500 million U.S. dollars. These differences are often used as a reason to deny the market the necessary maturity. The argument that the crypto market consists only of one or at best two assets, as can also be read from the distribution of market values, is aimed in a similar direction (see Figure 5.15).

The distribution of market values of crypto assets differs significantly from that found in numerous stock indexes. But the comparison of the crypto market with the stock market sectors tells a different story. Some industries, like manufacturing and utilities, have a relatively inconspicuous market cap distribution. The curves of the communication and IT industries on the other hand resemble the distribution of crypto market capitalizations (Figure 5.16). These sectors are dominated by a small number of constituents as well.

It is not uncommon for investors to have an anchor within an asset class that they prefer to look at, and by which they measure the development of other assets. In the stock market, it is the Dow Jones Industrial Average or the S&P 500; in the foreign exchange market, it is the U.S. dollar.

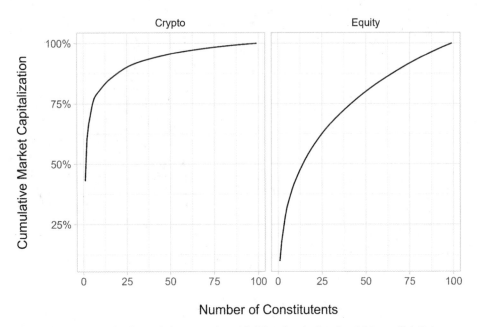

Figure 5.15: Distribution of market caps in the crypto market and the U.S. stock market. Data: NorgateData.com, MarketVector.

However, these anchors can change over time, as the example of the British pound shows. Just a few decades ago, it was at the top of the currency list. Today, except for Britons, it is almost meaningless.

In the equity area, investors often like to buy those stocks that they have at least heard of. Therefore, it is not surprising that many investors interested in digital assets initially focus on the biggest title in this area and simply divide the crypto biosphere into two groups. On the one side is Bitcoin, on the other side is everything else. This led to the still common classification into Bitcoin and the alternative coins, or Altcoins for short. This simple summary of everything that is not Bitcoin may be practical, but it is far too coarse, as the share of the best-known crypto asset has already decreased markedly. Therefore, as with conventional asset classes, a classification of tokens into overarching categories and sectors is gradually being established, as is explained in the chapter on the taxonomy of crypto assets.

The dominance of Bitcoin brings with it a strong influence of the token on the price development of the overall market. However, the segmentation of the new asset class, the filtering out of tokens that are no longer traded or represent a dead project, and the growing share of professional investors have led to greater independence of the Altcoins in recent years.

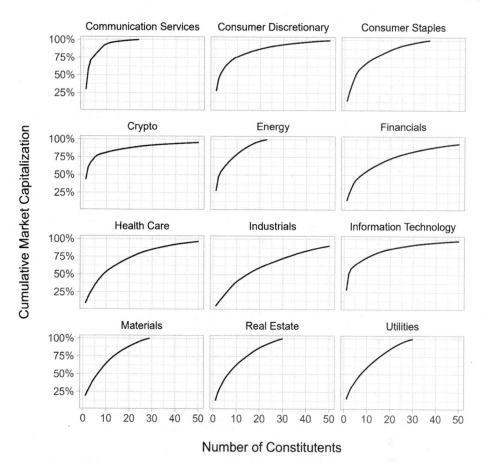

Figure 5.16: Distribution of market caps of crypto assets and in sectors of the U.S. stock market. Data: NorgateData.com, MarketVector.

Other factors such as sector affiliation or even the fundamental evaluation of individual projects are gaining increasing influence. These are signs of a gradual professionalization of the market.

5.3.1 Bitcoin as a Scarce Commodity

> "The gold standard has not collapsed. Governments have
> abolished it to pave the way for inflation."
> Ludwig von Mises

There are no technical limits to the multiplication of a fiat currency. Political and legal hurdles may pose a barrier, but they may change over time and are not insurmountable. There is always a compelling reason to deviate from former goals such as price stability or from rules such as the prohibition of state financing by the central bank. A financial crisis requires "special measures," the economy should be "stimulated" or the supposedly imminent "collapse of the system" should be prevented. Once the inhibitions to use the monetary means of the central banks have been overcome, the process is difficult to stop. In the long run, history shows that it is virtually impossible to control money creation without technical limits.

Bitcoin and numerous other crypto assets are the exact opposite of a politically influenced fiat currency, whose money supply can be increased without limit. The number of outstanding tokens of a digital currency can be technically limited. The maximum number of Bitcoins that can be produced is exactly 20,999,999.9769. The Bitcoin network started with a money supply of 50 Bitcoin, which were created with the creation of the first block. In the process of mining, new Bitcoin have been created ever since. With each verified block that is attached to the blockchain, new Bitcoin are created. However, the number of newly created Bitcoin per block is halved after every 210,000 new blocks. Since May 2020, only 6.25 Bitcoin are created with each block. Therefore, the growth rate of the Bitcoin money supply continues to decrease. By the end of 2021, more than 85% of all possible Bitcoins will have been created. In the year 2140, the last new Satoshi, the smallest unit of Bitcoin, will find its way into the network. The contrast to fiat currencies could not be clearer.

The Bitcoin protocol is just one of many ways to launch a cryptocurrency. Some are based on this example, but there are also completely different approaches. For instance, with some digital tokens, the entire money supply was created (pre-mined) and distributed from the beginning. Other protocols set a fixed inflation rate per year while many have no supply cap at all. An absolute upper limit of the tokens that can be issued, as with Bitcoin, is therefore not a general characteristic of crypto assets.

5.3.2 Bitcoin and Gold

Gold coins were an essential means of payment for thousands of years and continue to play an important role as a reserve asset of central banks. This is not changed by John Maynard Keynes's designation of the gold standard—not gold itself—as a "barbaric relic."

What makes gold so important and why is it so valuable? Academics Claude Erb and Campbell Harvey cite three reasons.[7]

1. The purchasing power of gold remains constant even over long periods.

2. Inflation is the main driver of gold prices.

3. Over very long periods, the real return on gold is 0%, it offers pure inflation protection.

So, according to Erb and Harvey, gold preserves purchasing power, no more and no less. A look at the history of fiat currencies shows how valuable such protection from inflation can be. However, the representations in the section on conventional investments show that gold could not always meet these expectations.

It is the physical properties that distinguish gold from other commodities. Gold is extremely inert, virtually indestructible, and not synthesizable with reasonable effort.[8] Furthermore, the metal is not a consumable good like oil. The annual production results in an average increase of all stocks of less than 2% and a sharply increasing demand cannot be met promptly with a corresponding increase in production quantities. Gold is and remains a scarce good that cannot be multiplied at will.

The famous scientist Isaac Newton recognized this as early as 1696. When his path at the Royal Mint in England began, the English monetary system was battered. It is estimated that every tenth coin in circulation was counterfeit. Newton quickly began a battle against counterfeiters and at the same time increased the requirements for the quality of the coins to make counterfeiting more difficult because every copy diluted the number of real coins. Therefore, combating counterfeiting was nothing more than the state-enforced guarantee of the scarcity of coins in order to maintain the value of money and thus trust in the currency system.

In the Bitcoin network, the maximum money supply is restricted by the protocol and thus programmatically implemented. After the halving in 2024, the stock of Bitcoin will increase more slowly than the global gold stocks.

---

7 See Erb and Harvey (2013).

8 Gold synthesis refers to the process of transmuting base metals into gold. Gold synthesis is possible with the help of particle accelerators or nuclear reactors, but in practice it is far too cumbersome.

"It's the same situation as gold and gold mining. The marginal cost of gold mining tends to stay near the price of gold. Gold mining is a waste, but that waste is far less than the utility of having gold available as a medium of exchange. I think the case will be the same for Bitcoin. The utility of the exchanges made possible by Bitcoin will far exceed the cost of electricity used. Therefore, not having Bitcoin would be the net waste."

Satoshi Nakamoto

According to the World Gold Council, the total amount of gold mined and still existing amounts to 197,576 tons. Between 2,500 and 3,000 additional tons, less than 2% of the stocks already mined, come to light each year.[9]

In comparison to the relatively stable amount of gold mined each year, the annual Bitcoin supply decreases significantly over time. Figure 5.17 shows how small the proportion of new coins to the already existing amount has already become. For gold, we assumed a constant increase

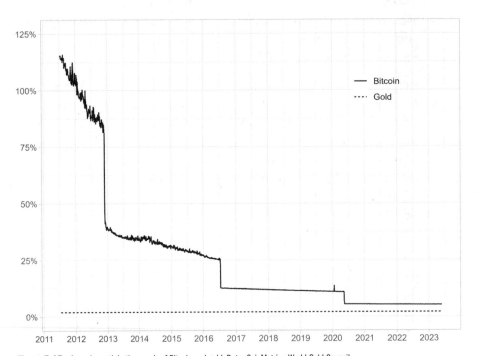

Figure 5.17: Annual growth in the supply of Bitcoin and gold. Data: CoinMetrics, World Gold Council.

9 See World Gold Council (2021).

in stocks of two percent per year. The graphic shows the effects of the rules-based reduction of Bitcoin's money supply expansion. There are no central bank press conferences, there is no opportunity for political and societal influence. The process continues unabated, thus forming a contrast to the world of politically influenced monetary policy.

Both gold and Bitcoin exist only in limited quantities. The raw material gold can only be mined to a limited extent, the number of Bitcoins that can be generated in total is limited by the protocol. What is special about Bitcoin and many other crypto assets is the algorithmically implemented scarcity of the supply of a digital good. For the first time, digital resources cannot simply be multiplied. As developments around NFTs show, this concept can be applied not only to a monetary system, but to any things, for example, art, music, or videos.

In times of expansive central bank policy, scarce goods become more attractive. The numerous acronyms with which the central banks' programs are labeled, such as QE, TLTRO, TALF, or TARP, simply refer to various ways of indirect corporate or government financing by the central bank. During the turbulence of 2020 alone, the Federal Reserve increased its balance sheet by four trillion USD with a stroke of a pen. That is about 12,000 U.S. dollars per capita resulting from just one of numerous actions by the U.S. Federal Reserve, which is not alone in its approach. All relevant central banks have been expanding the money supply in their respective areas of influence for years to an extent that bears no relation to the corresponding economic performance.

There may be understandable reasons to call on the central bank in a crisis to demand temporary monetary measures. The problem lies in the use of the word *temporary* and the associated uncertainty about the duration and final extent of monetary interventions. As can be seen from Figure 5.18, the trend towards expanding central bank balance sheets has been visible since the financial crisis of 2008–2009. Ironically, cheap money was one of the causes of this crisis.

Since inflation is a monetary phenomenon, this monetary policy will in the long-term lead to a significant loss of purchasing power for numerous currencies. This point is not disputed, as the increase in inflation was even chosen as a goal by central banks not so long ago.

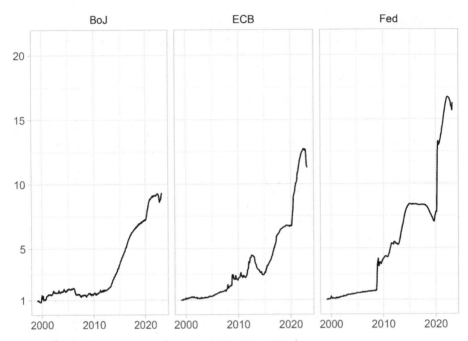

Figure 5.18: Development of central bank balance sheets, 1999 = 1. Data: BIS.

There is another point in which gold and Bitcoin are similar, and thus, differ from fiat money. Both do not rely on trust. This is an important advantage, as a typical financial crisis always goes hand in hand with a loss of trust. Promises are not kept, loans are not repaid, or rules are changed without inquiry as was the case with the haircut on Greek bonds in 2011, for example, that forced investors to take a loss of more than 50%. There is no guarantee that a certain crypto asset will be a success, but like gold crypto assets bear no credit risk.

In terms of technology, Bitcoin and gold have little in common. However, when looking at their characteristics as an asset class, they have many similarities. Bitcoin shares many positive aspects with gold and combines them with the advantages of the digital world, such as easier divisibility and both fast and cheap global transfers. The authenticity check is also much easier with the digital asset. Gold, on the other hand, scores with the at least theoretical possibility of anonymity and the resulting non-traceability of transactions. In the everyday life of institutional investors, these two points are not relevant, but they are noteworthy for private investors.

5.3.3 Crypto Assets and Money

> "Paper money eventually returns to its intrinsic value: zero."
>
> Voltaire

Central banks have also been looking into the possibility of using a fully digital currency for years. Statements by British central banker Marc Carney indicate a general openness, even if central banks are likely to have different reasons for using cryptocurrencies than many investors. However, one truth should be clear to investors not only in banking crises. Crypto and gold are money and have no issuer risk. Everything else is a liability.

Jon Cunliffe, as Deputy Governor of the Bank of England responsible for the stability of the British financial system, has been dealing with the rise of Bitcoin and other cryptocurrencies for years. About every 100 to 150 years, there is a revaluation of money, Cunliffe said in an interview,[10] and this is now imminent. He emphasized in the interview that cryptocurrencies reveal the inefficiencies in the existing financial system, which are shown, for example, in the high costs of cross-border money transfers. The crucial point, according to Cunliffe, is that citizens can rely on the security of their money, regardless of the technology used to create it.

First, however, the question should be answered whether Bitcoin or other crypto assets can be categorized as money at all. The German Bundesbank names three functions that money must fulfill for this purpose: the function as a medium of exchange, the function as a unit of account, and the function as a store of value.

5.3.4 Bitcoin as a Medium of Exchange

Bitcoin is durable. There is no way to destroy the blockchain, as it is stored decentral on thousands of computers worldwide. A central server and its backups can be destroyed, but not a peer-to-peer network with several thousand nodes.

Bitcoin is fungible. Regardless of who owns them or where they come from, every Bitcoin has the same value and can be exchanged for products and services. However, there is a limitation. Since every transaction

---

10 See Torsten Riecke (2020).

is publicly visible, there is the technical possibility not to accept bitcoin that are sent from certain addresses. Fungibility can therefore be limited at least theoretically.

Bitcoin can be transported. The coins can be transferred worldwide without problems. In the case of foreign transfers, the transfer is fast compared to existing systems and it is final, and therefore, irreversible after a short time.

Bitcoin is highly divisible. Each Bitcoin can be divided into 100 million units, the Satoshi.

Bitcoin cannot be counterfeited. Bitcoins are always assigned to a certain address and cannot be duplicated.

5.3.5 Bitcoin as a Unit of Account

The classification of Bitcoin as a unit of account is more problematic. In the world of fiat currencies, the volatility of the Bitcoin price is currently still too high to use it as a basis for price determination. An asset with an annual volatility of 70% is unsuitable for setting the price for a theater ticket for the coming months. In the universe of crypto assets, however, Bitcoin is already an important unit of account. On the common trading platforms, the counter value in Bitcoin and sometimes also in Ether is always displayed in addition to the quotation in U.S. dollars.

5.3.6 Bitcoin as a Store of Value

Opinions differ on the classification of Bitcoin as a store of value, again due to its high volatility. Let us therefore take another look at the perspective of the Deutsche Bundesbank, which says on its website: "Money must primarily function as a store of value, that is, retain its value over a longer period. This way it can be kept and used for a purchase later. To serve as a store of value, money must be durable and stable in value. Money owners must trust that they will be able to buy just as much for their money later as they can today. The purchasing power of money must therefore be preserved." The Bundesbank also addresses crypto assets with the following sentence: "Crypto assets are hardly suitable as a store of value because they are subject to strong price fluctuations."

This statement seems intuitively correct, which is due to equating volatility with downward volatility. Nobody wants to see their savings fluctuate downwards by 70%. If the fluctuation is upward, it is a different story. Therefore, it is more revealing to look at the price drops from the most recent highs, the drawdowns. While these maximum interim losses are often enormous, these declines are relativized by the often-dynamic recovery of the price losses and the price gains that preceded the downturns. According to the Bundesbank's interpretation, if everything that has shown strong losses over time compared to the U.S. dollar is no longer classified as a currency due to a lack of value retention function, the list of foreign currencies quickly empties.

There are a lot of established currencies that have fulfilled the value retention function much worse over time than Bitcoin and many other cryptocurrencies. Those who have so far allocated a portion of their assets to Bitcoin will not have complained about a lack of value retention of the cryptocurrency, at least so far.

> *"Inflation is always and everywhere a monetary phenomenon in the sense that it is and can be produced only by a more rapid increase in the quantity of money than in output."*
>
> *Milton Friedman*

The argument of value retention and the associated requirement of maintaining purchasing power always turns against fiat currencies in the long run.

The USD has lost more than 90% of its purchasing power over time (see Figure 5.19). This is a considerable loss for a supposed store of value. Because of the linear representation, the course of the last two and a half decades may seem less dramatic. However, since the mid-1980s alone, the U.S. dollar has lost more than 60% of its purchasing power. This development is no accident. It is not due to economic uncertainties or unforeseeable developments. It is, for better or worse, a characteristic of every fiat currency. In tech speak, one would say "Inflation is not a bug, it is a feature of every fiat currency."

Depending on the degree of political influence and global market power, losses of purchasing power occur at different speeds in different currencies. A particularly dramatic example of the collapse of the currency is provided by the Argentinian Peso (Figure 5.20). The currency did not free the people in the South American country from concern about value preservation, but to the contrary robbed them of all their savings within a few years.

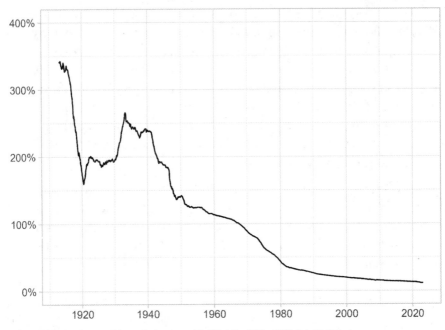

Figure 5.19: Development of the purchasing power of the U.S. dollar, 1967 = 100%. Data: World Bank.

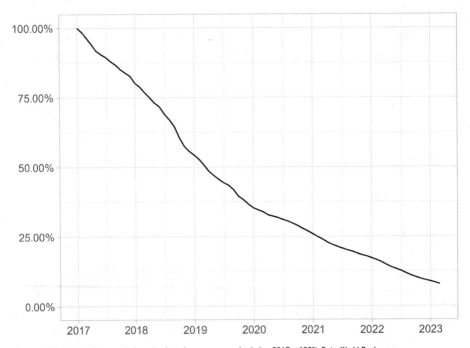

Figure 5.20: Purchasing power in Argentina based on consumer price index, 2017 = 100%. Data: World Bank.

A bitter experience that has destroyed prosperity and livelihoods and is likely to have shaken the trust of millions of people in paper currency over generations. People who have never experienced the collapse of a currency can hardly imagine the dramatic effects of such a development on all aspects of life. However, the list of countries in which such an event has taken place in the last 50 years is impressively long. Financial crises are not as rare as many people think. The International Monetary Fund (IMF) alone mentions 218 currency crises for the period from 1970 to 2011. A currency crisis is considered a minimum 30% drop in the respective currency in relation to the U.S. dollar. Moreover, this decline must be at least ten percentage points more significant than the depreciation measured in the previous year. Most of these currency crises occurred in so-called emerging countries, but industrialized countries like Norway or Sweden were also affected.[11]

With crypto assets, a technical limitation of the final amount of money is possible, but it is not a mandatory feature. While Bitcoin's supply is capped at 21 million, Ether and many other tokens have no upper limit.

Hal Finney, who developed the source code of Bitcoin together with Satoshi Nakamoto and was involved in the correction of errors, already described a scenario in January 2009 in which Bitcoin establishes itself as the dominant payment system. Finney wrote the following message as a reply to Nakamoto's email, in which he announced the release of the Bitcoin network.[12]

> "It's interesting that the system can be configured to only allow a certain maximum number of coins ever to be generated. I guess the idea is that the amount of work needed to generate a new coin will become more difficult as time goes on.
>
> One immediate problem with any new currency is how to value it. Even ignoring the practical problem that virtually no one will accept it at first, there is still a difficulty in coming up with a reasonable argument in favor of a particular non-zero value for the coins.
>
> As an amusing thought experiment, imagine that Bitcoin is successful and becomes the dominant payment system in use throughout the world. Then

---

11 See Valencia and Laeven (2012).

12 See Satoshi Nakamoto Institute (2021).

the total value of the currency should be equal to the total value of all the wealth in the world. Current estimates of total worldwide household wealth that I have found range from $100 trillion to $300 trillion. With 20 million coins, that gives each coin a value of about $10 million.

So the possibility of generating coins today with a few cents of compute time may be quite a good bet, with a payoff of something like 100 million to 1! Even if the odds of Bitcoin succeeding to this degree are slim, are they really 100 million to one against? Something to think about. . . ."

Hal

This is less a wishful thinking of Finney's than a consideration of the impacts of a development that seemed unlikely at the time. Without a technological layer extending the properties of Bitcoin by a scalable payment system, the likelihood of the network developing into the dominant money system is low. But Bitcoin is just one of many crypto protocols. The question of whether it is generally possible to build a secure, efficient, cost-effective, and scalable peer-to-peer payment system based on crypto assets can therefore be answered with "yes."

5.4 Crypto Assets in the Portfolio Context

In the portfolio context, the parameters total return, volatility, and correlation with other asset classes are particularly relevant. We present these three factors in this section.

First, we look at the total return and drawdown charts. The history of crypto assets is much shorter than that of conventional asset classes. We therefore make two adjustments. On the one hand, we switch to a nominal perspective, as the cumulative effect of inflation is negligible compared to the fluctuation range of crypto assets. Additionally, we look at daily data, which allows a more detailed view that is especially important when analyzing drawdowns.

The total return of Bitcoin is remarkable even considering the frequent deep drawdowns (see Figure 5.21). The development of the first years is mainly of theoretical interest because when the Bitcoin network started in 2009, there were no organized trading platforms where investors could buy Bitcoin. Trading took place primarily bilaterally, that is, buyers and

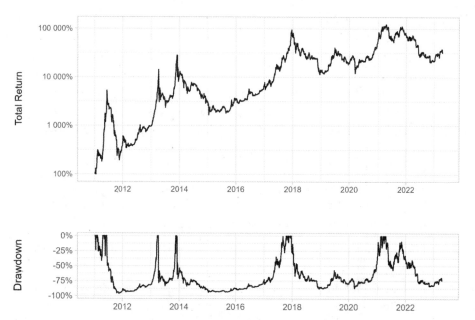

Figure 5.21: Total return and drawdowns of Bitcoin. Data: MarketVector.

sellers had to find each other and conduct the trade directly with one another. This process was often cumbersome, time-consuming, and insecure, as there were no standardized mechanisms for price discovery, the exchange of Bitcoins, and the processing of transactions.

Over time, centralized trading venues were created to remedy this lack. They offer users a platform on which they can buy, sell, or exchange Bitcoin and other cryptocurrencies. These trading venues represent an interface between traditional currencies and cryptocurrencies, and offer central price discovery as well as mechanisms for the processing of transactions.

Centralized trading venues have several advantages, such as increased liquidity, as they consolidate the trading activities of many users, thus enabling larger transaction volumes. They also offer an enhanced usability by providing user-friendly interfaces and features such as limit and stop orders. However, they are also more vulnerable to hacks and security risks, as in the case of Mt. Gox, which had to file for bankruptcy in 2014 after a large portion of the deposited Bitcoins was stolen.[13] In recent years,

13 See McMillan (2014).

decentralized trading venues (Decentralized Exchanges, DEX), which are based on blockchain technology and do not require a central entity, have also developed. In decentralized trading venues like Uniswap or SushiSwap, trading operations are carried out directly between users via smart contracts, which can increase security and reduce dependence on a central entity. Decentralized trading venues offer several advantages such as increased security, privacy, and a lower susceptibility to censorship. However, their liquidity is often lower compared to centralized trading venues, as they typically have fewer users and facilitate less trading. Overall, both centralized and decentralized trading venues have improved the liquidity and accessibility of Bitcoin and other cryptocurrencies by making it easier to buy, sell, and trade cryptocurrencies.

Looking not only at total return over the early days of the Bitcoin network, but as with conventional asset classes, at many possible paths, it is evident that the development was quite impressive even in later stages (see Figure 5.22).

In recent years, the conditions for the participation of institutional investors in the crypto market have improved. This is due to advances in regulation but also the emergence of professional and accepted custody

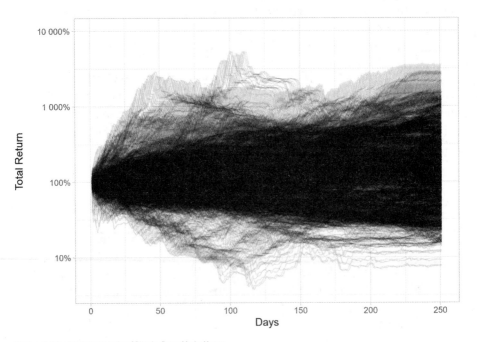

Figure 5.22: Total return paths of Bitcoin. Data: MarketVector.

solutions that enable institutional investors to store their crypto assets securely and in accordance with regulatory requirements. These advances led to an increasing interest of institutional investors, including pension funds, insurance companies, and wealth managers.

The participation of institutional investors is important for several reasons. First, their involvement increases liquidity and trading volume, leading to more efficient price formation. Second, the presence of institutional investors can contribute to broader acceptance of crypto assets, as they often serve as pioneers for other investors. Finally, the involvement of institutional investors can lead to the recognition of crypto assets as an established asset class that can be used in a balanced portfolio alongside traditional assets such as stocks, bonds, and real estate.

5.4.1 Correlations

In addition to expectations regarding profit opportunities and risks, correlations of crypto assets to other asset classes are the most important parameter of portfolio construction. The term correlation is used in the finance industry as frequently as it is used imprecisely. There is talk of correlated and uncorrelated assets, as if correlation were a static value. For example, it is often heard that stocks and bonds are negatively correlated. Anyone who does not merely declare the last decades of financial market history to be an overly long outlier cannot confirm this. It is also important when assessing the correlation of two asset classes to describe which returns are being considered. Two asset classes can be negatively correlated within the span of individual trading days, but show a positive correlation in the long term. The market regime is also important. If interest rates fall in the long term, stocks and government bonds rise at the same time. If there is a rapid crash in the stock market, the prices of government bonds often rise. In this case, the prices of bonds and stocks are temporarily negatively correlated, but this relationship is not set in stone.

Since correlation is a measure of the potential degree of diversification between investments, not only institutional investors need a clear picture of what correlation is and how it can behave over time. An asset that shows a low or negative correlation to other asset classes over as many different market regimes as possible has the potential to be an important portfolio building block.

What Is Correlation?

We consciously avoid formulas and derivations and focus on the practical significance of correlation. In capital markets, it represents the mutual relationship between the price developments of two investment instruments. These instruments can be anything from stocks and ETFs to digital tokens. The degree of correlation of the investment instruments is expressed by the correlation coefficient, which can take values between –1 and +1. Perfectly positively correlated assets have an exact synchrony and have a coefficient of +1. Uncorrelated assets show a value of 0. A coefficient of –1 describes perfectly negatively correlated instruments. A perfect synchrony does not mean, as is often assumed, identical changes. If stock Zig increases by 0.5% every day and stock Zag increases by 3.7% every day, then the daily returns of these two stocks are as perfectly correlated as the daily returns of two stocks that increase by 1% every day.

Correlations reflect a static and usually linear relationship between the price changes of two assets over a certain observation period.[14] Although such a snapshot is interesting, it can lead to incorrect statements due to rigidity. Anyone who uses only the result of a static view as an input value for the optimization of portfolios should be prepared for unpleasant surprises. For reasons of risk minimization alone, it is always advisable to look at the rolling correlations over time.

When considering and evaluating correlations, it is also essential to check their plausibility. A correlation does not imply causality. American Tyler Vigen[15] impressively demonstrates this on his website, where he has collected a lot of examples of so-called *spurious correlations*. This term refers to a correlation or correspondence between two quantities that is not based on a causal relationship, but only on a coincidental or indirect relationship. Two examples are the correlation of the development of the divorce rate in the

---

14 See Spiegelhalter (2020).
15 See Vigen (2021).

U.S. state of Maine with the per capita consumption of margarine (correlation coefficient: 99.26%) and that between fatal collisions of car drivers with trains and U.S. oil imports from Norway. While Tyler Vigen's website captivates with its entertaining content, at its heart, it provides a wealth of intriguing information.

A timeless example of why correlation values should not be interpreted without any context in a vacuum was provided by English statistician Francis John Anscombe. Anscombe's quartet, which shows the linear regression degrees and correlation coefficients for four different data sets[16] (see Figure 5.23), was first displayed in his publication "Graphs in Statistical Analysis" from 1973.

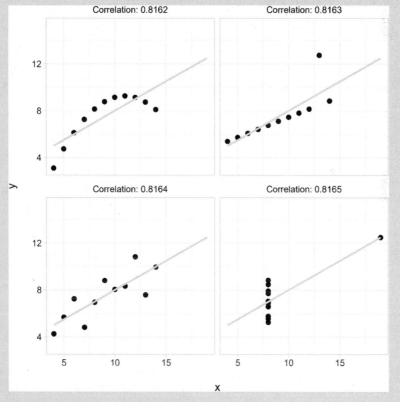

Figure 5.23: "Anscombe's quartet." Data: F. J. Anscombe.

16 See Anscombe (1973).

The presentation is astounding. While the data sets differ significantly from each other, the differences in the correlation coefficients only become apparent at the fourth decimal place. This example shows why it is advisable to perform a visual assessment in addition to examining numbers, whenever possible.

Both Tyler Vigen's expositions and Francis Anscombe's demonstration should remind investors to take correlation coefficients seriously, but not to view the metric as a static variable nor use it as the sole criterion for asset allocation.

5.4.2 Correlation with Conventional Assets

In the search for arguments advocating for the allocation of crypto assets in portfolios, correlation takes a prominent place. The long-term view of daily returns since 2015 shows why this is the case. Crypto assets were nearly uncorrelated with stocks, gold, and commodities during the observation period (see Figure 5.24).

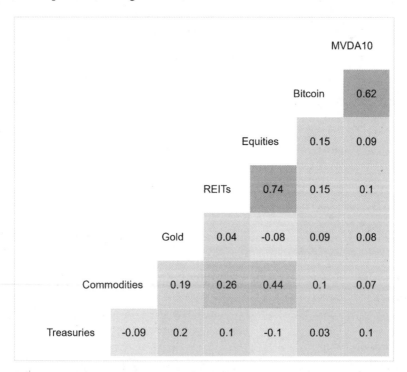

						MVDA10
Bitcoin						0.62
Equities					0.15	0.09
REITs				0.74	0.15	0.1
Gold			0.04	-0.08	0.09	0.08
Commodities		0.19	0.26	0.44	0.1	0.07
Treasuries	-0.09	0.2	0.1	-0.1	0.03	0.1

Figure 5.24: Static correlations of different asset classes, 2015–2023, monthly returns. Data: NorgateData.com, MarketVector.

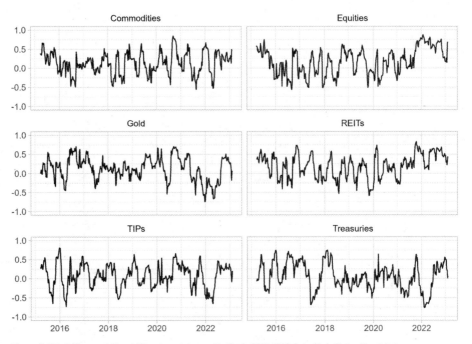

Figure 5.25: Rolling correlation of different asset classes with Bitcoin 2015–2023. Data: MarketVector, NorgateData.com.

The potential diversification of crypto assets is evident at first. However, cryptos did not provide a hedge against losses from other assets within a portfolio during the observation period. This would be expressed by a notably negative correlation. If we consider the rolling correlations, the impression conveyed by the static values is confirmed (see Figure 5.25).

The rolling correlations of crypto assets with conventional asset classes range from –0.5 to about +0.5. Figure 5.26 illustrates why the view of static correlations should always be supplemented by rolling correlations. On one hand, this review can prevent investors from drawing hasty, incorrect conclusions. A static correlation can be an artifact and may prove to be at best useless and at worst harmful in practice. The visualization of correlations over time reveals the risks of simple portfolio optimizations, which often stand on shaky ground due to simple return estimates. A look at the distribution of the correlations of cryptos with conventional asset classes (see Figure 5.26) shows a significant emphasis around the mark of zero as well as some clusters in the range between 0.25 and 0.5.

The rolling correlations of cryptos to conventional investments have confirmed its high diversification potential in recent years. This effect is not

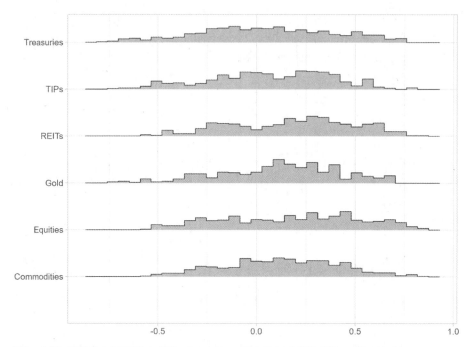

Figure 5.26: Distribution of correlations of different asset classes with crypto assets 2015–2023, monthly return data.
Data: MarketVector, NorgateData.com.

only seen in a static view, but is also evident over a longer period. The distribution of correlations does not show permanently negative correlations. Therefore, the classification of Bitcoin as an instrument to hedge against price losses of other asset classes cannot be deduced from the available data.

5.4.3 Correlation between Crypto Assets

The correlations within the crypto assets provide information about whether diversifying an investment into various tokens, compared to investing solely in Bitcoin, can lead to a significant diversification effect.

Bitcoin is currently the anchor currency of the crypto ecosystem. Therefore, the basic impression of many investors can be summarized in two sentences: A sustainable weakness in Bitcoin also negatively affects most other tokens. However, if Bitcoin is in a sustained bull market, most other tokens also perform positively. This perception is not wrong in a general

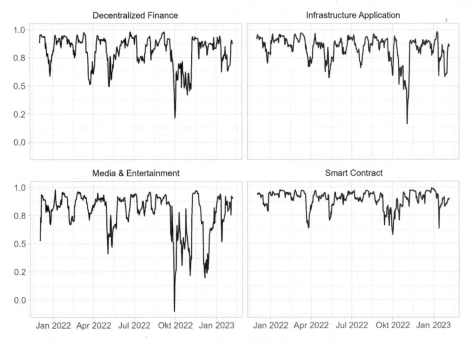

Figure 5.27: Rolling correlations of crypto asset sectors with Bitcoin 2022–2023, weekly data. Data: MarketVector, NorgateData.com.

sense, but neither is it particularly enlightening, as this pattern is also seen in the stock market. Comparable overarching tendencies should not lead investors to assume a permanent synchronicity of all crypto assets and thus ignoring potential opportunities for diversification.

To make a reliable statement, investors need to look at the correlations within the asset class. Figure 5.27 shows the rolling correlation coefficients of some sectors to Bitcoin.

The sectors presented show high, but by no means stable, correlations with Bitcoin. On the contrary, they clearly live their own lives at times. However, periods of negative correlation are not seen. Therefore, investors should not expect a hedging function through the combination of certain sectors.

As with the presentation of Bitcoin and conventional asset classes, we also want to look at the distribution of correlations within the crypto sector.

Figure 5.28 supports the thesis that the performance of Bitcoin is the dominant, but not the only factor influencing tokens from other sectors.

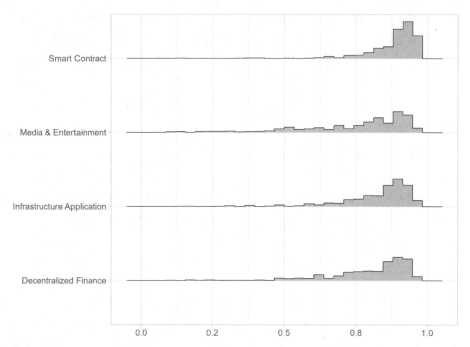

Figure 5.28: Distribution of correlations of crypto asset sectors with Bitcoin 2022-2023, weekly data. Data: MarketVector, NorgateData.com.

There are phases in which individual sectors can significantly decouple. Thus, the ongoing specialization in the crypto ecosystem with the increasing emergence of clearly distinguishable sectors and categories, to which projects and their tokens are assigned, is the logical next step.

5.5 Crypto Stocks: Alternative, Addition, or Neither?

The search for comparable characteristics of cryptos and other assets leads us to individual stocks from the technology sector. Amazon, Apple, Cisco, and Microsoft are some of the better-known companies whose stocks have made many investors wealthy. These are joined by companies popular among shareholders like Meta, Alphabet, and Tesla, whose IPOs are not that far in the past.

The characteristics of stocks and cryptos are different. Then why do we use stock prices as a proxy for past market movements? For one thing, some asset classes are not suitable for comparison. As interesting as the volumes in the bond market are, without derivative doping, the returns to be achieved in this market are usually comparably modest.

With commodities, there is only a limited supply of different contracts. The stock market, on the other hand, offers a huge investment universe, numerous sectors, and subsectors, and thus, an inexhaustible fund of remarkable price developments. This asset class lives between the extremes of a total loss and a hundredfold increase.

Figure 5.29 shows the trends of some well-known stocks from the start of their rise to the current value. Any dividends and stock splits were considered.

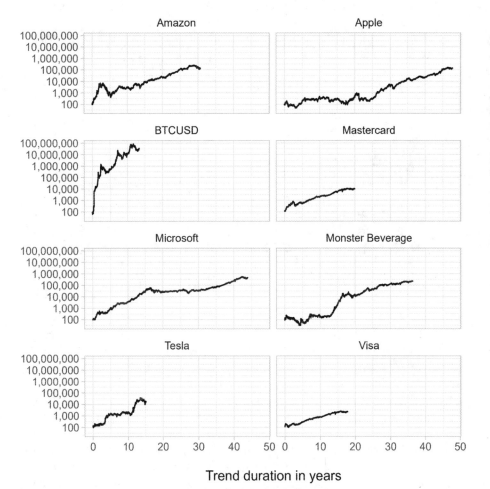

Figure 5.29: Trends of stocks and Bitcoin, Start = 100. Data: NorgateData.com, MarketVector.

In view of the impressive total returns, some may think how simple the investor's life could be. Figure 5.30 can help correct this misconception. The curves displayed in this diagram show the maximum interim price losses (drawdowns) that investors had to endure if they wanted to stay on board until the end of the uptrend.

Many crypto investors can tell you one or two things about drawdowns. Weak nerves and equally weak hands were put to some tough tests by the price fluctuations of digital assets. Surviving these distortions was probably mainly reserved for those who had temporarily forgotten their Bitcoin (but hopefully not their private keys).

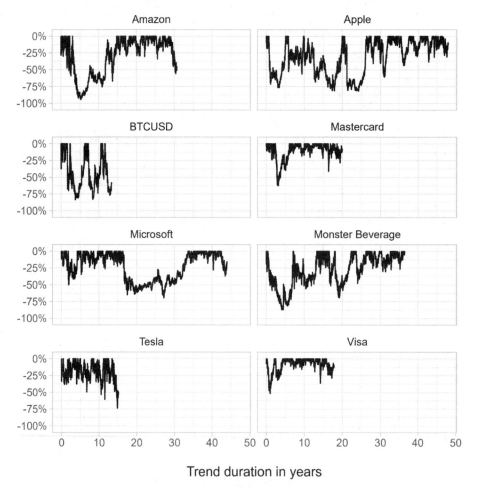

Trend duration in years

Figure 5.30: Drawdowns of stocks and Bitcoin. Data: NorgateData.com, MarketVector.

The phenomenal surges in prices, akin to those witnessed with Bitcoin and numerous other cryptocurrencies, partially offset the impact of the expansive volatility ranges. However, the realm of altcoins narrates a different story, with many assets suffering severe depreciation without any subsequent recovery. It is important to underscore that neither are windfalls distributed freely on the stock exchange. A multitude of small enterprises, once viewed as harboring great potential, faltered in their ability to sustain, a prerequisite for escalating prices. If one recalls the frenzy surrounding internet companies at the dawn of the millennium, every investor can likely recount a host of firms predicted to have a seemingly guaranteed successful trajectory, which ultimately capsized. At best, they were either absorbed through acquisitions or delisted from the stock market. However, there have been numerous instances where investors bore the brunt of stock value depreciation until the inevitable insolvency of the companies.

A similar picture can be expected for the stocks of the crypto sector should there be a significant boom in new issues. Despite the growth of the sector, such a development is not certain because the financing of crypto projects is not tied to the stock market. As early as 2017, projects were able to finance themselves easily through initial coin offerings[17] (ICOs). As the development status and quality of serious projects have made significant progress in recent years, financing through the sale of tokens is often the easier way compared to an IPO. Moreover, there are numerous ways to integrate ongoing financing into the protocols already in the implementation of a project.

Nevertheless, there are arguments for traditional IPOs as well. A stock exchange listing provides a legal framework for investors and issuers that has been tested over decades. This regulatory clarity is particularly important for institutional investors. This is especially true regarding the set investment guidelines, which define the limits of an investor's allocation. These investment guidelines usually include the typical asset classes of stocks and bonds. Until digital assets have found their way into the mainstream, stocks from the crypto sector represent a way to build positions in this segment, if the investment guidelines leave no room for a direct crypto exposure.

---

17 Initial coin offerings are a way of funding for crypto projects. Investors acquire coins of the corresponding project within the scope of an ICO (Momtaz, 2019).

The playing field has also widened for crypto stocks, as evidenced by the listing of crypto exchange operator Coinbase in the United States. In the early years after the launch of Bitcoin, investors who could not or did not want to invest directly in cryptocurrencies took the shortcut via one of the numerous stocks that adorned themselves with the then new label "blockchain." As in the years of the internet stock bubble at the turn of the millennium, there were also companies this time that simply changed their name.

5.5.1 Name Changers and Game Changers

In 2000, not only small firms wanted to catch some of the internet's shine. Countless company names were supplemented with the domain ending ".com" or with terms like "online." Established corporations were also not immune to the hype. In 2017 as well, some executives could not resist choosing a new name for their company that included the modern-sounding term blockchain. This often happened regardless of whether the companies had anything to do with the development of blockchain applications or not.

Probably the best-known example is the company "Long Island Iced Tea" that renamed itself "Long Blockchain Corp." (see Figure 5.31). The story

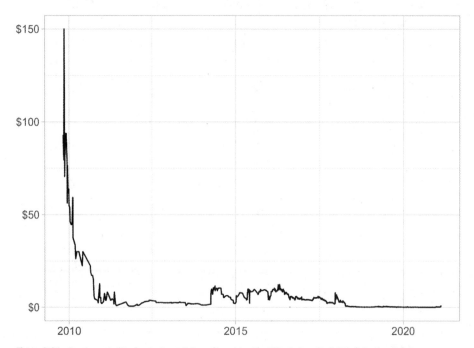

Figure 5.31: Development of the "name changer" share of Long Island Iced Tea aka Long Blockchain Data: NorgateData.com.

of this name changer did not end well. After an enormous price increase following the renaming, which should give pause to fans of the so-called swarm intelligence, the stock price initially fell back to the starting level. This was followed by the delisting from the U.S. technology exchange, Nasdaq, because the company no longer met the minimum requirements for a stock exchange listing. The decision of the exchange operator Nasdaq was succinct: "The Nasdaq Stock Market, Inc. (the Exchange) has determined to remove from listing the common stock of Long Blockchain Corp. (the Company), effective at the opening of the trading session on June 18, 2018. Based on review of information provided by the Company, Nasdaq Staff determined that the Company no longer qualified for listing on the Exchange pursuant to Listing Rule 5100."[18]

The change of company names to appear more attractive is often associated with so-called "pump and dump" schemes. During such activities, fraudsters stock up on illiquid shares of small listed companies and then fuel demand for the papers with rumors and absurd stories in forums and networks. Due to the illiquidity of the papers, just a few unlimited orders from unsuspecting investors are enough to trigger an enormous price increase (pump). The pump 'n' dumpers sell their papers into this increase (dump). This is usually followed by the collapse of the price.

There are also more harmless examples of companies that changed their business purpose more than once. One such is the Canadian Northern Peak Resources, which started out as BTL Group, dealt with blockchain applications in the energy sector, and apparently even completed a pilot project with BP, Eni Trading & Shipping, and Wien Energie.[19] There was a first renaming to Interbit Ltd. and finally the name was changed to Northern Peak Resources. The company now deals with mining in the traditional sense. The company's website states that the management team is aiming to acquire long-lasting, low-cost gold mining projects.[20] We keep our fingers crossed, but the company's paper is no longer a candidate for a crypto stock watchlist.

Such anomalies, or even unethical practices, are prevalent across all economic sectors. Unsurprisingly, fraudsters tend to target subjects that are currently trending or in vogue. In 2017, it was the stocks that could be

18 See SEC.gov (2021).
19 See DSA Corporate Services (2017).
20 See North Peak Resources (2021).

linked in some way to the topics of blockchain and cryptocurrencies. Around the turn of the millennium, it was stocks related to the Internet. The equivalent of the years 1959–1962 was the appendix "tronics." For investors, it is important to avoid such things while remaining open-minded to the opportunities that present themselves. Not every internet stock is backed by a fraudster and the abbreviations "24" or ".com" are demonstrably also found in the names of reputable and successful companies.

In addition to the isolated name changers, there are many serious companies that deal with applications of the blockchain in various areas from logistics, through the energy sector, to the financial industry. The requirements for using a blockchain within a trusted network pose different demands on the platform used than a public network, which is about getting by without trusted third parties. Many companies therefore rely on permissioned blockchains such as the Linux Foundation's open-source framework Hyperledger[21] when restructuring internal processes. Hyperledger and similar frameworks are better suited for many tasks than some would like to admit. Public blockchains have their place, but they will not be used in all economic processes because they are not the best solution for every purpose.

The core operational sectors of publicly traded companies engaged in cryptocurrencies and blockchain applications are as diverse as the categories within the crypto-biotope itself. The pioneering companies in this field, unimpeded by conventional thinking or organizational barriers and committed to advancing technologies and business models, harbor immense potential. If these companies can secure large-scale financing without significant hurdles, they can revolutionize the industry. A review of ecommerce illustrates the potential trajectory of a stock when conventional rules are deemed flexible. As the concept of decentralization and the ensuing elimination of intermediaries transcends industry boundaries, we can anticipate parallel transformations across various sectors. This shift ushers in the next logical phase, aligning the internet more closely with its original vision of a global, decentralized network. Consequently, the stakes are high, with substantial opportunities for those who adapt and significant risks for those who resist change.

---

21 See Hyperledger.org (2021).

5.5.2 Crypto Assets versus Blockchain Applications

Crypto-related companies can be clearly separated based on a dividing line between the ones focusing on crypto assets and the others that are developing blockchain-based applications for other use cases. Companies specializing in crypto assets engage in processing, trading, and consulting. Examples include trading venue operators and specialized investment firms.

As in other industries, there are broadly positioned companies and those that focus on one task. The latter include mining companies. Others operate exchanges, bilateral trading venues, or are on their way to becoming a diversified investment bank in the field of digital assets.

Despite crypto assets being just one use-case for blockchain technology, the companies operating in this field dominate the sector. But other players will likely catch up. Even today the major cloud platform providers already provide blockchain-as-a-service products, which, like the introduction of other cloud solutions, enable small start-ups to enter the blockchain application development market with minimal organizational overhead.

The possibilities for using blockchain-based software solutions are not limited to individual sectors. Almost every industry offers a potential use, and as in the early days of the internet, short-term potentials are often overestimated, while long-term changes are significantly underestimated. This also applies to the speed at which these new developments will take place once they have gained a foothold. For instance, Kodak had its very own experiences with digital photography, and those who scoffed at streaming services like Netflix only a few years ago and instead preferred to rate the good old video rental as undervalued hopefully did not put too much money on their forecast. How quickly and comprehensively initially ridiculed business models can prevail, and what they do to old structures, is shown by the stock prices of Netflix and Blockbuster Inc., the former largest video rental company in the USA (see Figure 5.32).

When evaluating stocks from sectors that are subject to complete change, the assessment "surprisingly low valued" is often followed by insolvency. Betting on changes carries risks, and it is not about reacting immediately to every idea. However, hoping to sit out any change can potentially be existence-threatening.

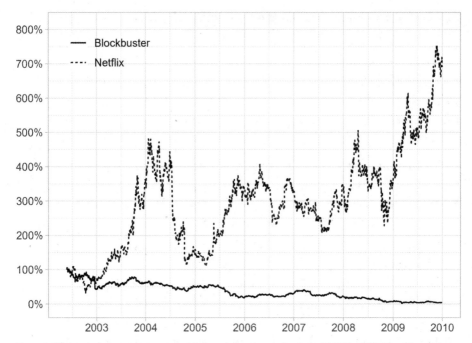

Figure 5.32: Impact of technical disruption on stock prices of affected companies, Netflix IPO 2002 = 100%. Data: NorgateData.com.

Since we are dealing with the topic of asset allocation in this book, we also want to look at possible changes in the financial sector beyond trading or mining, as this sector forms the intersection of classic blockchain applications and digital assets. Even the foreseeable impacts will be enormous. The obsolescence of central authorities, instant settlement, and the programming, and thus, automation of almost any process will enable the comprehensive digital representation of most services in the financial system. The concept of an autonomous, fully automated, and self-learning asset manager, for example, we would not even call a vision. It is more of a conservative design of what is to be expected in the coming years. Already now, it is possible to launch investment vehicles on the blockchain in a short time, which enable rule-based control of investments and do not neglect the integration of various fee models. Also, topics such as an investment limit check can be explicitly defined by program code, thereby technically excluding the violation of investment guidelines. These methods do not account for all financial market complexities. This may still be insufficient to cater every unique need of individual investors, but for straightforward investment strategies, and thus, for the bulk market, such structures are perfectly adequate.

That said, one should not underestimate the massive efficiency gains brought by a full transparency of the transaction history in areas like taxes and accounting. Providers who are currently conducting their business in the conventional manner can substantially streamline certain aspects of their operations. Many business models will be profoundly altered by the elimination of specific procedures. The proportion of processes that can be automated will increase significantly.

This approach is currently limited to crypto assets, but this is no reason to underestimate the potential. If the tokenization of conventional assets gains momentum, there is technically nothing standing in the way of a completely digital representation of comprehensive asset management. Since tokenization will also affect illiquid assets such as artworks, the possibilities of blockchain-based asset management significantly exceed those of conventional procedures.

The impacts of progress will also affect the administrative aspects of many financial products. What will happen to the classic setup of investment funds, which so far have been based on the interaction of investment management company, custodian, and portfolio management? Is this prime example of central authorities in asset management still viable? Instant settlement and an inherent control of transactions by the network will render many tasks that today constitute the core business of service providers obsolete. As in other industries, this opens new opportunities and brings enormous potential for the democratization of asset management. The extent to which this transformation in the financial industry mirrors the disruption experienced in the media industry hinges on regulatory decisions. Despite the potential challenges of market entry in certain regions, there lie opportunities for players unencumbered by legacy systems to establish and scale novel structures swiftly, potentially outshining the established norms.

In any case, numerous traditional back-office tasks that can be eliminated will be affected. Given this evolution in fast forward, some job descriptions already seem outdated today. A central ledger with delay-free settlement and no counterparty risk makes centralized controls obsolete, and in addition to higher security, enables a tremendous acceleration of processes in asset management. In this complete overhaul of the infrastructure, a classic case of creative destruction, large companies are already driving developments. Therefore, not only startups will benefit from the developments, but also many existing companies.

5.5.3 Crypto Stock Returns

Compared to the several thousand crypto assets, the selection of stocks in this segment is modest. Initially, mining companies like Marathon or Riot were in focus, but also companies with more comprehensive business models entered the stage. The field of listed stocks offering services outside the financial sector is dominated by large software houses and cloud platforms. We would not consider these papers as crypto stocks, as they only have a limited connection to digital assets. We classify as crypto stocks the companies that are active in the field between mining, investment, and consulting. A significant correlation of these titles to the development of the crypto market is plausible, so they allow, an albeit inaccurate, representation of crypto risks in portfolios.

The progress of two mining stocks in comparison to Bitcoin is shown in Figure 5.33. The time series begins on the date of the start of the first Bitcoin futures at the Chicago Mercantile Exchange.

The performance of the mining equities in this period is comparable to that of Bitcoin. By including more mining equities, it is possible to construct a portfolio with a high correlation to Bitcoin. Thus, investors could indirectly move toward a crypto allocation without altering the investment guidelines. Obviously, the fundamental characteristics and hazards of an equity investment are notably different from those of a portfolio of digital assets. Therefore, a crypto portfolio cannot be wholly replaced with crypto stocks.

Nevertheless, investment opportunities in the sector are diverse. By adding further titles, a broadly diversified portfolio can be built, which, while having a lower correlation to Bitcoin, is not largely dependent on the development of the very price-sensitive miners. This will probably be the preferred route for many investors who cannot directly invest in cryptos.

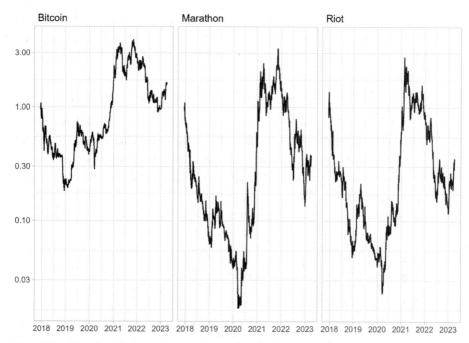

Figure 5.33: Bitcoin and crypto stocks performance. Data: NorgateData.com, MarketVector.

Warren Buffett famously only buys companies that an idiot could run because sooner or later an idiot will run a particular company. With a semi-talented top management, a quick and profitable exit from a private investment via an IPO might be possible in a boom. However, building a long-term successful company in a very dynamic sector like crypto assets will not succeed without capable management. Nevertheless, in addition to the digital assets themselves, it is worth keeping an eye on the publicly traded corporations. Important and free sources of information accessible to everyone are the daily published positions of exchange-traded funds like the VanEck Vectors Digital Transformation ETF.

5.6 Interview with Jan van Eck

Jan F. van Eck, CEO of Van Eck Associates Corporation, has a distinguished career in financial services, joining the firm in 1991 and leading its Executive Management Team since 1998. An industry innovator, van Eck established the firm's ETF business in 2006, making it one of the world's largest

ETF sponsors. With a knack for predicting asset classes and trends, his strategies span strategic beta, tactical allocation, emerging markets, and commodities. A Stanford Law graduate and Williams College alum, he is also a director at the National Committee on United States–China Relations and a regular contributor to CNBC and Bloomberg Television.

Q: **The VanEck website carries a provocative message: "Don't settle for the conventional; dare to be different." This certainly aligns with VanEck's impressive track record. Could you take us back to the beginning and explain how VanEck's history and its unique investment philosophy, established by your father in 1955, have shaped the company's approach and strategies over the years?**

A: Certainly. Fundamentally, we are what you might call "macro investors." In the investment industry, when people ask if we focus on growth stocks, value stocks, or something else, I usually respond that VanEck's perspective is macro. What that means is that we examine the big global trends and evaluate how they will impact financial markets, as well as the potential opportunities and risks for your portfolios. For example, throughout the company's history, which began in 1955, we have looked at various macro trends. Although this type of macro investing might be relatively unique in the United States, I believe it's a more natural approach for European investors who have a long historical perspective. Americans tend to harbor a bias that equities are always a good bet, but investors from other countries recognize that various factors, such as wars, political instability, and technological change, can dramatically affect their portfolios.

The firm was founded on the premise that, particularly after World War II, international stocks—specifically from Europe, Germany, and Japan, as well as Asia—were growing at a faster rate. Their revenue and profit growth was more rapid, and their valuations were more attractive. This is the perfect combination that every investor wants: an affordable investment with a substantial tailwind. In our case, that tailwind was the growth and rebuilding that took place after World War II.

Sometimes, however, when we look at trends, we see more risks than rewards. In 1968, despite the U.S. performing well economically, there were concerns due to its large government spending policies and the rapid expansion of its money supply. My father foresaw the risk of inflation in the United States and started looking for ways to hedge against that risk. One such option was investing in gold.

Interestingly, at that time, it was illegal to invest in gold bullion in the United States, so people turned to gold coins. This was due to the banking reforms initiated by FDR to stimulate inflation and curb private sector gold ownership. Another interesting point is how different the future can look from what you might imagine. At that time, no one thought the price of gold could reach $800 per ounce. This sort of dramatic change is often not on people's radar unless they have a historical perspective that allows them to entertain a wide range of possibilities.

Looking ahead, we have to consider different asset classes—stocks, bonds, gold, or other stores of value—in our portfolio. For instance, with the rise of China over the past 30 years, investors had to consider how to include this new market in their portfolios. When China first emerged as a global economic power, it did not even have a well-functioning stock market, and there was no asset class known as "emerging markets." These considerations make investing a fascinating and ever-evolving challenge, a subject perhaps for another interview.

Q: **Before we delve into the topic of cryptocurrencies, I understand that you have a chart of old railway stocks, which you've said illustrates how disruptive this sector was in its early days. Could you explain this chart to us and what lessons it might hold for investors looking at the disruptive potential of cryptocurrencies? In particular, could you discuss the dangers of investing too early in new and disruptive markets and how one might mitigate those risks?**

A: Absolutely, I'd love to. The chart you're referring to portrays the sector weights of the U.S. stock market since its inception. The first stocks were primarily financial or banks, such as the Bank of New York founded by Alexander Hamilton. Interestingly, the transport section of this chart, primarily railroads, saw a massive surge before the railroads were even fully built.

Railroads, a vital technology of their time, were essentially complete around the 1860s in the United States. What you'll notice, however, is the substantial increase in the market cap and stock prices of these companies preceding the full implementation of this technology. Investors had arguably correctly anticipated the potential profits from this new technology, but the risk lies in being too early. Even if your fundamental premise is correct, you can still experience significant losses, as railroad stocks peaked before 1860 and subsequently fell by over 50%, despite the continued development of the technology.

Now, you might view railroads as outdated technology, but I urge you to think of them as the first iteration of the internet. Before the advent of railroads, there was no national consumer market or business market in the United States. Farmers typically had to sell their goods within a 10- to 20-mile radius, as transporting goods over long distances was cost prohibitive. The railroad revolutionized this, enabling the transport of goods and communication at an unprecedented speed.

How so? By facilitating the stringing of telegraph wires along the railroad lines. During the Civil War in the 1860s, President Abraham Lincoln could communicate with his generals in mere seconds via the telegraph. That's why I equate it to the first version of the internet, as it allowed data to be transported at a speed that was hitherto unattainable.

I reference this history when discussing cryptocurrencies because, like railroads, cryptocurrencies could potentially be highly disruptive. However, it's essential to be cautious of the volatile investment cycles, a lesson from the past that holds relevance even today. Even if your investment thesis is correct, you could still lose money as an investor, making it a cautionary tale worth remembering.

Q: **When did you first notice Bitcoin or crypto assets? When did you realize that they might be interesting?**

A: I believe it was around 2015 or 2016. As an investor, part of our job, and what makes finance so intriguing to me, is that you need to keep up with various types of news, not just political, but also technological advancements. We're all children of this technology age, so I was naturally tracking the progress of Bitcoin. By early 2017, I began questioning whether this could be a potential competitor to gold. I found myself constantly hearing about it and started wondering whether I should shift my personal interest and investments toward it, and possibly even present it as a viable investment opportunity for VanEck's clients.

As you can imagine, even in 2017, there were plenty of skeptics. I sought opinions from my colleagues, but they didn't have much insight into this emerging asset. I realized that if I wanted to understand it better, I would need to do the research myself. So I dived into the world of cryptocurrencies—listening to podcasts, reading white papers, trying to grasp the technology behind it. Although I'm not a computer scientist, I am familiar with how computers and databases are structured, which helped in my understanding.

Finally, in early 2017, I concluded that Bitcoin indeed had the potential to rival gold. That was when we embarked on the project to file for one of the first Bitcoin Exchange-Traded Funds (ETFs) in the United States.

Q: **What's the main reason, apart from historical performance, you found that Bitcoin or cryptos should be a part of an investor's portfolio, whether it's an institutional portfolio or a private one?**

A: Well, I believe cryptocurrencies can fit into different parts of your portfolio. It's crucial to clarify that what I'm about to share cannot be empirically proven because we can't predict the future definitively; it's more of a mental model that guides my thinking.

Firstly, Bitcoin acts as a competitor or companion to gold. This is due to its scarcity value that mirrors that of gold—indestructible not because of physical limits (like the finite amount of gold in the ground) but because of the algorithms underlying Bitcoin. So, it represents a store of value and offers protection against fiat or government-controlled supply of money.

Secondly, beyond Bitcoin, other cryptocurrencies represent applications akin to any other type of growth or technology investment. Be it healthcare, science, databases, cloud computing, 5G, or 6G, these cryptocurrencies play a similar role. So, the inclusion of cryptocurrencies in an investor's portfolio would depend on their concerns about inflation—that's where Bitcoin comes in, and also their time horizon and appetite for growth investments, which is where the rest of the crypto market fits in.

Q: **Could you share your experience of launching a Bitcoin ETF or other crypto-related products, considering the difficulty private investors or consultants may have allocating Bitcoin in a portfolio?**

A: From a business perspective, in the United States, we've only been allowed to launch a Bitcoin Futures ETF. In Europe, we found a way to offer Bitcoin safely with proper custodial services and made it tradable with in-kind creations and redemptions. We've also managed to list it in Germany and other markets.

Our journey with these initiatives started around 2020. After becoming pro-Bitcoin in 2017, we dove deeper into the crypto space during the DeFi summer in 2020. That's when we decided we wanted to go more aggressively into this space, offering not just Bitcoin but also Ethereum and other growth-type investments.

Q: **Would you say it's like an internal venture capital approach where you allocate some parts of your asset base into disruptive technologies like Bitcoin and Ethereum, not knowing if they will end up constituting a significant portion of your business? Is it a bet on the future, as Gretzky said, "I skate to where the puck is going to be, not where it has been?"**

A: Yes, I think that's an apt analogy. One of my colleagues refers to these non-Bitcoin software projects, often labeled as "cryptocurrencies," as a kind of call option on future adoption. They essentially represent growth investments. In the context of crypto and blockchain technologies, the obvious sectors for adoption would be finance, which explains why many projects are financial in nature, and technology and database management because, fundamentally, something like Ethereum is a database technology. These are the traditional sectors that seem ripe for disruption.

Q: **A year ago, people expressed reluctance to buy cryptocurrencies because they were outside the system. With recent banking issues, interest has shifted toward these cryptocurrencies, like Bitcoin, for the same reason. As disruptive future technologies, the precise impact and probability of cryptocurrencies are uncertain. What are your thoughts on this?**

A: Yes, we have seen significant changes in the adoption of these technologies, particularly in the summer of 2023. Although the Bitcoin code itself hasn't changed drastically, its adoption has varied.

Consider it as an eight-year-old child; it is still maturing. Millions of retail investors and some macro hedge funds and crypto funds have adopted Bitcoin, but the majority of Pensions and Investments have no exposure to it.

Major institutional gold buyers like central banks, especially from developed markets like France, the UK, Germany, and the US, haven't shown much interest in Bitcoin yet. Their credibility was established based on gold reserves a hundred and two hundred years ago. However, we're now seeing emerging market central banks and frontier banks, like Russia and China, buying gold and possibly Bitcoin to enhance their credibility. Some countries in Central America, Africa, Middle East, and Asia involved with Bitcoin mining could already be accumulating Bitcoin, although they haven't announced it.

The investor adoption curve for Bitcoin is still unknown, as is the evolution of the Bitcoin ecosystem. Block rewards for network validation will change next year, but the ability to earn transaction fees is gaining importance. The latter rose from 7% to over 30% of Bitcoin revenue earlier this year, indicating a healthy ecosystem.

There are concerns about what will happen to Bitcoin when it must rely exclusively on transaction fees by 2100. This is why I liken it to an eight-year-old child; it has a lot of potential and many interesting dynamics that have yet to manifest.

Q: How do you perceive cryptocurrencies' impact on finance?

A: The financial ecosystem has transitioned from paper-run in the 1950s to programmed mainframe computers in the 1970s. Now, we face the question of whether a new decentralized financial ecosystem can be built. However, my main concern is the fragmentation of the financial system due to blockchain. Major financial institutions are working on blockchain applications, but having their private blockchain would be no different than having their private mainframe.

Regulatory bodies are moving at different speeds. Europe and Brazil, for instance, are advancing toward adopting tokenization and blockchain technologies to reduce costs for investors, while other countries like the US are at a standstill. The structural centralization of liquidity pools and the issue of fragmentation in decentralized finance (Defi) also raise numerous questions.

The bottom line is that we must recognize that things are changing. Although we can't exactly predict how they will evolve, we must stay aware and open to these developments.

Q: **It's always a question of what a country stands to lose, and in regards to currency, some countries have nothing to lose. Some Southern African nations, for example, have already faced severe economic problems. What could possibly go worse than it has already? But if you are in the United States, you've got the dollar, a major asset. This, I believe, is a reason for Americans to be more cautious. It's interesting to see these developing countries taking bold steps toward change. I'm not sure if they will be successful, but how do you see these developments playing out between the Western world and developing countries?**

A: It's crucial to not dive too deep into macro or philosophical aspects, but I believe the key question here revolves around the concept of financial freedom. In an economy where cash was king, people had a certain degree of privacy. Today, with every transaction, even a cup of coffee purchase, being recorded in a database, the level of surveillance has increased dramatically. This capability has fostered an environment similar to a large-scale police state, causing concern across the globe, and rightly so, as such tools have been used against citizens before.

This surveillance state, enabled by technological advancements, has escalated to an unprecedented level. And surprisingly, there are people, even in the United States, known for its love of individual liberty, who appreciate this. They see the potential for limiting activities they disagree with, like the purchase of firearms, by using the financial system.

So, the power of government extends beyond the financial sector alone. The financial sector can be weaponized to exert government influence in ways we haven't seen before, even in U.S. history, let alone in other countries. That's a bit of a philosophical standpoint, but it's a real concern.

The political control of the banking system is another crucial point. Banks play a significant role in an economy, and the importance governments attach to this control cannot be understated.

Q: In terms of adoption, when I meet institutional investors, a major concern is volatility. This can be managed by position sizing and active risk management. However, another big argument is always reputational risk. We've seen that recently with Temasek, the Singaporean wealth fund, who invested in FTX and lost almost everything. Despite it being less than 0.1% of their assets, they announced that they will stop investments in crypto. So, how do you handle the reputational risk? Are you afraid of it, given you're a thought leader in this space? What advice would you give to an institutional investor who is concerned about reputational risk?

A: Our business is fundamentally simple: we are fiduciaries and must act in our clients' best interests. When we structure a fund or investment vehicle for clients, we aim to do so in the most optimal way. Although future prospects of investments are uncertain, it's crucial to explain both the upside and downside. That's why I use my railroad chart to remind people that things don't always skyrocket.

Setting expectations and managing operational risk is important, and safeguarding fund assets is paramount if you're concerned about investors. One way we have familiarized ourselves with this new industry is by meeting people, the old-fashioned way. This method might harken back to my roots in Wall Street and dealing with various markets, but there's no better way to understand the inner workings of an industry than by meeting people involved in it.

Regarding FTX, our company, using company funds and not client money, invested a small amount. This was a risky move and wasn't included in client portfolios. That's how we deal with it.

Ultimately, reputational risk is about how well your funds perform and whether they meet the expectations you set for your customers, both on the upside and downside. I don't believe you can let governments dictate your portfolio construction, nor have I ever been concerned about reputational risk. If you're a gold investor, you're practically betting against central banks because you're expressing doubt about their ability to control the money supply. Therefore, it's never been an issue for us, and I don't think it should be a problem for any investor to express skepticism about anything that could affect their portfolio. It's part of the job.

Q: **Absolutely, it makes sense. In terms of the other big argument, the volatility argument, we write about it in our book, of course, and discuss simulations in terms of allocation. So, what's the optimal allocation? How do you approach clients? I understand it depends on their risk aversion and wealth, but do you have a rough guideline or recommendation of how much to invest? I can imagine you're not all in; this would surprise me. Can you make a recommendation? Especially from a volatility perspective?**

A: To answer this, I need to revisit what I've mentioned earlier. If you think about Bitcoin as an eight-year-old child, its behavior will change over time, especially in terms of its volatility. There have been periods in the last 12 months where it's been less volatile than the S&P.

In terms of traditional measurements, if Bitcoin is a counterpart to gold, the biggest macro concern for any investor in Germany, China, the United States, and developed market countries is the amount of debt they carry. This is where something like gold or Bitcoin becomes interesting. If you're not concerned about the debt or believe it won't affect you in your lifetime, then you may not need to invest in these assets. But if you're at all concerned, it becomes essential. It's the biggest risk in global financial systems.

The second major criteria for Bitcoin is the central bank cycle. The Federal Reserve in the United States was behind on inflation and is now trying to regain credibility, which isn't a great time for gold or Bitcoin. However, this is likely to end in the next 12 to 24 months. At that point, you'd want to increase your holdings of gold or Bitcoin. But timing it is challenging.

That's why I've recommended getting involved now, as it's hard to predict. It rallied for two months and is now correcting. You have to look at the longer fed cycle and consider the global synchronization of developed markets.

Then, if you look at blockchain technology adoption and the price movement, we're clearly in a bear market for these types of investments, except for AI and growth investing in general. I would suggest a normal allocation in your growth portfolio. Say you own 50 stocks, with a split of 25 for growth and 25 for value. I would include crypto in that growth allocation, around 5%.

I believe you need it as a hedge to your financials and technology equity exposure. So, in a sense, like Argentinians would rather hold U.S.-dollar–linked stable coins than the Argentinian peso that has almost 100% inflation, in your growth portfolio you'd like to have some allocation to a technology that could disrupt you.

Q: **I guess you're referring to a diversified crypto basket, or are you specifically talking about Bitcoin?**

A: Yes, I was indeed talking about a basket of crypto assets. I find this area to be fascinating and I plan on closely watching it, perhaps for the rest of my career. My attention is particularly drawn towards the actions of the government and central banks, their policy choices, and how they navigate these high levels of debt.

I envision two potential scenarios playing out. Either none of this will significantly impact my lifetime, or we will face some significant financial or inflationary challenges. If the latter scenario comes to pass, I would likely allocate more than 5% of my assets in Bitcoin or gold.

I've made a prediction that Bitcoin could easily become half the market cap of gold, which would result in a valuation of around $250,000 per Bitcoin. This may seem like a bold prediction, but I believe it's entirely possible. This potential is one of the reasons why one might want to own Bitcoin as well as gold.

That said, I'm not entirely certain that gold would perform as well as Bitcoin in this scenario.

Q: **I think it's still a conservative estimate for Bitcoin because not only is it a type of money, but with its whole ordinal inscription thing, it could also have other use cases. In that regard, it's also a long call option on technology. If you look at the whole sectors, we do all the categories. It's interesting the value accrual so far in crypto is with Bitcoin, with the layer ones, especially Ethereum. If you look at DeFi and Metaverse or media infrastructure, it's all super tiny. The future is still uncertain as to who will capture the value. Where do you see most of the value capturing?**

A: There's a big war between Web2, like Apple, for example, and Web3 kind of shareware software. Let me give you an example because I don't think people understand how inefficient the financial system can be. The costs, for example, if we list an ETF on an exchange, the exchange owns all the transaction information and all the price information for that ETF. They charge a lot for that information to everyone in the ecosystem, including investors, brokers, banks, and what have you. And they keep increasing those costs at 10% a year. It's sort of this hidden tax.

I'm not saying that these costs can go to zero in a crypto world, but there's a definite possibility of having a much more price competitive and customer-friendly ecosystem. These costs are very hidden in the financial system, but they're very real.

To go on a slight tangent, we had the largest Russian ETF, and you couldn't trade them after the sanctions. But banks were still charging depository receipt fees in the millions of dollars. They were charging for this depository receipt, which is supposed to be more liquid than the underlying stock, but neither was trading and they were still charging their fees. It's an unbelievable business model.

Even though there is no progress with DeFi right now, and as you pointed out, no value creation for the people in those ecosystems today, that's not to say that there isn't a lot of excess inefficiency and expense in the current system that can't be disrupted.

Q: **We often find ourselves eager for results, don't we? In this context, the requirement for patience can be a challenge. With respect to research, VanEck has a significant research department and a commendable reputation for it. If you were to focus your research on crypto assets, would it be from a technological perspective or a macroeconomic view?**

A: Well, as I mentioned before, our primary task at VanEck is to provide solid investment funds for our clients. A substantial part of this involves elucidating both the potential and the risks involved. The educational role we play around Bitcoin, Ethereum, other blockchain technologies, and digital assets has evolved over time.

In 2017, it was all about simplifying the technology for investors, explaining what it is. Now, we find ourselves in a different era where tens of millions of investors are familiar with the technology. Our focus is more on clarifying what a particular project can achieve, the possibilities of its success or failure, and the developments surrounding it.

Generally speaking, I notice three distinct types of audiences. The first group is the "never crypto" audience, who will never get involved in crypto investments. The second is the "100% convinced" group who are completely sold on crypto. The third group, whom I call "the persuadables," are somewhere in the middle.

Our communication is primarily with "the persuadables" and the "100% convinced," as the "never crypto" audience is largely unreachable in this context. Interestingly, even the persuadables are quite knowledgeable now, having years of investment scrutiny under their belts.

For example, many institutions in the United States indirectly got involved in crypto through venture capital funds like Andreessen Horowitz. They're familiar with the crypto landscape, having discussed blockchain and other related topics in their investment committee meetings for the past two or three years. Therefore, the concept of blockchain and cryptocurrency is not a novelty for them anymore.

Q: **As we approach the end of our discussion, I'd like to hear your thoughts on tokenization. I personally believe that, in the future, everything will be tokenized, including identity, real estate, tickets, and OTC derivatives. How do you view the future of ETFs in your business in this context? In Germany, we've already seen the tokenization of bonds, and there's a new legislative initiative for equities, but overall, it seems to be a distant reality. So, what are your views on tokenization in your daily fund business?**

A: First and foremost, the path towards tokenization or decentralized finance (DeFi) has to be clear, and above all, cost-effective. Technology, generally, either does something amazing or is simply cheaper. But when it comes to tokenization, regulation is a significant driver of its structure. My major concern here is to comply with various countries' regulatory systems, which might lead to a very fragmented ecosystem around tokenization.

For tokenization to take off, it needs to demonstrate a cost advantage. This is something I am continually trying to understand, and I believe we are learning every day. Furthermore, from my perspective as an ETF provider, liquidity is another significant concern.

Q: **Could you expand more on why you're stressing liquidity?**

A: The beauty of ETFs is not only in their cheap fees but also in the narrow bid-ask spreads. This is something we have yet to see in tokenization. It's easy to lose sight of the fact that while I can fractionalize various assets, the liquidity of these assets is crucial. If I ever want to sell that ownership interest, I don't want to lose a significant portion of its value. Therefore, marrying the concept of tokenization with liquidity is essential. The theory of tokenization needs to align with its practical aspect, such as liquidity. Also, the technology's adoption has to benefit consumers. There's always excitement about the potential of technology, but we often overlook the secondary market and liquidity, which are vital issues to address.

Q: **Before we end this discussion, could you highlight the major macro trends our readers should pay attention to?**

A: I'd like to share two significant trends that I believe will shape our future. The first one relates to longevity. During a board meeting four months ago, we discussed the outlook for the 2023 economy. However, I believe the future beyond that is more important and somewhat predictable. One of the major changes we can expect by 2030, as U.S. financial advisor Rick Edelman has said, is that if you live to 2030, you're likely to live to a hundred. This is due to expected medical breakthroughs in treating cancer and cardiac diseases in the next five to seven years. This will increase average lifespans significantly, affecting investors as their savings horizons for retirement could be much longer than they currently anticipate.

The second macro trend is the declining population in China. It is predicted that their population will drop from 1.4 billion to approximately 700 million by 2100. This decline is not just a future prediction; it is already underway. Last year, China had 10 million live births, and this year, that number will decrease to 8 million. In fact, they are predicting only 7 million live births next year at the current pace. The number of marriages year-to-date has also fallen by 25% from last year, which could be seen as a significant indicator of consumer confidence.

These trends will have major implications for various sectors, including housing. For instance, every province in Japan, except for Tokyo, had fewer residents this December than the last. Understanding these irreversible trends will be crucial when considering the future and how it might impact your investment portfolio.

Q: **Thank you very much for your time and insights, Jan. It has been an absolute pleasure speaking with you. Your perspective has certainly enriched this discussion and I'm sure our listeners will appreciate it as well. We look forward to possibly having you again in the future.**

You can watch the full video of our conversation with Jan VanEck on our website by scanning the QR Code below.

5.7 Conclusion

Digital assets or crypto assets represent a standalone asset class. They offer participation in price developments but, depending on their design, also interest-like returns within the scope of lending and staking. Since their inception, they have shown a low correlation with conventional asset classes. A hedging function against general market stress cannot be derived from the developments.

In evaluating crypto assets, the focus of a portfolio manager responsible for asset allocation is not solely on returns and absolute price fluctuations. The correlations of cryptos with other asset classes are hardly less relevant when constructing diversified portfolios. As the previous section shows, not only Bitcoin has a lot to offer in this respect. The growing interest of institutional investors, who are concerned with capital preservation over generations, is therefore not surprising. Important developments bring great opportunities. However, there will be no proverbial free lunch this time either. For investors interested in digital assets, it is therefore important to approach the topic with a healthy mix of openness, discipline, and sobriety.

New developments need time. This was no different with the railroads or the World Wide Web than with smartphones and will also be the case with digital assets. The speed of mass adoption depends on two points. The basis for broader use is a reliable legal framework to be created by the legislator and the regulatory authorities. The second point is the further development of the technical biotope with the aim of making both the acquisition and the handling of crypto assets easy for the average citizen. Whoever cannot sleep for fear of losing their private keys or placing their tax consultant in front of an unsolvable task will rather adopt a wait-and-see stance.

The price growth of Bitcoin and numerous other cryptocurrencies is unmatched by conventional asset classes. However, these offer a lengthy history that in the case of Gold even dates back thousands of years. Therefore, it is ineffective to cite Bitcoin's past enormous growth and declare other asset classes obsolete. Similarly, it is not beneficial for investors to disregard the development of digital assets solely because their history is so brief and at times chaotic.

Stocks from the crypto sector are not a perfect substitute for a direct investment in crypto assets. However, traditional securities can serve as a complement. For investors who will have no access to digital assets in the foreseeable future, a diversified and actively managed portfolio of crypto stocks may even be the only possibility of allocation in this sector for the time being.

For both private and institutional investors, the question arises as to how and to what extent digital assets should be integrated into a portfolio. This is the topic of the following chapter.

5.8 References

Anscombe, F. J. (1973). "Graphs in Statistical Analysis." *The American Statistician 27*(1): 17–21. https://doi.org/10.2307/2682899.

Benartzi, Shlomo, and Richard H. Thaler. (1995). "Myopic Loss Aversion and the Equity Premium Puzzle." *The Quarterly Journal of Economics 110*(1): 73–92. https://doi.org/10.2307/2118511.

DSA Corporate Services. (6 May 2017). "BP, Eni Trading & Shipping and Wien Energie Successfully Complete BTL Group's Interbit Energy Pilot." GlobeNewswire News Room. https://

www.globenewswire.com/news-release/2017/06/05/1280801/0/en/BP-Eni-Trading-Shipping-and-Wien-Energie-Successfully-Complete-BTL-Group-s-Interbit-Energy-Pilot-Additional-Participants-Invited-to-the-go-to-Production-Phase.html.

Erb, Claude B., and Campbell R. Harvey. (2013). "The Golden Dilemma." Working Paper 18706. Working Paper Series. National Bureau of Economic Research. https://doi.org/10.3386/w18706.

Gorton, Gary, and K. Geert Rouwenhorst. (2004). "Facts and Fantasies about Commodity Futures." Working Paper *10595*. Working Paper Series. National Bureau of Economic Research. https://doi.org/10.3386/w10595.

Hyperledger.org. (2021). "Hyperledger—Open Source Blockchain Technologies." https://www.hyperledger.org/.

Mahar, Maggie. (2004). "Bull: A History of the Boom and Bust, 1982–2004 (9780060564148): Mahar, Maggie: Books." https://www.amazon.com/Bull-History-Boom-Bust-1982-2004/dp/0060564148.

McMillan, Robert. (2014). "The Inside Story of Mt. Gox, Bitcoin's $460 Million Disaster." *Wired*. https://www.wired.com/2014/03/bitcoin-exchange/.

North Peak Resources. (2021). "North Peak Resources." https://northpeakresources.com/.

Satoshi Nakamoto Institute. (2021). "[bitcoin-list] Bitcoin v0.1 released | Satoshi Nakamoto Institute." https://satoshi.nakamotoinstitute.org/emails/bitcoin-list/threads/4/.

SEC.gov. (1 July 2021). https://www.sec.gov/Archives/edgar/data/1629261/000135445718000184/lbccdelistreason.txt.

Shafir, Eldar, Peter Diamond, and Amos Tversky. (1997). "Money Illusion." *The Quarterly Journal of Economics 112*(2): 341–374.

Spiegelhalter, David. (2020). *The Art of Statistics: Learning from Data*. Pelican.

Torsten Riecke. (2020). "Libra zwingt uns, über die Rolle des Geldes neu nachzudenken." *Handelsblatt.com*. https://www.handelsblatt.com/finanzen/maerkte/devisen-rohstoffe/vizechef-der-bank-of-england-libra-zwingt-uns-ueber-die-rolle-des-geldes-neu-nachzudenken/25665566.html.

Valencia, Laeven. (2012). "Systemic Banking Crises Database: An Update." *IMF*. https://www.imf.org/en/Publications/WP/Issues/2016/12/31/Systemic-Banking-Crises-Database-An-Update-26015.

Vigen. (2021). "Spurious Correlations." Spurious Correlations. https://tylervigen.com/spurious-correlations.

World Gold Council. (2021). "How Much Gold?" https://www.gold.org/about-gold/gold-supply.

6 Asset Allocation

"Yes, risk-taking is inherently failure-prone.
Otherwise, it would be called sure-thing-taking."
Jim McMahon

Since the advent of capital markets, investors have been deeply involved in attempts to find the best single investment. Which stock will rise the most? Will gold rise more than silver? Will value stocks wake up from their slumber, and if so, when and for how long? Except for a few professional traders for whom investing is not a sideline, the answer is: it does not matter. Admittedly, this is a short and unsatisfactory statement for many, so we complement it with the long version. Investors should care about asset allocation and abide by the basic rule to first and foremost do no harm.[1]

Asset allocation is the overarching division of wealth into different asset classes. What should be the proportion of equities, how high the bond quota? Is it sensible to own gold, and if so, how much room should it take up in a portfolio? Once these decisions are made, time becomes the investor's greatest friend, and one should not disturb it at work. If there is neither time nor desire to develop such a plan and follow it, then further thoughts are obsolete. If after three months, one throws over a capital allocation aimed at several decades because another approach or some particular investment theme has performed better in this short period, then a strategic approach is evidently not the right one.

Focusing on the basic orientation rather than individual bets serves, not least, to reduce drastic price losses at the level of total wealth. Private investors often consider fluctuation risks irrelevant. However, this often only applies until the eventuality occurs. When markets are falling, most people make equally unpleasant and costly experiences with their emotions. A single rash decision made at the wrong time then causes more damage than a previously perceived profit-reducing equity ratio that was allegedly too low. The old rule applies: when stocks rise, you always have too few; when they fall, always too many.

For institutional investors, the situation is more complicated. Besides human psychology and various committees, regulation plays a dominant

1 See Goyal and Wahal (2008).

role here. Therefore, the expected fluctuation ranges are, for risk management reasons, a metric that must be considered by this group of investors for regulatory reasons. Whether someone considers the respective
metrics meaningful in a technical sense or not does not always matter
in practice.

In this chapter, we embark on a journey to explore the principles of
asset allocation and unveil various approaches to establish allocation
proportions for individual investments. As we delve into the integration of crypto assets into a well-diversified portfolio, it is important to
note that, unless specified otherwise, we employ the MVDA10 Index
as our representative benchmark for the captivating realm of crypto
assets. Furthermore, we analyze the repercussions of incorporating
these digital assets into the risk-return dynamics of a balanced portfolio comprising bonds and equities. Let us start with the tension between
the expectations of many investors and the reality of the financial
markets.

6.1 Foundations of Asset Allocation

> "The secret to happiness is having low expectations."
> Warren Buffett

The importance of reasonable expectations cannot be overstated. These
are often in contrast to repeatedly reiterated mantras that represent hopes
rather than realistic assessments. Over time, even the experience of the
1970s slowly but surely faded, and after decades of declining yields, bonds
were once again labeled as "safe." Investors who recalled the inflationary
past and understood the distinction between nominal and real returns
could only shake their heads at this reclassification during a period of low
and sometimes negative returns. In 2022, the event ultimately occurred.
Beginning at a very low level, yields increased rapidly and significantly.
The concurrently high inflation caused the sharpest real price decline in
U.S. Treasury bonds since the 1970s. This was a hurtful reminder of the
fact that even if the reported yield of a bond can be realized over the term,
it says nothing about interim fluctuation risks.

While high expectations and a healthy ambition can promise success
in personal matters and can also motivate and inspire others, they can

quickly lead down a dangerous path when it comes to capital investment. Emotions that the branch of behavioral economics deals with often exert a stronger influence on the long-term investment success of many investors than the markets themselves.

6.1.1 Use of Return and Risk Projections

> "Time is your friend; impulse is your enemy."
> Jack Bogle

The construction of an asset allocation depends on five factors: (1) the investment horizon, (2) the expected return, (3) the permissible risk, (4) the correlation of investments with one another, and (5) any investment policy restrictions. When using forecasts, it is important to be clear about the period to which these refer. If you plan to invest for only 10 more years, expected averages over 30 years are of no help since the investment horizon[2] and the expectation horizon are not congruent. If an investment is not aimed at achieving a savings target, but at long-term wealth accumulation, then the time horizon includes long periods, and therefore, several economic cycles. As the compound interest effect increases with the duration of the investment, the rule for choosing the investment horizon is "the longer, the better".

The dependence of the meaningfulness of expectations on the chosen investment horizon is immediately apparent as the expected returns for the next few years also depend on the developments of the past years. In the stock markets, the tendency for mean reversion comes into play after strong directional moves, and for bonds, the expected return depends directly on the current yield level.

For estimating expected returns, investors use different approaches for different asset classes.[3] For bonds, the matter is simple. Over a certain period, they can expect to get the yield that is currently reported on the bond market for the corresponding term. These values can be adjusted for historical default rates, which is not only a sensible approach for high yield bonds. For stocks, there are various models that are largely similar.

---

2 An investment horizon is the period over which an investment is expected to be held.

3 See Leinweber and Willig (2021).

A common method determines the expected return based on the sum of the dividend yield, the real earnings growth, and the expected percentage change in the valuation level of a stock.

While there is at least methodological agreement in determining the expected long-term returns of individual investments, the discussion about the correct and universally valid risk indicator will probably never end. Since investors cannot wait for the final consensus on this matter, they must pragmatically deal with this issue and use one of the existing approaches or an aggregation of different indicators. The pragmatic solutions do not include the simple Value at Risk or more complex indicators, like the Conditional Value at Risk. Both indicators play a role primarily for regulatory reasons. Practitioners rather use fluctuation ranges or historical drawdowns.[4] As with other pragmatic approaches, the advantages of any method used are offset by weaknesses. For example, the determination of standard deviations of returns assumes a certain mathematical distribution of these returns, which is not given for most investments in the capital market. However, these and other weaknesses of the usual approaches are known, and investors can deal with them, which of course, does not mean that all investors do this in a meaningful way. A transparent process with known weaknesses is usually better than a complex approach that nobody knows about if, why, and especially how long it works.

The correlation or covariance of an asset class with other asset classes is the most essential determinant of its contribution to the portfolio's diversification. The correlation between two assets expresses, in simplified terms, their tendency to move in the same direction. If the prices of two assets tend to move in the same direction, the correlation of these asset prices is positive and the stronger this parallel movement, the higher the correlation. If the prices tend to move in opposite directions, their correlation is negative. The compilation of investments whose price developments have low correlations with each other reduces the fluctuation risk of the portfolio compared to investing in individual assets, and thus, also reduces the potential emotional stress of investors.

---

4   The term *drawdown* refers to the extent of losses from the previous maximum portfolio value.

6.1.2 Behavioral Finance

> "If you are wearing yellow goggles, every blue thing will appear
> green to you. It is your perception, and it is your reality."
>
> Naved Abdali

There are numerous emotional obstacles that prevent investors from effectively implementing a rational investment strategy. This varies from person to person, making it difficult to identify the solitary most significant factor. Consequently, we would like to highlight a few of the reoccurring thoughts that virtually every investor has.

The fear of losses and the fear of missing out (FOMO) are two unequal siblings, but both have cost investors a lot of money. Fear of losses leads to either constantly postponing investments or aligning a long-term portfolio in such a way that short-term fluctuations are minimized. However, anyone who invests their entire investor life exclusively in T-bills and avoids fluctuating investments like stocks piles up assets that over time have a much lower expected return than an allocation that also includes other investments. Fear of missing out, on the other hand, frequently leads to uncontrolled jumping on developments that have recently received a great deal of attention due to their exceptional performance. Frequently, each factor follows the other. First, the investor repeatedly delays the decision to purchase an asset. If they find themselves watching these investments surge over an extended period, the emotional pressure eventually leads to a purchase—usually at the temporary peak of a development. Confirmation bias and overconfidence are other factors that frequently occur together. Confirmation bias is exhibited by investors' preference for information that supports their preconceived opinions. Other arguments are not considered. Coupled with the overconfidence that can quickly develop after a few successful transactions and the ensuing perception of easy money, investors frequently purchase assets that they only believe to comprehend. Since they also disregard risks and criticism, they take on excessively large position sizes. If losses ensue, the position is neither reduced nor liquidated. In contrast, errors are frequently not acknowledged and additional funds are invested, which is euphemistically termed "averaging down" because the average entry price decreases as a result of the additional purchases. However, as the losses accumulate, so does the emotional burden on the investor because there is more and more capital at stake. A vicious circle.

All the negative effects of emotions on investing are supported by the human herd instinct. The social environment and media coverage can mutually reinforce each other, causing investors to be influenced by the behavior of other investors. Decisions are then made not rationally based on one's own strategy, but purely emotionally in order to belong to the group of other investors. To avoid these and other emotional problems, or at least to reduce their influence, it is important for investors to choose an asset allocation that matches their needs and risk tolerance and to stick with it in the long term. This increases the probability of achieving long-term investment goals. Investors should therefore soberly confront the opportunities and risks of the financial market.

6.1.3 The Price of Procrastination

"The best time to invest is several years ago. The second-best time is now."
Warren Buffett

Diverse factors make it difficult for investors to implement an investment decision once it has been made. The news is frequently too negative, the risks appear too great, and the returns appear eternally distant. Due to an overemphasis on short-term fluctuation risks and a disregard for the long-term compound interest effect, many individuals choose to delay their investments. This is not only a poor choice, but an exceptionally poor choice.

Treasury bills, which are frequently selected as an alternative, have much lower expected returns even over periods of just a few years than, for example, stocks. During the period in which an investor purportedly invests more cautiously (i.e., out of dread), opportunity costs are incurred. This is evident when examining the distribution of stock outperformance relative to treasury bills for periods between 1 and 10 years (see Figure 6.1).

Admittedly, there have always been phases when it would have been advantageous to wait a bit longer. However, these are rare. Much more common, however, were periods when hesitant investors just watched the significant price increases in the stock market and then entered at much higher prices later. Accepting reasonable expectations for the returns of

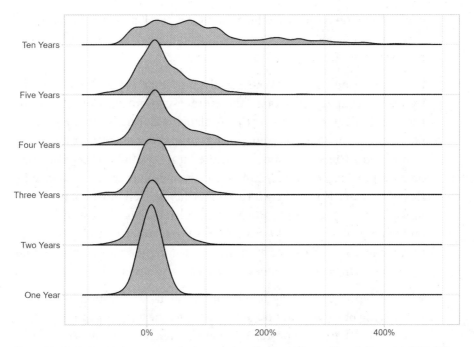

Figure 6.1: Distribution of final excess returns of an investment in equities versus T-bills over different holding periods (1900–2023, monthly data). Data: NorgateData.com, Ibbotson SBBI® data.

a long-term investment is more essential than trying to precisely time the investment's inception. Due to the larger capital base, the volatility of returns toward the end of the investment horizon is far more important than at the initial stages.

6.1.4 Rebalancing: Buy Low, Sell High

> "The act of rebalancing forces the disciplined and systematic buying low and selling high."
> David Swensen

Private investors usually let their portfolios drift freely. This inactivity leads to a steady over-weighting of the strongest asset class. At the end of a long upward trend in the stock market, a 60/40 portfolio can become an 80/20 portfolio, and investors find themselves at the peak of the stock market with the highest equity quota. The impact is correspondingly hard when the stock market finally drops. Anyone who chooses a certain risk profile for good reasons should prevent the portfolio from deviating too far from this target value by rebalancing regularly. This approach is common practice in institutional asset management.[5]

For cost reasons, reallocations should only take place when there are significant changes in quotas. Therefore, a combination of timing and threshold values for triggering the rebalancing is usually used. For example, a review can take place once every quarter to see whether the deviation of the current allocation from the target portfolio exceeds or falls below a previously defined threshold value. Quotas are only adjusted if this is the case. This approach can be further broken down. Some investors adjust the portfolio to the original values, others orient themselves on the range defined by the maximum values and bring the quotas back to these levels. In terms of accurately reflecting the chosen risk profile, returning to the original values is the cleaner solution.

William Bernstein, among others, investigated the question of whether rebalancing portfolios is good or bad, coining the term *rebalancing bonus*. In an article, Bernstein postulated that rebalancing portfolios could lead to over-returns compared to passive portfolios in most cases.[6] The correct answer from practice, however, is often: it depends. Certain conditions must be met in order to increase the potential return or a reduction in risk through regular rebalancing. One such condition is sufficient volatility of the individual asset classes. High variances lead to phases in which certain asset classes significantly outperform the development of the overall portfolio, followed by periods in which the same assets perform significantly below average compared to other components. An outperformance leads to profit-taking through sales due to a reweighting. An underperformance triggers a purchase at a lower price.

Furthermore, uncorrelated, or negatively correlated assets are the basis of effective rebalancing. A lower correlation of the constituents of a portfolio leads to a reduction in aggregated volatility at the portfolio level and can accelerate the accumulation of returns through low drawdowns and contribute to the increase in portfolio value over time. In addition to the purely monetary aspects this also reduces the emotional pressure on the investor as lower drawdowns can protect investors from imprudent actions.

---

5   See Ang (2014).
6   See Bernstein and Wilkinson (1997).

Portfolios that are regularly adjusted tend to exhibit notably lower draw-downs in comparison to static allocations. The term drawdown refers to the decline in an investment's value from its recent peak to a subsequent lower point. In Figure 6.2, positive values indicate that the rebalanced portfolio experienced a greater drawdown than the non-rebalanced portfolio, whereas negative values represent a deeper drawdown for the non-rebalanced portfolio. Analyzing the chart, we observe that the line depicting the differences predominantly resides below the zero line, signifying negative values. This suggests that the non-rebalanced index generally encounters more significant drawdowns compared to the rebalanced index. It is worth noting that deviations above zero are noticeably less pronounced than deviations below zero, underscoring the considerably higher risk associated with the non-rebalanced index. In essence, the rebalanced strategy demonstrates a propensity for experiencing milder declines in value during market downturns, thus offering a more resilient and stable investment approach.

However, over the very long term, investors should keep in mind that the much higher expected return of an asset class such as stocks is likely to

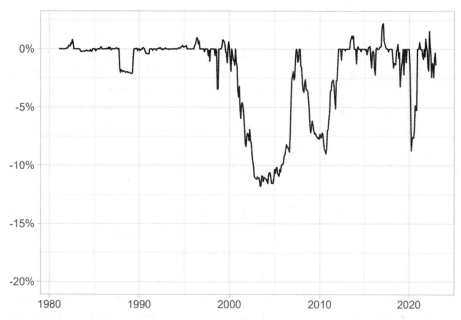

Figure 6.2: Relative drawdowns of a quarterly rebalanced versus a non-rebalanced portfolio initially containing 50% equities and 50% government bonds, 1980–2023. Data: NorgateData.com.

prevail. Therefore, rebalancing is less important for investors who are just beginning an investment period spanning three or four decades than for investors who plan to start drawing money from their savings in five years and are therefore more focused on risk than on the maximum earnings potential. For professional investors, rebalancing portfolios is the standard approach. Only the frequency of adjustments is a matter of disagreement. Even Meb Faber, in his book on tactical asset allocation,[7] cannot name an adjustment rhythm that generally proves superior. Ultimately, the frequency also depends on transaction costs and the tax situation of the investors. Rebalancing strategies can be perfected by aligning the reallocation cycle with market cycles, for instance, by integrating a trend analysis.

Consistent rebalancing can have a long-term risk-reducing effect. However, regular transactions incur costs and investors must also consider tax considerations. Therefore, the frequency of adjustments should not be too high. In general, a pragmatic approach is better than a dogmatic one.

6.2 Approaches to Asset Allocation

> "Short-cuts are timesavers for a reason: they omit details that can differentiate a profitable decision from one that you regret."
> Coreen T. Sol

In any asset allocation, two tasks need to be accomplished. The first step is to identify the relevant asset classes. This is followed by their weighting within the portfolio in accordance with the applicable investment limits. There are various methods for determining the shares of individual asset classes, some of which we briefly describe.

6.2.1 The Bearable Loss-Method

> "It's an insurance policy in case inflation comes back again as it did in the 1970s. I would say that if that's a sensible thing to do, then, certainly to have 1 to 2% of your assets in Bitcoin makes great sense here."
> Bill Miller, Founder, Chairman and CIO, Miller Value Partners

The first attempt to determine the proportion of digital assets in a portfolio is very simple and intuitively understandable. You choose the maximum loss that you are willing to accept for the allocation of crypto assets. If this

---

7   See Faber (2013).

value is 1%, then this is the allocation ratio. Since such an approach assumes the risk of a total loss, unpleasant surprises are ruled out. Given the historical crypto asset drawdowns of sometimes more than 80%, this approach is not overly cautious, but simply pragmatic. If the threshold has been chosen carefully, it also saves a lot of work and need for adjustment. Only the handling of increased quotas triggered by price rises needs to be clarified. This can easily be achieved by setting a fixed threshold. If the proportion of crypto assets, for example, increases from 1% to 1.5%, their share is then returned to the original value. Such clear rules save discussions and reduce the influence of emotions, which are rarely helpful in the financial market.

Even professionals usually start with small volumes in the face of uncertainties that are difficult to quantify. For example, hedge fund manager and "Market Wizard" Paul Tudor Jones announced that he would initially start his crypto investment with a ratio in the low single-digit percentage range. Investors who laugh at this should ask themselves whether they can handle risks better than managers who know their craft inside and out. Bill Miller, the former CEO of Legg Mason and responsible portfolio manager of the Legg Mason Capital Management Value Trust, is undoubtedly one of these. From 1991 to 2005, Miller significantly outperformed his benchmark, the S&P 500, with his fund. The probability of the outperformance he achieved was 1 in 2.3 million. Like Tudor Jones,[8] Miller also has a clear opinion and invested in Bitcoin at an early stage.

The difference between long-term successful managers like Paul Tudor Jones or Bill Miller and mere market shouters becomes immediately apparent in the mentioned allocation ratios. When Miller says that 1% to 2% Bitcoin in the portfolio could well make sense, you are dealing with a professional risk manager. Whether and how an allocation of this magnitude makes a difference in the portfolio, we consider later in this chapter.

6.2.2 The Global Market Portfolio

> "I think it's hard enough to predict the present. It is very hard to
> step out of your context and see what is happening."
> Lloyd Blankfein

The Global Market Portfolio (GMP) is intended to represent the entire global investable capital market. Therefore, the identification of relevant

---

8   See Letters (2020).

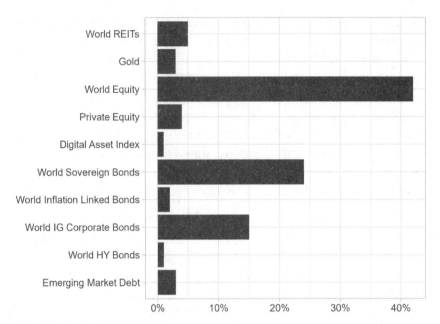

Figure 6.3: Exemplary Global Market Portfolio.

asset classes is generally simple, but varies depending on the size of the portfolio and the opportunities of the individual investor. Anyone who wants to build a GMP (see Figure 6.3) has no problem determining investment ratios. The approximated values for the size of individual capital market segments are relatively easy to find. We rely on the MVDA10 index, a modified market cap-weighted index that measures the performance of the 10 largest and most liquid digital assets for all subsequent allocations

In determining the final investment ratios, however, pragmatism is required. For example, due to costs, it does not make sense to replicate every detail of the global asset class distribution in a very small portfolio. The larger a portfolio becomes, the more investors can consider smaller aspects.

An advantage of the GMP is the automatic adjustment of the investment ratios. Once such a portfolio is set up cleanly, the ratios change roughly in line with the corresponding market segments. This is not exactly the case, as there are other influencing factors besides prices, such as new bond issues or strongly fluctuating volumes of new deals in the private equity sector. However, these changes are cyclical movements that do not change the character of a portfolio within a few months. A GMP can therefore be managed with a steady hand. As the portfolio grows over time, the granularity and diversification can be modified by a more detailed representation of the asset classes.[9]

Let us now depart from immediately intuitive paths and consider the contribution of financial science to this topic. What kind of allocation is the product of a portfolio optimization according to "Modern Portfolio Theory"?

6.2.3 The Markowitz Approach

> "Advisors can create the best portfolios in the world, but they
> won't really matter if the clients don't stay in them."
>
> Harry Markowitz

In 1952, Harry Markowitz laid the foundation for a new era of risk management. In his work, the economist described the construction of so-called efficient portfolios[10] that maximize the expected return for a given fluctuation risk. For his work, Markowitz was awarded "The Sveriges Riksbank Prize in Economic Sciences." However, it took a long time before the necessary computing power was available and affordable to practically implement his theory. Nowadays, optimizations according to Markowitz are part of everyday life in the financial industry. The use of optimized portfolios is not limited to individual asset classes, but can be applied to a pure equity portfolio as well as to a mix of different asset classes. The greatest challenge, and thus, the primary source of error is the estimation of expected returns as the most important input value of the optimization. Although risk parameters and correlations also need to be estimated, their impact on the result of the portfolio optimization is less than that of expected returns.

According to the supporters of Harry Markowitz's theory, the minimum variance portfolios determined based on his approach dominate all other risk-equivalent portfolios as it offers the highest return per unit of risk. The significance of Markowitz's approach is not clear to everyone. At its

9 Butler, Philbrick, and Gordillo (2016).
10 See Markowitz (1952).

core, the theory says that higher risk in the financial market does not necessarily lead to higher returns because the overall result comes from the interplay of returns, fluctuation risks, and correlations of the individual components of a portfolio. A haphazard expansion of risk positions, for example, through aggressive positions in sectors or even individual titles, therefore only guarantees investors a higher overall risk.

The result of the optimization are the weights of the portfolio and the expected values for its range of fluctuation and return. Since all parameters are changing all the time and these changes can occur very quickly in certain market phases, portfolios constructed in this way must be constantly monitored and adjusted if necessary. The turnover of such strategies can therefore be very high.

The proportion of digital assets in the resulting minimum variance portfolio is manageable (see Figure 6.4), but it is significantly higher than the corresponding value of the Global Market Portfolio. This is mainly due to the combination of historically very high returns of crypto assets and their low correlations with other asset classes.

Both the theory and the necessary calculations for determining efficient portfolios are simple. The major weakness of this approach is the dependence on estimates in several dimensions. While an estimate or modeling of fluctuation risks is feasible, return forecasts are notoriously prone to error. The need for reliable estimates of the correlations between

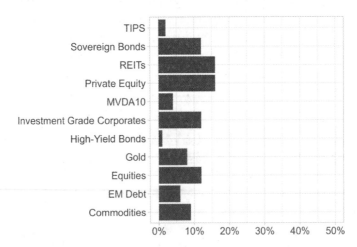

Figure 6.4: Exemplary minimum variance portfolio based on mean return and risk values.

numerous asset classes does not make the task easier. In practice, therefore, the Markowitz approach is frequently more of a mental model than a direct method for portfolio construction.

6.2.4 Risk-Parity Approach

> "He who lives by the crystal ball will eat shattered glass."
> Ray Dalio

The risk-parity strategy gained prominence largely due to the hedge fund, Bridgewater Associates. In this strategy, the overall risk of a portfolio is spread uniformly across different asset classes. Unlike a portfolio where each asset class is equally weighted by its amount, in risk-parity, each asset class is weighted by its contribution to the portfolio's overall risk. The aim is to construct a portfolio in which no component dominates the risk of the overall portfolio (see Figure 6.5). For example, stocks have significantly higher fluctuation ranges than short-term U.S. government bonds. If a risk-parity portfolio is to be formed from these two asset classes alone based on volatility, then the proportion of stocks will be relatively low, so that the risk contribution of both asset classes is the same.

The relevant variable parameter of this methodology, besides the decision on the permitted asset classes, is the selection of the risk measure used.

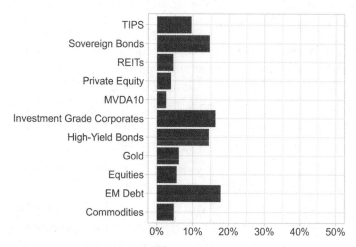

Figure 6.5: Exemplary risk-parity portfolio.

In the simplest case, the volatility of the respective assets is used (vola-parity), but there are numerous alternative indicators.

As with the efficient portfolios in the sense of portfolio theory according to Markowitz, the pure risk-parity portfolios are rather theoretical constructs, as there are usually side conditions to be observed in practice. Regardless of the chosen optimization methodology, minimum and maximum weights for individual investments must be observed. Also, a restriction of the total risk or a minimum targeted return can lead to sometimes significant deviations from the pure doctrine of risk parity.

Since not only the price levels, but also the fluctuation risks of the investments are constantly changing, a stringently managed risk-parity portfolio must be regularly rebalanced in order to bring the allocation back to the correct target quotas.

6.2.5 The 1/N Portfolio

The 1/N portfolio is constructed without future price forecasts. This straightforward allocation divides all asset classes equally. When multiple investments are combined, determining the significance of the investment universe is the most crucial step. Since each asset class is weighted equally, only certain investments can be chosen. For instance, it would be difficult for investors seeking a balanced portfolio to construct a portfolio with equal weightings of equities, bonds, gold, and gold mines, as the proportion of assets related to the development of the gold price would account for half of the portfolio.

Consequently, the broad asset classes of equities, bonds, and real assets are typically weighted equally. For larger portfolios, the ability to employ equal weighting at lower levels of allocation, such as in the sectors of the equity share, is of particular interest. This approach is not only easy to maintain but also highly flexible and adaptable to expanding portfolios and rising investor demands despite or precisely because of its simplicity.

The 1/N strategy is intriguing because of its simplicity. This technique is simple to implement and immediately reveals any deviations from the desired quotas. The classic variant of such a portfolio consists of 50% equities and 50% government bonds. In the sections that follow, we examine this portfolio in the context of integrating crypto assets.

6.3 Navigating Crypto Cycles—More Than a Story

Marcel Kasumovich boasts over 25 years of experience in financial markets, beginning at the Bank of Canada and progressing through roles at Goldman Sachs, Merrill Lynch, and Soros Fund Management, where he played a vital role in the firm's preparation for the financial crisis. He was a founding partner of the macro hedge fund Woodbine Capital and later helped grow Tse Capital's assets from $200 million to $1 billion. He currently partners with Semanteon Capital, focusing on machine-learning portfolio management, and advises Predata, an enterprise predictive analytics software firm. He also established Pure Macro Capital Advisors, engaging in cryptocurrencies since 2012, and published significant research, notably a 2015 warning about liquidity challenges in fractured markets.

The following paragraphs illustrate Marcel's stance on cycles in the crypto market.

Navigating Crypto Cycles

It is early. Crypto asset rails are built. They are demonstrably resilient. But they are also just tracks. What is built to ride those rails will matter most to adoption and value. Integration into any portfolio will require dynamism.

We aim to provide a glimpse of such dynamism—both in narrative and analytics.

The Story of Mike Hearn

Bitcoin has a historic return of more than twice its volatility. Running numbers to show Bitcoin was additive to past portfolios is obvious. Exploring where crypto assets fit into a portfolio takes more nuance, subtly, and dynamism that mirrors the assets.

A story. It is a less conventional path to portfolio analyses. But machines are increasingly adept at handling rote intelligence. To target an audience, to influence learning, to motivate discussion, and to encourage thought—a rich story wins the day. Stories like the one of Mike Hearn. Mike was one of the earliest Bitcoin developers and users in the ecosystem. His prescient vision of the future of money imagined financial cryptography and advanced robotics merging, with a reshaping of capital formation and the distribution of its returns. It is as relevant today as the date of its publication in 2013.

Mike sold his Bitcoin and left the network in 2015. He deemed hashing power as too concentrated, a long way from Bitcoin's decentralized vision. It is easy to run numbers and say that a portfolio "would have" earned extra risk-adjusted return being long Bitcoin. It is another matter altogether to hold the position.

Of course, we know that Bitcoin thrived. Hashing power diversified. Adoption broadened. It is not that Mike was right or wrong. The integration of any new technology, especially one with transformative vision, requires constant reassessment of risk and reward. Mike's assessment of the risk influenced the community to ensure they were not realized.

Mike's story is a reminder that when evaluating the role of crypto assets in historical portfolios, we are importing a bias—a survivorship bias. We should treat any such analysis with the humility it deserves.

Resilience—Crypto Assets Are Here to Stay

Bitcoin has had six drawdowns of more than 50%. We know the story—it lived to reach new highs in the first five. Most assets do not get a chance to experience a second let alone a fifth drawdown of such magnitude. It is not just a classic bubble.

Still, it is asking a lot for any portfolio manager to weather such downturns. After all, in each instance, there was a real threat to its survival. Just ask Mike. There are much more than just numbers—the fundamental thesis needs to be intact. And plenty of crypto assets have been rendered worthless on each downturn.

But several have endured. Even if skeptical, crypto assets demand your attention as an investor. They are technologies with chameleon portfolio properties. Bitcoin as a commodity. Ethereum as a bond. Stablecoin as low-risk collateral. NFTs as art. Metaverse as gaming. Wallets as banks. Tokenized assets as a bridge between digital and traditional worlds.

Of course, this is entirely consistent with historical analyses. Bubbles do not repeatedly reflate. The history of the world's biggest bubbles is documented in Table 6.1, courtesy the Man Institute. Bubbles burst and destroy all objects in their immediate orbit with rare occasions of resurfacing decades later. That is not Bitcoin's story.

That is not to say companies are not harmed on downturns. Bitcoin miners Compute North, Celsius Mining, and Core Scientific all declared

Bubble	Period	Duration in years	Max. multitude of starting price	% decline from peak
Dutch Tulips	1634–1639	0.9	39.9×	−93%
Mississippi Company	1718–1720	2.3	36.9×	−64%
South Sea Company	1719–1720	1.3	8.4×	−81%
DJIA	1921–1932	11.0	5,6×	−89%
U.S. rail stocks	1923–1932	8.8	2.4×	−92%
Gold	1977–1982	3.8	6.3×	−60%
Oil	1973–1986	7.2	2.8×	−73%
Nikkei	1982–1992	10.5	5.1×	−59%
Japan Real Estate	1982–1992	10.5	6.5×	−74%
Polish equities	1992–1995	2.8	28.7×	−70%
Developed Market Tech	1995–2002	5.7	7.9×	−78%
U.S. Real Estate	2000–2009	9.3	2.9×	−73%
Saudi equities	2003–2007	5.1	8.5×	−66%
U.S. Financials	2002–2009	6.4	1.9×	−78%
Gold	2002–2015	14	6.8×	−44%
Japan Real Estate	2003–2009	6.0	5.9×	−76%
Copper	2004–2008	3.5	4.1×	−66%
Uranium	2005–2010	5.2	6.6×	−70%
Oil	2006–2008	2.2	2.5×	−69%
China A-Shares	2005–2008	2.9	6.7×	−71%
Median		5.4	6.4×	−72%

Table 6.1: History of bubbles.

bankruptcy in the 2022 downturn. But the Bitcoin network functioned safely and soundly. There was no interruption of service, and no downtime.

It Is Not Just the Bitcoin Network, Either

Ethereum migrated away from proof-of-work to proof-of-stake—a brutally complex engineering change—during a period of severe weakness in asset prices. There was no interruption in operation. Dominant U.S. dollar stablecoin—Circle and Tether—also held their unit values to the U.S. dollar through wild swings in assets under management and extinction of other stablecoin.

Bitcoin, Ethereum, and the U.S. dollar stablecoin constitute more than three-quarters of the crypto asset ecosystem as of May 2023. Their resilience is undeniable, a strong sign that the assets are here to stay. How they integrate into investment portfolios is another matter.

Portfolio Analysis—A Pinch of Salt

Historical analysis argues for a substantial allocation to crypto assets. It is just math. Since 2010, Bitcoin has returned two times its realized volatility, outsized compared to equity, fixed income, and commodity markets that have ranged from 0 to 1.6 times. Figure 6.6 illustrates that cryptocurrencies, as measured by the MVDA10 index, also have a low average correlation across a variety of assets.

The combination of a high Sharpe Ratio and a low cross-asset correlation makes for a simple statistical case of the past—any optimizer will tell an investor to add crypto, and handsomely. But it comes with a tradeoff of larger drawdowns. Even optimizing to minimize the greatest drawdowns

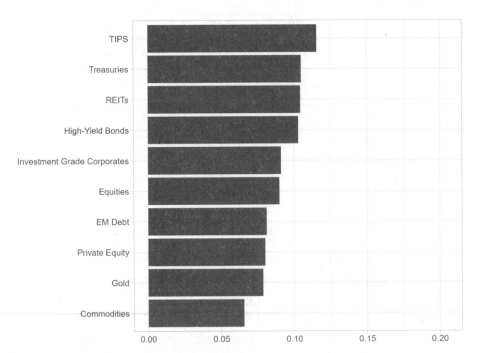

Figure 6.6: Average pairwise asset correlation for the MVDA10 Index with different asset classes, 2015–2023, weekly returns. Data: NorgateData.com, MarketVector.

is merely a disguise—drawdowns still would have been larger and more frequent on average.

Of course, the past is not indicative of the future, especially with nascent technologies. After all, high return-risk strategies cannot be sustained. Capital enters the ecosystem and competes away returns. Volatility declines. This is precisely the hope and expectation of crypto adoption. The historic analysis cannot be extrapolated, so we do not dwell on them here.

The dynamism of crypto assets is more relevant to the future, clearest when evaluating risk episodes instead of longer period averages.

We isolate 13 well-known periods covering macro and crypto events, from the collapse of FTX in November 2022 to the Covid Economic Crash in March 2020. Figure 6.7 shows the scatter diagram of S&P 500 returns on the x-axis against crypto assets on the y-axis. There is virtually no correlation. Crypto assets are not just beta to equities. Dispersion

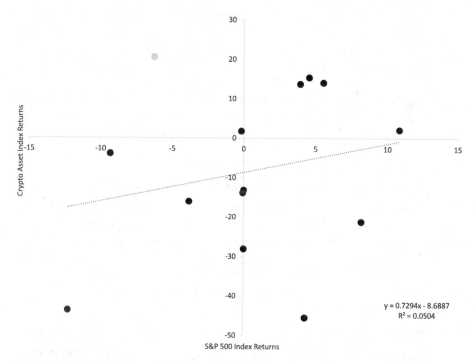

Figure 6.7: Crypto asset returns versus U.S. equities across 13 risk episodes.
Source: Coinbase Asset Management.

is considerable over episodic cycles. That is when the dynamism of risk management becomes key.

Naturally, when there is a common, negative shock, like the Covid economic downturn, crypto assets were beta to equity markets, declining 44% with the S&P 500 off 12% (leftmost dot in Figure 6.7). However, equity markets remained in negative territory during the subsequent phase of emergency Fed rate cuts whereas crypto assets rose 21% over the same period (highest dot).

There is a lot more to the story. Like fundamental matters. Take the latest crypto winter that descended on the market in 2021, bringing with it a chilling wave of uncertainty. The rapid expansion of micropayments integrated into the Bitcoin protocol serves as a powerful reminder that innovation does not hibernate in winter.

The rise of micropayment capacity is just one of the many a-cyclical indicators in the digital asset market. It defies the boom-and-bust cycles that often plague traditional markets. While Bitcoin's price had more than halved, the depth of layer-two micropayments had steadily advanced. The Lightning Network capacity had nearly doubled, driven by compelling user experience and organic growth. Companies like Block had made significant strides in delivering near-costless micropayments on digital rails.

The potential of digital assets extended beyond mere single price representation of fluctuations. There are asset classes within the class of crypto assets.

Portfolio Dynamism—Thought Experiment

The wide range of variation across equity and crypto asset markets is intriguing. Drivers of crypto assets are diverse. Momentum, growth, credit, and fundamental factors are all at work. Adding crypto assets to a portfolio demands a framework to consider its diverse properties.

The analysis asks the question: could an "all-season" strategy be developed to capture the different factors and mitigate the cyclicality of digital asset markets?

That would convert crypto asset as a blunt tool in a portfolio into an "alternative strategy" bucket. After all, the world of finance has already witnessed the creation of strategy tools to navigate different risk cycles.

The initial results of this thought experiment are encouraging. Well-designed stablecoin and digital income strategies proved their mettle during market downturns, providing a safe harbor asset to reduce risk. This is a natural starting point for an all-season strategy.

The chameleon nature of crypto assets means that they can play different roles at different times. We evaluate an "all-season" benchmark built on four digital asset strategies: income, credit, active, and passive.

- The income strategy involves generating short-term yield in U.S. dollars on OTC lending to digital asset counterparties. The return stream is simulated from three-month 150% overcollateralized Bitcoin loans, fitted to the Bitcoin forward curve to interpolate to daily data.
- The credit strategy is an unsecured lending into the digital asset ecosystem, calibrated to the equivalent of being long the five-year bond of Bitcoin mining companies.
- The active strategy is a systematic trend, a long-short strategy across multiple assets based on short-, medium-, and long-term price trends where risk is endogenous, rising and falling with conviction in the trend.
- Finally, passive beta is represented by the Coinbase Core Index or "the Index," a multi-asset, dynamic index based on fundamental and market-based factors that is published by MarketVector recalibrated quarterly.

Although the historical data spanned only from 2018 to 2022, it was a concentrated period that condensed the cycles of digital asset markets.

Figure 6.8 shows the return and volatility profiles across the four strategies. The x-axis is the daily return of the Index, and the y-axis is the daily returns of income, credit, and active strategies. The most striking observation is the significant dispersion among them. It reinforces that there are unique return characteristics within crypto asset markets.

Income, as designed, assumes the role of the lowest-volatility asset. Credit returns are overshadowed by the negative outcomes endured by Bitcoin miners last year, which was more attributable to the prevailing cycle than the strategy itself.

The passive long strategy, true to the high-volatility nature of digital assets, exhibits 80% annualized volatility. On the other hand, the active strategy stands in the middle, reducing passive beta volatility by three-quarters while delivering roughly half of the return.

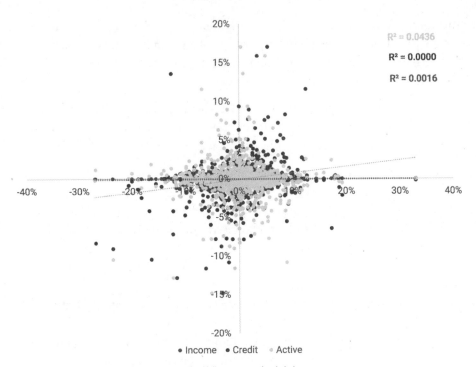

Figure 6.8: Uncorrelated dispersion across strategies (daily returns, x-axis = Index).
Source: Coinbase Asset Management. Coin Metrics. MVIS. Bloomberg LP. January 2018 to December 2022.

Again, applying traditional portfolio metrics to the data and running it through an optimizer is inadequate. And again, digital history cannot be extrapolated in the same manner—the correlations are simply not as stable as more mature markets.

It is inconceivable for credit to yield negative returns in the future, for example. Financial intermediation to crypto asset markets would cease to exist. Similarly, income cannot sustain a double-digit return-to-volatility ratio. Capital would flood the strategy, eroding returns and raising risk.

Such an exercise demands more creativity in analytics, requiring a comprehensive evaluation of patterns across cycles and an assessment of their potential persistence.

All-Season Crypto Benchmark

This brings us to the creation of an "all-season" benchmark. An effective all-season strategy should possess a high degree of upside capture while offering improved downside risk management. Achieving this goal relies primarily on integrating active strategies and income into the portfolio.

Take an initial static benchmark allocation that consists of 20% to passive, 20% to income/credit, and 60% to active strategies. The simplicity of this allocation reveals compelling results.

While the Index experienced a 27% decline over the 2018 to 2022 period, the all-season portfolio advanced by an impressive 61%.

However, it is not the return expectations that poses a challenge to investors; rather, it is the management of downside risk. And the all-season approach successfully trims the downside risk.

A closer examination of the three largest peak-to-valley drawdowns for the Index is shown in Figure 6.9. It unveils an average decline of 74% during the 2018 to 2022 period. In contrast, the all-season benchmark suffers drawdowns of 28%. Although not trivial, the benchmark represents a significant improvement.

The all-season characteristic also exhibits positive implications for broader portfolios. Over the same period, the S&P 500 experienced three large peak-to-valley declines averaging 26%. In comparison, the Index recorded a sharp 50% decline. However, the all-season benchmark demonstrates resilience with a modest 14% drop.

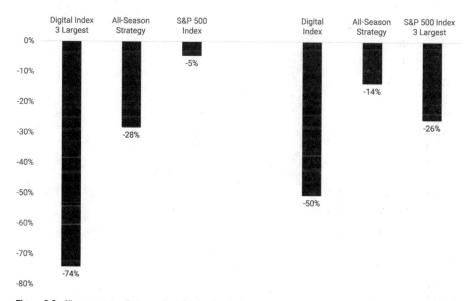

Figure 6.9: All-season strategy better weathers digital and equity drawdowns.
Source: Coinbase Asset Management. Coin Metrics. MVIS. Bloomberg LP. Metrics are average index and strategy returns during the three largest Digital Index drawdowns and during the three largest S&P 500 drawdowns over the period January 2018 to December 2022.

All-Season Dynamism

But what if the allocation across crypto seasons was not static? Could a dynamic asset allocation strategy further enhance the all-season approach? This question pushed the boundaries of the thought experiment to explore the benefits of dynamic allocation.

The seasons in the crypto market are defined as follows: winter follows a 50%+ drawdown lasting longer than one month; spring commences after a sustained one-third retracement from the lows; summer denotes a phase of rapid price increases toward the end of a cycle; and fall marks the acute phase of a drawdown.

Dynamism brought about notable improvements. During the spring stages of the cycle, a larger allocation to directional beta naturally proves beneficial, enhancing returns. A dynamic all-season strategy, with its ability to adapt, achieves a 91% increase during spring, outperforming the static benchmark, which recorded a 52% rise, illustrated in Figure 6.10.

This phase also provides an opportunity for credit strategies to shine, emerging from distress with renewed strength. Importantly, the dynamic approach does not necessarily result in larger drawdowns when the

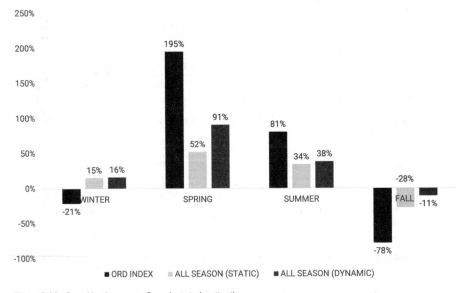

Figure 6.10: Smoothing the seasons–Dynamic strategies attractive.
Source: Coinbase Asset Management. Coin Metrics. MVIS.

allocation shifts aggressively to income strategies during the fall phase, characterized by acute market declines.

All about Drawdowns

One of the toughest decisions an investor faces is whether to stick with a strategy through a drawdown. Portfolio managers must contemplate exposure, just as Mike Hearn did as a core developer. The cyclical nature of markets, particularly in the crypto asset realm, is well-known. The solution lies in building tools that can proactively identify asset seasons and have scalable, familiar strategies ready for implementation.

Volatility and cyclicality in digital asset markets can be managed more effectively than a single blunt instrument. However, it requires a deep understanding of the market's seasonality and the development of fundamental tools to navigate the terrain successfully. The journey has just begun, and there is much more to explore.

6.4 Influence of Different Crypto Asset Allocations

> "If you can't sleep at night because of your stock market position, then you have gone too far. If this is the case, then sell your position down to the sleeping level."
>
> Jesse Livermore

Few investors will fall into the category of those who desire to invest nothing or their entire investment portfolio in crypto assets. Therefore, the most important question is not whether an investment should be made, but rather how much should be invested. In the following sections, we therefore discuss the allocation of crypto assets within a portfolio.

6.4.1 Evaluating Portfolios

In this forthcoming analysis, we aim to explore the potential implications of integrating cryptocurrency assets into a traditionally balanced portfolio comprised of bonds and equities. Beginning with a 50/50 bond-equity split as our baseline portfolio, we incrementally incorporate cryptocurrency assets, adding 1% per step equally derived from both bonds and stocks, until we reach a portfolio composition with a 25% allocation to cryptocurrencies. Through this approach, we calculate key metrics to discern the influence of varying cryptocurrency proportions on the portfolio's total return and drawdowns.

Our initial visual representation features a six-panel chart depicting the total returns of portfolios with cryptocurrency allocations ranging from 0% to 25% in 5% increments. This graphic intends to vividly illustrate the profound impact of cryptocurrency integration on a portfolio's overall performance (see Figure 6.11).

The impact on the allocations' volatility and drawdowns is inherently tied to the growing influence of cryptocurrencies on the overall portfolio trajectory. Importantly, the practice of quarterly rebalancing has

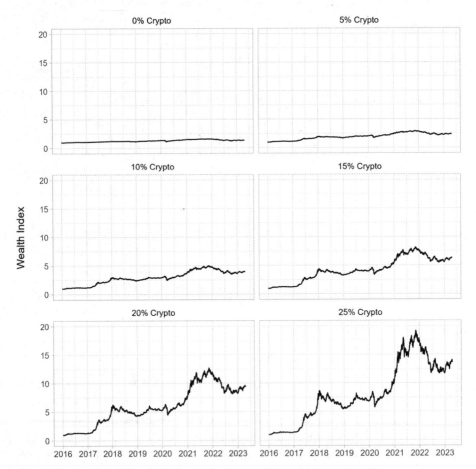

Figure 6.11: Performance of balanced portfolios with shares from 0% to 25% crypto assets. Data: MarketVector.

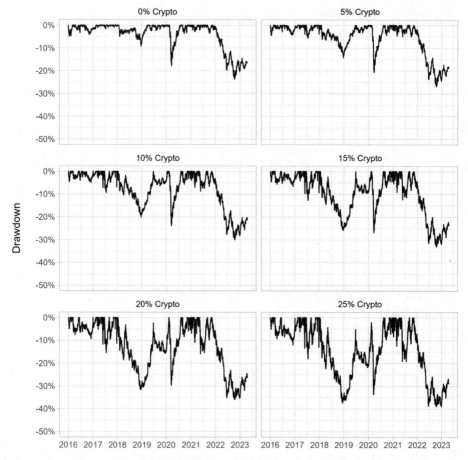

Figure 6.12: Drawdowns of a balanced portfolio with a share of 1% to 25% crypto assets. Data: MarketVector.

notably cushioned the periodic price dips since the prior all-time high (see Figure 6.12).

Had investors allowed the allocations to fluctuate unchecked, a more substantial cryptocurrency proportion would have etched deeper imprints on the key metrics over time. It is for this reason, among others, that the consideration of rebalancing strategies proves to be judicious. It is through this methodology that a consistent evaluation of specific allocations can be achieved, the results of which attenuate the influence of both the entry point and transient extreme phases.

As the proportion of cryptocurrency assets within a portfolio rises, both the cumulative return and its associated volatility see a corresponding increase. However, it is important to note that the risk-adjusted return does not scale linearly with this increased allocation. The historical out-performance of cryptocurrencies compared to other asset categories may paint a misleading picture if used as the sole basis for future performance projections. Instead, to generate a more accurate, representative metric, it is prudent to evaluate the historical return paths available.

In this light, we have conducted an in-depth analysis of all plausible 250-day periods across 26 portfolios, each with varying allocations of cryptocurrency assets. Figure 6.13 graphically represents the total return at the conclusion of each observation period for every portfolio. Each black dot signifies the median of all individual data points for each allocation.

Figure 6.13 depicts, for each portfolio and individual return path, the total return at the conclusion of the respective observation period for each of the portfolios. The black dot represents the median of all indi-vidual point values for each allocation. It is evident that the dispersion

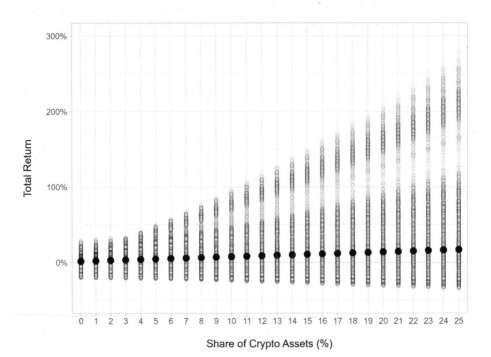

Figure 6.13: Total return of all crypto allocations over every rolling 250-day period between 2015 and 2023. Data: NorgateData.com, MarketVector.

of returns increases more than the median with increasing allocation. This is due to the exceptionally positive outliers, which can be enjoyed by investors who purchased crypto assets at precisely the right time. This obviously only applies to a small portion of investors.

A clear observation from the chart is that the scatter of returns expands more dramatically than the median as the allocation increases. This wider dispersion is largely attributable to the outstanding positive outliers brought on by those investors fortunate or prescient enough to time their cryptocurrency purchases impeccably. Yet it is vital to remember that such fortunate timing is a rarity, and only a small fraction of investors may boast such successes.

Considering this, it becomes clear why it is more sensible for investors to shape their future expectations based on the median rather than the mean value. The median, being less influenced by extreme values, offers a more realistic expectation of returns, and discourages falling into the trap of inflated expectations driven by rare, highly positive outliers.

Figure 6.14 provides a drawdown plot analogous to the total return path plot previously discussed. This plot, inclusive of all potential paths, demonstrates significant dispersion, and highlights the median values for each scenario. The primary distinction between these two charts lies in the median drawdown's heightened sensitivity to increased cryptocurrency allocation, compared to the median total return.

This finding underscores a critical point: while heightened returns are certainly attainable with a larger cryptocurrency allocation, the likelihood of enduring more substantial drawdowns is substantially increased. Therefore, investors must be prepared for larger downturns as they increase their crypto asset positions, reinforcing the importance of balance and risk management in portfolio construction.

Assessing an optimal cryptocurrency allocation within a portfolio, as indicated by the evaluation of all return paths, is a challenging task. Resorting to using average returns and risks for decision-making is discouraged due to the unique asymmetrical return distribution characteristic of crypto assets. Such a method would invariably favor the highest allocation of crypto assets, an approach that may not mirror realistic

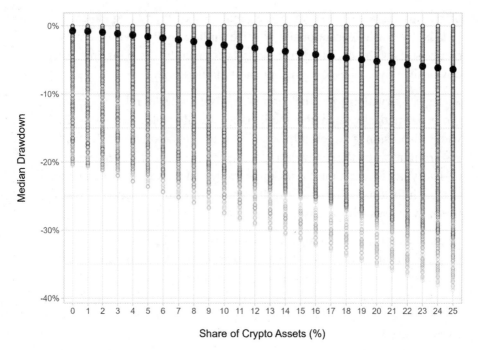

Figure 6.14: Maximum drawdowns of all crypto allocations over every rolling 250-day period between 2015 and 2023. Data: NorgateData.com, MarketVector.

scenarios. It would equate to an overly optimistic gamble on a recurrence of the extraordinary market trends of recent years.

To address this, we adopt a balanced and conservative metric: the ratio of the median total return to the maximum portfolio drawdown across all 250-day periods during the observation window. Given the vast number of scenarios under consideration, the median remains resilient to the numerous positive outliers in performance. By leveraging the maximum drawdown as opposed to its median equivalent, we underscore the prudent perspective of our analysis.

This metric not only reflects the remarkably positive contribution of a moderate addition of crypto assets to the portfolio, but it also emphasizes the element of risk. This risk-focus is most noticeable at a 7% cryptocurrency asset allocation, which is defined as the inflection point. Beyond this allocation, as shown in Figure 6.15, the quality of the portfolio begins to progressively deteriorate when evaluated on this basis.

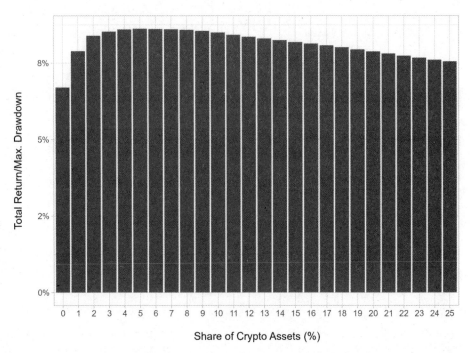

Figure 6.15: Influence of different crypto allocations on the ratio of median total return in relation to maximum drawdowns (all rolling 12 months periods between 2015 and 2023). Data: NorgateData.com, MarketVector.

The historical patterns of return contributions from cryptocurrency assets provide a cogent argument against the reliance on persistently high values. Much like any other asset class, the performance of cryptocurrencies is cyclical in nature. Within the period under scrutiny, the extraordinary contributions between 2017 and 2018 are as conspicuous as the subsequent plateauing of contributions (see Figure 6.16). Yet, at no point did these additional assets significantly detract from the overall portfolio performance. This observation can be attributed to the fact that sharp price declines have typically been preceded by even more potent price increases, leading to the accumulation of profits over time despite intermittent drawdowns.

It is, therefore, logical to conduct a more detailed investigation of the portfolio with a 3% cryptocurrency allocation. This allocation sits comfortably below the 7% inflection point, thereby offering a better balance between potential rewards and manageable risk. It also avoids the portfolio quality deterioration that becomes evident with higher allocations.

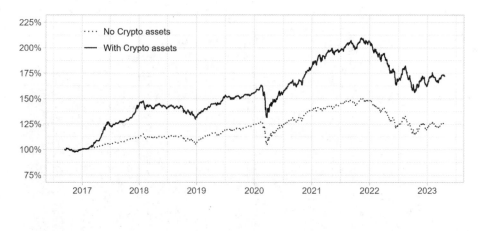

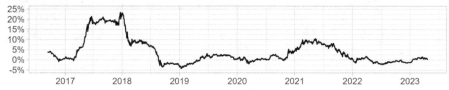

Figure 6.16: Total Return of a balanced portfolios with and without a 3% allocation of crypto assets and rolling contribution of the crypto allocation. Data: MarketVector.

A deeper analysis of this allocation could yield valuable insights into its potential benefits for risk-averse investors seeking exposure to crypto assets without significantly jeopardizing their portfolio's overall health.

It is crucial to understand that not every investor is perfectly positioned at the ideal time to maximize returns. Therefore, assessing performance based solely on the development over an entire period could lead to a skewed understanding. Instead, a more meticulous approach would be to examine all possible 250-day periods since the start of 2015, specifically for the portfolio with a 3% cryptocurrency allocation (as represented in Figure 6.17). This tactic enables us to glean a comprehensive understanding of its performance across a variety of market conditions, reflecting the realistic investment experience more closely.

This approach reaffirms the integral role that correlation plays in the crafting of a well-balanced portfolio. High volatility of individual assets shouldn't invariably be seen as a shortcoming. In fact, a portfolio composed of volatile assets can indeed prove to be an advantageous choice, particularly if these assets exhibit low correlation to each other. This principle can also be

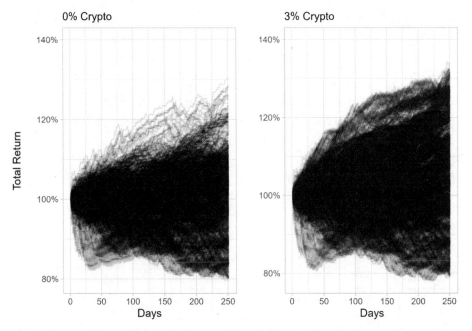

Figure 6.17: Total return paths of two portfolios with shares of 0% and 3% crypto assets. Data: MarketVector, NorgateData.com.

harnessed within highly active trading strategies, particularly when paired with rigorous money management.

An insightful resource exploring this theme is the paper "Growing Wealth with Fixed-Mix Strategies" authored by Dempster, Evsitgneev, and Schenk-Hoppé.[11] Their work presents a deeper understanding of how a diverse mix of volatile, yet weakly correlated assets can contribute to wealth accumulation, thereby further underlining the value of scrutinizing all possible 250-day periods since 2015 for our portfolio of interest.

6.4.2 Key Metrics

> "If you can't measure it, you can't improve it."
> Peter Drucker

Owing to the distinctive asymmetric earnings profile of cryptocurrencies, the likelihood of experiencing larger drawdowns grows at a rate that outpaces the probability of reaping higher returns as the crypto allocation

---

11 See Dempster, Evstigneev, and Schenk-Hoppé (2009).

expands. It is imperative to weigh both the respective probabilities of occurrence and the impact when considering these factors. The occasionally substantial returns of crypto assets, as a result of their asymmetric risk profile, may indeed warrant an increased portfolio allocation.

Table 6.2 presents a comprehensive outline of key metrics for portfolios with cryptocurrency asset allocations ranging from 0% to 25%.

Crypto (%)	Return	Sharpe Ratio	Volatility	Sortino Ratio	avg. Drawdown	max. Drawdown
0	2.66%	0.39	6.83%	0.036	1.08%	23.63%
1	3.84%	0.55	6.96%	0.049	0.95%	24.28%
2	5.00%	0.69	7.24%	0.061	1.07%	24.93%
3	6.14%	0.80	7.64%	0.071	1.26%	25.57%
4	7.27%	0.89	8.13%	0.079	1.50%	26.21%
5	8.38%	0.97	8.69%	0.085	1.69%	26.84%
6	9.48%	1.02	9.29%	0.090	1.79%	27.47%
7	10.56%	1.06	9.94%	0.094	2.02%	28.10%
8	11.63%	1.10	10.60%	0.097	2.27%	28.72%
9	12.69%	1.12	11.29%	0.100	2.48%	29.34%
10	13.73%	1.14	11.99%	0.102	2.73%	29.96%
11	14.76%	1.16	12.70%	0.103	2.95%	30.57%
12	15.77%	1.18	13.41%	0.105	3.34%	31.18%
13	16.78%	1.19	14.12%	0.106	3.51%	31.78%
14	17.77%	1.20	14.84%	0.107	3.62%	32.38%
15	18.75%	1.21	15.55%	0.107	3.71%	32.98%
16	19.72%	1.21	16.27%	0.108	3.81%	33.57%
17	20.67%	1.22	16.98%	0.109	3.94%	34.18%
18	21.62%	1.22	17.69%	0.109	4.09%	34.79%
19	22.55%	1.23	18.39%	0.109	4.25%	35.39%
20	23.47%	1.23	19.09%	0.110	4.41%	35.99%
21	24.38%	1.23	19.79%	0.110	4.56%	36.59%
22	25.28%	1.23	20.48%	0.110	4.76%	37.18%
23	26.18%	1.24	21.18%	0.110	4.50%	37.77%
24	27.06%	1.24	21.86%	0.110	4.76%	38.36%
25	27.92%	1.24	22.54%	0.111	4.86%	38.96%

Table 6.2: Key metrics of all portfolios. All metrics, excluding drawdowns, are annualized; Sharpe Ratio and Sortino Ratio are calculated using a risk-free rate of 0%.

Of particular note among these metrics are the average drawdown values for different strategies. Contrary to most other key figures that tend to rise in parallel with an increased crypto allocation, the average drawdown initially exhibits a decreasing trend. Remarkably, a portfolio with a mere 1% allocation of crypto assets exhibits the lowest average drawdowns. While this solitary data point should not be viewed as a sufficient foundation for allocation decisions, it certainly offers invaluable insight. This metric underscores the contribution of cryptocurrency assets toward diversifying a portfolio. Furthermore, this understanding might serve to assuage the fears of more conservative investors, illuminating how a modest crypto addition can enhance portfolio resilience without exposing it to significant risk.

As investors contemplate the appropriate asset allocation, the long-term key risk indicators should be accorded significant importance. Although historical evaluations cannot provide absolute certainty about the precise risks a given strategy might pose in the future, the wisdom of past market behavior should not be dismissed when predicting future trends. Equity markets have witnessed declines of 50% or more on several occasions, and such fluctuations are unlikely to be eradicated in times ahead. Similarly, if a cryptocurrency has previously suffered drawdowns of 80% or more, it would be ill-advised to presume such occurrences will be categorically eliminated in the coming years. The same principle applies to dramatic increases in interest rates, an eventuality that many considered implausible until confronted with the stark reality.

Ultimately, the winners in the long-term investment game are those investors who approach the financial markets with an open mind, maintaining steadfast discipline in their strategies. Their success is anchored not in attempting to predict the unpredictable, but in preparing for a range of possible outcomes and ensuring that their portfolio is resilient enough to weather the ever-changing tides of the financial markets.

6.5 Dynamic Risk Management

> "Everyone has a plan until they get punched in the mouth."
> Mike Tyson

The strategic asset allocation, for which we have introduced several methodologies, can be augmented with tactical elements. These can lead to adjustments within individual sectors as well as at the macro level of the total allocation. Generally, these modifications are less about maximizing profit potential and more focused on curbing fluctuation risks and draw-downs inherent in a strategy. As is typically the case, minimizing these risks correlates with lessening the emotional stress experienced by investors.

For institutional investors, implementing such measures often holds significance not only from a regulatory standpoint, but also in terms of reputation and marketing. Frequently, it involves adherence to non-binding threshold values that have gradually cemented themselves as industry norms over time. For instance, if one is pitching a hedge fund, the process becomes simpler if the maximum drawdown of the proposed strategy is less than 20%. This approach is widely accepted, despite not being legally mandated, as it bolsters credibility and ensures alignment with industry expectations.

6.5.1 Trend Filter

> "If you diversify, control your risk, and go with the trend, it just has to work."
>
> Larry Hite

While phrases such as *dynamic risk management* may sound complex and daunting, many strategies aimed at mitigating risk are rather straightforward. As is often the case, elaborate concepts can be appealing in theory. but particularly when factoring in costs, prove to be either challenging to execute, costly, or both in practice. Consequently, we focus our attention on a selection of uncomplicated approaches that are accessible to all.

One such basic risk management technique for asset allocation employs a crossover strategy predicated on moving averages. The premise behind these strategies is to avoid investing during deep, potentially prolonged downtrends in specific markets. An investment in a risk asset like stocks, for instance, is only made if the market demonstrates an upward trend. This trend is determined by whether the closing price of a broad stock index exceeds its long-term moving average.

In its most rudimentary form, this strategy would entail a full investment in the risk asset during an upward trend, with a shift to purchasing treasury bills in a downturn.

There is a plethora of variations of this approach, with endless debates waged over the optimal length of the moving average and whether closing prices or average prices should serve as the reference. Furthermore, this strategy can be employed not solely as a binary "stocks or treasury bills" decision, but also as a means to control the stock allocation between 0% and 100%.

6.5.2 Momentum Filter

> "Not losing big is the single most important factor for winning big.
> As a speculator, losing is not a choice, but how much you lose is."
> Mark Minervini

The terms *trend* and *momentum* are frequently conflated, which is not entirely accurate. A trend filter, such as a 200-day moving average, gauges price trends across the entire period. In contrast, simple momentum evaluates the absolute progression of an investment relative to itself (absolute momentum) or other investments (relative momentum) over this time. As such, momentum could still be positive even if a stock, after a 190-day downtrend, experiences a dramatic rise over the subsequent 10-day measurement period that outpaces the beginning of this period. This occurrence is particularly common in instances of moderate downward movements. In this scenario, a trend filter would take longer to identify a positive trend. Hence, while trend and momentum often align, this is not invariably the case.

Trend filters typically monitor an investment's trajectory, whereas many momentum-based approaches utilize both absolute and relative progressions. Therefore, in its simplest form, the strategy measures not only the development of a stock index, but also the index's progress minus the T-bill return. Here, the index has positive momentum if the total return over the lookback period surpasses the total return on treasury bills. In other instances, such as Gary Antonacci's well-known "Dual Momentum" approach, the asset demonstrating the strongest absolute momentum is selected from the investment universe. If it also outperforms T-bills in total return, it receives a full 100% allocation.

Both trend and momentum filters are intuitively comprehensible and easy to implement. Both result in considerably lower maximum drawdowns and lower volatility compared to full investment, as investors tend to avoid volatile bear markets. Consequently, the risk-adjusted return of such an approach usually outperforms a simple full investment.

However, this advantage is not without drawbacks. Notably, the transactions occurring during reallocations, which generate costs and tax implications, can vary depending on the individual investor's circumstances. Furthermore, the strategy's key advantage of reducing the probability of extreme drawdowns also has a downside. In a market trending sideways without a clear trajectory, numerous false signals often trigger losses. Although these losses are significantly smaller compared to potentially avoided drawdowns, maintaining discipline in following a strategy that can generate multiple consecutive "false" signals poses significant emotional challenges for many investors. It's not unusual for investors to abandon the long-term risk-reducing approach just as a new downtrend begins. This level of discipline isn't within every investor's reach. Institutional investors, who may find implementing a trend filter straightforward, can face pressure from clients in sideways markets. Moreover, it's harder for fund investors to weather the phases at the end of a bear market when the market is rapidly rising but the trend filter has not yet signaled re-entry. For those who can handle these factors, trend filters can simplify the investment process by significantly reducing interim drawdowns.

6.5.3 Dynamic Crypto Strategy in Practice

> "What does his lucid explanation amount to but this: that in theory there is no difference between theory and practice, while in practice there is?"
> Benjamin Brewster

As an illustration of pragmatic implementation, let us explore a momentum-based cryptocurrency trading strategy—a quintessential instance of a dynamic strategy. This methodology endeavors to capture pronounced uptrends and deftly sidestep lengthy, hefty downturns.

Various mechanisms can be employed to deploy such a strategy, but the essence of these systems invariably converges to a dyad of signals—an entry signal grounded in trend or breakout parameters, and an exit signal designed to curtail losses. The showcased technique makes use of absolute momentum and assesses the relative robustness of individual tokens vis-à-vis Bitcoin, utilizing weekly data sets (see Figure 6.18).

A critical caveat to bear in mind while assessing such strategies is that real-world trading outcomes carry a greater worth than mere back tests.

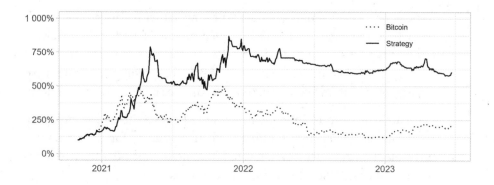

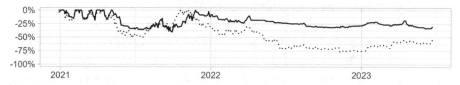

Figure 6.18: Total returns and drawdowns of an active strategy compared to a Bitcoin buy-and-hold approach.

These simulations can certainly offer illuminating insights and help craft hypothetical scenarios, but it is an idealized construct that may not fully encompass the actual complexities of live trading environments. Real-world costs, potential slippage, and other practical issues often get overlooked in simulations. Hence, while back testing offers a valuable launching pad, it is the real trading that ultimately delivers the genuine verdict. Nothing replicates the veracity of actual trading—where theory collides with reality, forging a more dependable measure of strategy effectiveness.

Upon scrutinizing the trajectory of the total return, the advantage of evading prolonged and significant drawdowns becomes manifest (refer to Figure 6.14). Despite the considerably enhanced risk and return characteristics offered to an investor who managed to sidestep significant losses, this strategy is not universally applicable. More specifically, not all investors are apt for such a strategic implementation.

A significant factor here is the investor's psychological resilience. Particularly in the incipient stages of rising markets, when a trend is too nascent to trigger an entry signal, many investors are persuaded that their chosen strategy has become ineffective, and they fear missing out on a potential windfall. There are either no discernible trends or they are too ephemeral to be exploited profitably. Rather than viewing this as a flaw, it should be understood as an inherent characteristic of the strategy. This inherent latency is the price paid for avoiding drawdowns. No strategy offers a miraculous solution or a cost-free benefit in such a context.

Ultimately, it is up to individual investors to assess their psychological resilience and determine the most effective strategy for their personal investment journey. However, it is paramount to remember the overarching benefit of significantly reduced drawdowns.

6.6 Interview with Peter L. Brandt

Peter L. Brandt entered the commodity trading business in 1976 with ContiCommodity Services, a division of Continental Grain Company. From his start in the commodity industry, Peter's goal was to trade proprietary funds. But he first needed to learn the business.

From 1976 through 1979, Peter handled large institutional accounts for Conti, including Campbell Soup Company, Oro Wheat, Godiva Chocolate, Swanson Foods, Homestake Mining, and others.

In 1980, Peter founded Factor Trading Co., Inc. In his capacity as CEO, Peter was primarily engaged in trading proprietary capital. Factor Trading also produced market research and managed the trading activities of several large institutional clients. Among Peter's institutional trading clients was Commodities Corporation ("CC") of Princeton, New Jersey, at the time one of the world's largest trading houses.

In 1990, Peter published his first book, titled Trading Commodity Futures with Classical Chart Patterns. *In 2011, John Wiley and Sons published Peter's second book,* Diary of a Professional Commodity Trader. *The book became Amazon's No. 1 ranked book on trading for 27 weeks. His first book,* Trading Commodity Futures with Classical Chart Patterns, *was published in 1990 and is considered a classic by many traders.*

Q: **Could you begin by briefly discussing your personal experience and journey in trading, particularly how you became interested in cryptocurrency? Despite your well-known reputation as a commodities trader, it seems that not many people are aware of your active involvement in the crypto markets.**

A: Yes, indeed. I began my trading career, or "gig" as you might say, back in 1975. Prior to '75, I was introduced to the world of commodity trading because I lived in Chicago and had friends involved in the business there. This sparked my interest, leading me to frequently visit the floor of the Chicago Board of Trade, which I found absolutely enthralling. In my 20s, with a youthful sense of invincibility, I decided to quit my salaried job to try my hand at commodity trading, despite having a wife and two kids.

I joined Continental Grain Company, then the second-largest grain merchandiser in the world, and received training from them. From the very beginning, my goal was to become a proprietary trader—to learn the art of trading, generate enough capital to fund a trading business, and then trade for my own account. This meant learning the ins and outs of the trading business.

In the early years, I had some rough patches. I didn't know what a futures contract was in 1975 and I had to learn the hard way. I blew up some accounts and had to experiment with different trading approaches, but I was determined. I wasn't suited to be a pit trader, despite the success of many in the pits at the Chicago Board of Trade and the Chicago Mercantile Exchange.

It wasn't until around 1978–1979 that I started gaining some traction when I stumbled upon the book *Technical Analysis of Stock Trends* by Edwards and McGee. This opened up a new perspective for me. I realized that there are as many ways to trade as there are professional career traders; no two traders operate in the exact same way. This realization helped me to solidify my approach.

Looking back, I think I was at the right place at the right time, with the right mentors, and good markets that charted well. I launched Factor Research and Trading at the Board of Trade in October of 1981, and it's been a great journey since then. It seems surreal to me at times that I've made my living trading futures contracts.

To me, it doesn't matter whether I'm trading corn, soybeans, copper, gold, or crude oil. As long as the market has liquidity and a clean contract, I can trade. I don't need to understand any market in detail, except maybe the grain markets, which were my origin. I don't need to delve into supply and demand or know the fundamentals of the market in order to trade it.

Then in 2016, a friend of mine, Raoul Pal from Real Vision, introduced me to Bitcoin. At the time, I had only vaguely heard of Bitcoin, but there was no futures contract, so futures traders weren't really paying attention to it. Raoul sent me a chart of Bitcoin, and I was fascinated by how well this market charted. I opened an account, started buying Bitcoin probably around the four- or five-hundred-dollar levels, and took a position.

Having a position in a market piques your interest in it. Consequently, I spent some time learning about Bitcoin, its existence, and its significance. I started believing in the narrative and realized that Bitcoin had the potential to be a massive disruptor of the economic system.

During 2018, my understanding and appreciation for Bitcoin deepened. However, I want to clarify that when you say "crypto," for me, Bitcoin is crypto. If it wasn't for Bitcoin, all these other cryptocurrencies wouldn't even be around. So, while I'm aware of other tokens and have traded them from time to time, my primary focus is on Bitcoin.

Q: **Having witnessed various market trends in the traditional finance world, would you say that charting Bitcoin is comparable to the Commodities Market in the 1970s, given our early stage and the lack of numerous market participants and players, or is it a unique entity of its own?**

A: While it's true that the commodity markets charted remarkably well in the 1980s and 1990s, to the point where we started having liquid electronic markets with platforms like Globex, I believe that Bitcoin has charted even better. In my opinion, the Bitcoin market is superior to the commodity markets of that time. It's unique and stands on its own as the King of the Hill.

The thing about Bitcoin that astonishes me is that it has gone through four parabolic advances, not just regular parabolic advances, but parabolics on a logarithmic scale (see Figure 6.19). This is extraordinary, a three or four standard deviation event. I can find no other commodity or stock that can make the same claim. Even tech stocks like Apple and Microsoft, which have seen parabolic moves, haven't experienced this on a logarithmic scale. There's nothing like Bitcoin that has existed in my time as a trader (see Tables 6.3 and 6.4).

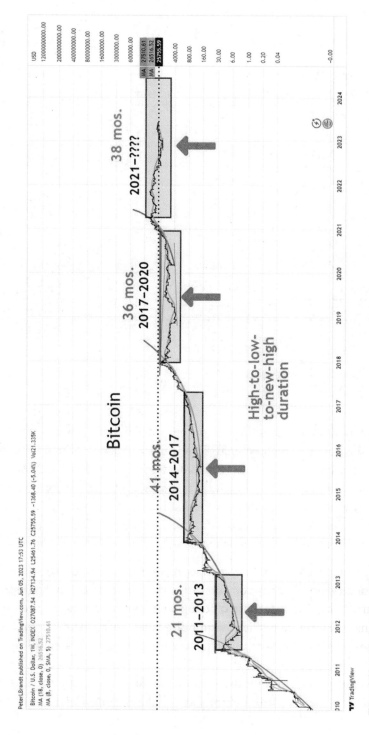

Figure 6.19: Parabolic advances of Bitcoin.
Source: The Factor Report.

Bitcoin in USD			
Date	Low	High	Advance
Jul 2010–Jan 2011	0.05	24.15	483-fold
Oct 2011–Nov 2013	2	1,142	571-fold
Jan 2015–Dec 2017	164	19,531	119-fold
Dec 2018–Nov 2021	3148	69,000	21-fold
Oct 2011–Nov 2021	2	69,000	34,500-fold

Table 6.3: History of Bitcoin advances.
Source: Factor LLC May 2023.

Comparison with other Assets			
Asset	Low	High	Advance
Dow Jones Ind. Avg.	30.088 (1903)	36,952	1,196-fold
Apple	0.04 (1982)	182	4540-fold
Amazon	0.07 (1997)	189	2694-fold
Gold (100 years)	20.67 (1919)	2,078	100-fold

Table 6.4: History of advances of different assets.
Source: Factor LLC May 2023.

When I think about the magnitude of what Bitcoin has accomplished, it's just phenomenal. This is not just about adoption by the masses, but by individuals who understood financial markets. At one point, I was curious if I could find another market that has had the same kind of magnitude advance that Bitcoin has. The only thing that came close was the interest rates in Germany during the hyperinflation in the mid-1920s, which of course, was even more dramatic.

That alone should inform people. It should be telling that we don't just have another random market, but a market with a significant story behind it. Bitcoin is quite unusual, but that doesn't lessen my interest in trading other commodities like soybean meal, gold, or sugar. I still find those markets very interesting, but Bitcoin is definitely special.

Q: **It's interesting to note that despite the significant movements in Bitcoin, there is still a great deal of skepticism. Often, after the**

second wave or so, the broader public is cheering along. Yet when I speak to individuals outside the financial sector, they perceive Bitcoin as a shady corner of the market that they prefer not to enter. They label it a scam and are not convinced. Despite these parabolic moves, the broader masses remain unconvinced. What do you make of this?

A: Indeed, we've witnessed this remarkable movement, yet skepticism abounds. Interestingly, this might actually be a positive thing. Markets often do well when climbing walls of uncertainty and worry. We should be more concerned when we witness large scale FOMO (Fear of Missing Out) and the influx of new participants. This was evident in 2020 and 2021 when family offices began getting involved in Bitcoin.

The push into Bitcoin was primarily driven by their clients, who were seeing the continuous rise of Bitcoin while their investments were tied up in traditional 60/40 portfolios. In the U.S., at least, it wasn't the family office advisors who were introducing their clients to Bitcoin, but rather, the clients pressuring their family offices to find a way to invest in Bitcoin.

There will always be doubters and reasons to question the legitimacy of Bitcoin, but this skepticism may be a good thing in the long term.

Q: **You refer to yourself as a "glorious order enterer" on your website. As a technical trader, what would you say are the most widespread misconceptions regarding technical analysis or trading?**

A: I believe there are numerous misconceptions about technical analysis. One major misconception is that charts can predict the future, which they cannot. Charts are a reflection of where prices have been and where they are at the moment. They can, however, indicate the path of least resistance and, with enough familiarity, present asymmetrical risk-reward trading opportunities.

For me, technical analysis primarily involves charting, following the classical charting principles originally defined by Richard W. Schabacker in 1933 and codified by Robert Edwards and John McGee in 1948. Chart patterns aren't magical; they're simply geometric forms that occur as a market consolidates and goes into a trading range. These patterns can indicate which side—buyers or sellers—is likely to prevail in their ongoing battle and can give some advance warning of when that victory will start to manifest.

So, while some people may believe that if a market doesn't move as predicted by a chart, it means that charting doesn't work, I've never claimed that charting is a guaranteed prediction tool. Charting, for me, simply represents the supply and demand of contracts, revealing the underlying supply and demand economics. It's another way to study fundamentals, but it focuses on the buying and selling activities of those who are truly informed, those who use the product, and it can hint at macro influences.

In terms of my role as an "order enterer," I don't need to predict where the market is going. I just need to be disciplined in placing orders where they make sense based on the chart. I could make a good trade that loses money, or a bad trade that turns a profit. A good trade, for me, is one where I can look at a chart in the future and understand why I bought and sold at specific points, based on classical chart principles.

My goal is to gain an edge over time, much like a casino does with its games. Just as a casino becomes profitable when a lever is pulled repeatedly, I aim to be profitable over the long term by consistently making orders that make sense. I believe this gives me an edge, which will lead to net profitability over time.

Q: **Could you describe your approach to risk management in trading, particularly how you apply technical charting to manage your portfolio?**

A: I look for pivots on a chart, particularly during phases of development similar to historical patterns. For instance, when a market experiences a significant advance and then enters a consolidated price range equivalent to about 8% of the underlying value for three months. History suggests that if the market breaks out of that range, it has better than a 50–50 chance of further extension or thrust in the direction of the breakout.

Now, this approach applies to conventional markets. My strategy concerning cryptocurrencies varies slightly, and I want to be clear here, *strategy* or *scheme* doesn't have a negative connotation in this context; it refers to my systematic approach or algorithm for trading. I monitor 40 to 60 markets and typically observe a tradable chart pattern a few times a year in each. When I identify a tradable setup, I want to avail myself of potential thrust by setting orders.

If I decide to engage, I aim to risk no more than .5% to 1% of my total capital on a single bet. Using the language of interest rates, that's roughly 50 to 100 basis points. If, for example, I'm considering entering soybeans at a particular point and I anticipate that I might need to exit at another point if the trade goes against me, I can do the simple math to determine how many contracts I need to equal my 70 basis point risk.

Then, it's mostly about using open orders; I typically use stop orders or stop loss orders. However, in thinly traded markets or during low-volume trading hours, I set alerts instead. These alerts, audible on my phone, iPad, or computer, warn me when an order is hit so I can avoid having an order just sitting there susceptible to high-frequency trading operations.

Q: **Regarding risk management, it seems that discipline and patience—the ability to wait and do nothing—plays a significant role. Would you agree?**

A: Absolutely, it's a two-edged sword. On one hand, you must be disciplined enough to pull the trigger when the market meets your criteria. However, it's crucial not to be overly eager. Early in my trading career, I made the mistake of jumping into trades prematurely, which usually led to losses. The danger is that you can become so disillusioned by a particular market that you miss out when it finally moves because you've depleted your capital by trying to anticipate the move.

It's a common pitfall new traders need to overcome—avoid wasting ammunition on every minor fluctuation while a market is discovering its price zone. For me, patience is key, and I need the market to make a significant statement before I enter, understanding that even then, there's at least a 50% chance I'll be wrong and take a loss.

From time to time, I need to relearn this lesson, which always stings. Even after 45 years, some lessons need repeating.

Q: **Peter, you've previously mentioned your transition from trader to investor and educator. How has this shift impacted your approach to trading and investing, particularly with regard to your Bitcoin holdings and risk management?**

A: That's an excellent question, Martin. In essence, I've become a bifurcated trader. Bitcoin, to me, is so special that it represents a unique asset class, distinct from traditional contracts such as European Milling wheat or the Dow Jones. While I might trade these markets a few times a year based on the right timing, Bitcoin has a different role in my portfolio due to its potential to disrupt the world.

When I trade a traditional market, I usually target a 10% change in price. For instance, when trading soybeans, I might aim for a $1.50 change per bushel, or a $100–$200 change when trading gold. Bitcoin, however, is not about chasing small profits for me. I view it as a vehicle for wealth preservation, thus shifting it from the trading category into wealth preservation. This mindset places Bitcoin in a class of its own.

That's not to say I wouldn't trade Bitcoin based on my usual market signals. When it comes to trading, it could be Bitcoin, oats, or anything else—it doesn't matter. What matters is that I treat Bitcoin with the same discipline and strategy as any other market when trading through my company's proprietary account.

For my personal account, which also covers my family trust, Bitcoin represents wealth preservation and acts as an insurance policy against potential economic calamity. When I was born in 1947, a dollar was a dollar. Now, it buys only five to six cents worth of goods. That's why I believe in the long-term value of Bitcoin—it's my insurance policy against the continuing devaluation of fiat currencies. Bitcoin's role in my portfolio is akin to a life vest on the *Titanic*.

At the same time, I'm gradually shifting my trading approach to a longer timeframe, not just for Bitcoin but for other markets as well. I pay more attention to weekly charts and take signals based on these longer patterns. This change doesn't mean I'm risking more than 50 to 100 basis points. However, it does affect my position sizing because I allow more room for the trade to play out over time.

Within my Bitcoin portfolio, there are three distinct buckets. One bucket treats Bitcoin like any other market. It could be a weekly or a daily chart; I'll enter and exit trades with no attachment or sense of pride.

The second bucket is strictly for holding. I'm willing to risk a certain amount of Bitcoin all the way back to zero because I believe in its long-term potential. It's like buying a life insurance policy—a protection against calamitous situations.

Finally, the third bucket involves timing the market. While I have no desire to short Bitcoin, I utilize charts and a long-term trend model unique to Bitcoin to maximize potential profits. This approach aims to catch big movements. For instance, I anticipate the next big parabolic movement will take Bitcoin up to $200,000.

Nevertheless, I recognize that a major rise in Bitcoin's price could invite government opposition, especially during a fiat currency crisis. Bitcoin might have to fight against such pressure. That's why a third of my portfolio aims to balance the potential rewards with risk management, not allowing the investment to fall back to zero.

Currently, I'm two-thirds committed to Bitcoin. I maintain the long-term trend position, which activated in February at about $23,000. Then there's the third bucket, which I treat as any other market. For these reasons, I'm willing to risk more on Bitcoin. I believe it not only has the potential to generate significant profits but also to preserve my wealth in the face of fiat currency devaluation.

Q: It's fascinating to observe the evolving perception of Bitcoin. Just a few years ago, many were hesitant to invest in Bitcoin precisely because it operated outside the traditional financial system. Nowadays, this very characteristic is what is driving people toward it. This shift, I believe, has been significantly influenced by the recent banking crisis and similar incidents.

Now, people are viewing Bitcoin as a form of insurance—a just-in-case measure against possible future upheavals in the traditional financial sector. It's almost as though Bitcoin, once seen as a risky venture into unknown territory, is now being viewed as a refuge

or safe haven, especially during times of economic instability. It's a truly remarkable transformation in public sentiment.

A: Throughout my years of involvement in this market, I've observed people crafting all sorts of inter-market correlations that, honestly, border on the absurd. When I first started trading, the talk of the town was the wheat-gold ratio, with assertions such as "if gold does this, wheat will do that." Then came OPEC and the claims about the interplay between oil prices and other markets. Such relationships, however, typically lack long-term validity and are eventually dismantled.

Lately, questions on the impact of high inflation on Bitcoin or how to position Bitcoin in the light of an upcoming Federal Reserve meeting have been prevalent. There's also been a surge in inquiries about the relationship between the U.S. stock market and Bitcoin. However, if Bitcoin's narrative holds true, none of these questions will matter. Bitcoin will eventually separate from these other markets, taking on a life of its own, and people will start to appreciate it for what it truly is. Ultimately, Bitcoin serves as a tool for preserving net wealth. It's important to remember, though, that it's not an asset to recklessly invest in. Bitcoin has seen four significant parabolic increases, but also four drastic 80% corrections. It's a volatile market, with huge parabolic advances that can reach 10×, 20×, or even 5× multiples, but these are often followed by dramatic downturns (see Table 6.5).

Bitcoin in USD					
From	To	High	Low	Drawdown (%)	Weeks to new highs
4/14/2021	06/22/2021	64,900	28,800	55.60%	26
06/24/2019	09/03/2020	13,831	3,858	72.10%	69
10/11/2021	present	69,000	15,639	77.30%	open
08/04/2013	04/15/2013	269	51	81.00%	30
12/17/2017	10/12/2018	19,765	3,148	84.10%	156
11/25/13	12/01/2015	1,177	164	86.10%	169
06/06/2011	11/14/11	32	2	93.80%	81

Table 6.5: History of Bitcoin declines.
Source: Factor LLC, Coinbase, Bitstamp, Bitfinex, Mt. Gox, Bitcoincharts, historical prices vary significantly by exchange.

It's not something you should impulsively buy, especially not with borrowed money.

In my view, the best strategy is to be smart about your timing. After Bitcoin has had a significant correction, it may be an opportune moment to consider buying. The last time, it didn't quite reach an 80% correction, but it was close enough and provided a buy signal on long-term moving averages.

Bitcoin is a unique market, one that I believe in for its long-term value. However, I don't share the same enthusiasm for other cryptocurrencies. I believe 99% of all coins, especially amid the current NFT craze, will ultimately be worthless. I've seen people pay astronomical sums for a JPEG, only to lose it—a situation that reminds me of the pet rock fad.

Even though some altcoins may become macro caps for a time, most will eventually lose their value. Perhaps a case can be made for the long-term future of platforms like Ethereum, but I hold steadfast to my belief: Bitcoin is synonymous with cryptocurrency, and vice versa. All other tokens will have their moment, but they will also fade. Bitcoin, in my opinion, is here to stay.

Q: So, do you see a parallel between the early internet and the current state of Bitcoin?

A: Absolutely. In my view, Bitcoin is where the internet was in the 1990s. Think about the potential if, instead of buying items from early online retailers in the late 90s, you could have purchased a share of ownership in the internet. That's essentially what Bitcoin offers—it's another chance to own the underlying mechanism of commerce.

Before, we could only invest in companies providing internet functionality. Now, we have the opportunity to invest in companies that will provide functionality to Bitcoin, and we can essentially own the equivalent of the internet in its infancy. This prospect is what makes Bitcoin so exciting.

While there will be challenges, such as government pushback, I believe these issues will be resolved over time. However, this isn't about charts; it's about the potential that Bitcoin holds.

Q: **Many institutional investors are intrigued by blockchain technology but remain skeptical of Bitcoin and tokens. You've mentioned that you're interested in Bitcoin not for multiplying your wealth, but rather for preserving it. Would you consider an allocation comparable to gold?**

A: Yes, that's one way to think about it. It's important to remember that we're not talking about investing all your wealth in Bitcoin. Instead, it's about making a careful allocation, perhaps comparable to gold.

If you look at Bitcoin's history, it's remarkable. In 2011, it was traded at $2, and now we've seen an almost 38,000-fold increase. In comparison, gold has had a 100-fold increase in its hundred-year history, and even superstar tech stocks like Amazon, Microsoft, and Apple have only achieved a tenth of what Bitcoin did.

For early Bitcoin investors, it's undoubtedly been a massive wealth builder, but for the majority, I think it has to be viewed more as a wealth preserver.

Q: **Can you share some of your experiences in crypto trading?**

A: Certainly, one of my most successful trades was when I bought Bitcoin at $400 and held onto some of it until it surpassed $19,000. On the other hand, one of my least successful trades occurred during the Covid-19 market crash. I had thought Bitcoin was poised for a major upward move in late 2019 and early 2020, so I bought more than I should have based on the pattern I was observing. When the breakout I anticipated didn't happen, I took a significant loss.

However, these experiences remind me of the importance of not buying into my own hype. Even with years of trading experience, it's essential to remember that the market can always surprise you. It's reassuring to know, though, that we all make mistakes and can learn from them.

Q: **You have mentioned that position sizing is one of the hardest components of trading, and it's something that you never fully master. Do you have any guidelines you use for position sizing?**

A: Yes, I tend to trade with far less size than most people would expect given the amount of capital I manage. One rule I follow is always to be undersized. For instance, even though I hold a sizable position in

Bitcoin, it's not overwhelmingly large considering the asset's volatility. This approach helps protect against significant drawdowns, which can damage both your financial and emotional capital.

For me, the "Holy Grail" is finding a way to achieve risk-adjusted returns. That means obtaining a return that I find acceptable, that can grow and accumulate over time, but without experiencing significant drawdowns. My aim is to keep drawdowns below 4% per year, which may seem shallow to many traders but it fits my approach.

In my early trading days, I had a lot of drawdowns in the 30% range and lots over 20%. But as I've gained experience and perhaps due to my age, I have no desire to experience such extreme swings anymore. Instead, I focus on trading metrics reflecting risk-adjusted performance. This approach keeps me willing to pull the trigger on trades without becoming gun shy.

The analogy for this could be a disciplined German ice skater performing with a free spirit. They maintain their technique while also expressing themselves artistically. It's about finding the right balance between control and freedom.

Q: **Peter, thank you so much for taking the time to share your insights and experiences in this interview. Your perspectives on Bitcoin, the evolution of markets, and your personal trading strategies are deeply enlightening. We appreciate your generosity with your time and knowledge.**

You can watch the full video of our conversation with Peter L. Brandt on our website by scanning the QR Code below.

6.7 Conclusion

> "The problem with long-term investing is the short term."
> Richard A. Ferri

The meticulous preparation of long-term asset allocation decisions is of utmost importance, as highlighted by various portfolio evaluation methodologies. In order to avoid costly and irreparable lapses in discipline, investors must honestly address key questions to determine the level of risk they can undertake. Likewise, it is crucial to establish reasonable performance expectations. For institutional investors, considerations surrounding regulations and the feasibility of incorporating crypto assets into their portfolios must be considered.

Both private and institutional investors can rely on a set of fundamental principles to guide their decision-making process, irrespective of individual circumstances. Over the past years, the inclusion of crypto assets, albeit modest, has made a significant impact on overall portfolio performance. However, due to the limited historical data available, evaluation possibilities are confined to a manageable timeframe. Notably, crypto assets have undergone multiple market phases, including severe drawdowns of 80% or more.

An examination of balanced strategies employing crypto allocations ranging from 0% to 25% reveals that incorporating crypto assets does not significantly heighten the overall risk of diversified portfolios, despite the inherent volatility of this asset class. While portfolios with smaller proportions of cryptocurrencies display minor deviations in average and maximum drawdowns compared to those without such additions, the Sharpe ratios of portfolios with increasing crypto allocations witness a substantial increase. However, it should be noted that an excessive allocation dominates the portfolio, which is unlikely the objective of the average investor. Remarkably, a significant portion of the positive effects can be observed with relatively small additions. Maintaining a disciplined approach to limiting crypto assets proves beneficial even during periods of volatility, as it helps mitigate emotional pressure.

Additionally, regular portfolio rebalancing plays a vital role in limiting risks—a factor that is frequently undervalued. By avoiding lump-sum risks, investors can safeguard themselves against missing out on opportunities arising from sharp price increases in certain asset classes. Given the dynamic nature of the cryptocurrency market, traditional trading strategies can also serve to mitigate long-term risks. Even a simple momentum strategy can prevent crypto asset investors from passively enduring an extended bear market. It is undeniable that all asset classes, including crypto assets, experience periods of weakness spanning several years. In this regard, professional risk management does not involve downplaying negative developments and hoping for a reversal. Instead, professional managers adhere to lucid rules and implement them rigorously.

6.8 References

Ang, Andrew. (2014). *Asset Management: A Systematic Approach to Factor Investing.* 1. Aufl. Oxford University Press.

Bernstein, William J., and David J. Wilkinson. (1997). "Diversification, Rebalancing, and the Geometric Mean Frontier." SSRN Scholarly Paper ID 53503. Rochester, NY: Social Science Research Network. https://doi.org/10.2139/ssrn.53503.

Butler, Adam, Michael Philbrick, and Rodrigo Gordillo. (2016). *Adaptive Asset Allocation: Dynamic Global Portfolios to Profit in Good Times—and Bad.* 1. Aufl. Wiley.

Dempster, M. a. H., Igor V. Evstigneev, and Klaus Reiner Schenk-Hoppé. (2009). "Growing Wealth with Fixed-Mix Strategies." SSRN Scholarly Paper ID 1479444. Rochester, NY: Social Science Research Network. https://doi.org/10.2139/ssrn.1479444.

Faber, Meb. (2013). "A Quantitative Approach to Tactical Asset Allocation." SSRN Scholarly Paper ID 962461. Rochester, NY: Social Science Research Network. https://papers.ssrn.com/abstract=962461.

Goyal, Amit, and Sunil Wahal. (2008). "The Selection and Termination of Investment Management Firms by Plan Sponsors." *The Journal of Finance* 63(4): 1805–1847. https://doi.org/10.1111/j.1540-6261.2008.01375.x.

Leinweber, Martin, and Joerg Willig. (2021). *Asset-Allokation mit Kryptoassets: Das Handbuch.* Wiley-VCH.

Letters, Fund. (2020, May). "Paul Tudor Jones: The Most Compelling Case for Owning Bitcoin (Cryptocurrency: BTC-USD)." Seeking Alpha. 9. https://seekingalpha.com/article/4345426-paul-tudor-jones-compelling-case-for-owning-bitcoin.

Markowitz, Harry. (1952). "Portfolio Selection." *The Journal of Finance*, 7(1): 77–91.

7 From Staking to Earning

The influx of institutions into the Web3 industry is fueled by the pursuit of secure and reliable ways to generate rewards from their digital assets. Among the myriad of mechanisms available, protocol staking is emerging as the most attractive and effective one as it provides a steady flow of rewards.

7.1 Background of Crypto Staking

Protocol staking is firmly rooted in the proof-of-stake (PoS) consensus algorithm, a mechanism that was conceived as an alternative to the energy-intensive proof-of-work (PoW) algorithm that Bitcoin and many early cryptocurrencies utilized. PoS was first introduced by Peercoin in 2012 as a means of securing the network and validating transactions, while also minimizing the computational power required. Under a PoS system, the creation of new blocks (also known as minting or forging) is not determined by who has the most computational power, but by the number of tokens a person holds and is willing to "stake." This mechanism of staking provides security to the network and creates a system where new tokens are distributed to those who are already invested, thereby incentivizing participation.

In 2014, BitShares further developed the concept with delegated proof-of-stake (DPoS), where stakeholders elect representatives or "witnesses" to validate transactions and maintain the blockchain. This approach was designed to improve the efficiency and democratic nature of the consensus process.

Ethereum, the world's largest smart contract platform, has transitioned from a PoW to a PoS model, dubbed Ethereum 2.0, reflecting the growing recognition of the benefits that staking brings to scalability, security, and sustainability.

Today, protocol staking is practiced widely across various blockchain platforms, each with its unique mechanisms and rewards. Token holders are supporting the networks further by locking their assets for the protocol to run effectively and the system is designed to reward their confidence. As blockchain technology and digital assets continue to evolve, so too will the methods and motivations for staking, making it a critical area of understanding for anyone interested in the digital currency landscape.

7.2 The Case for Staking

As we delve deeper into the world of decentralized finance and blockchain, the term *staking* frequently comes up, often leading to a considerable amount of confusion. It is not uncommon for staking to be associated with any activity that promises rewards for locking up tokens over a certain period. However, this interpretation falls short of accurately capturing the full scope of staking, particularly when we talk about PoS protocols.

In essence, when we talk about staking in this chapter, we focus on protocol staking. This does not include activities such as liquidity provisioning or lending, which are referred to as staking in the DeFi landscape.

7.2.1 Demystifying Protocol Staking

Networks applying proof-of-stake are rapidly becoming the dominant form of blockchains in use today. Compared to traditional proof-of-work (PoW) networks such as Bitcoin, PoS networks use significantly less energy and computational power to secure the network, while offering investors the ability to participate in governance and earn rewards. Staking provides a steady stream of rewards, independent of underlying token prices.

PoS enables token holders to earn rewards by "staking" their tokens in order to validate transactions on the underlying blockchain, which helps maintain the security and integrity of the network. Depending on the underlying protocol, token holders can either (1) stake their own digital assets or (2) delegate their validation rights to a Staking-as-a-Service provider (validator) to validate new transactions. In both cases, token holders maintain custody and always retain ownership of the staked tokens.

When a new block is created, Validators and token holders receive staking rewards in the form of newly minted tokens as well as transaction fees as rewards for adding valid blocks to the network. Staking rewards serve as the primary incentive mechanism to encourage participation in validating transactions on proof-of-stake networks, which in turn, helps secure and decentralize the networks. The rules with respect to protocol staking, including the rewards generated, are set by the underlying protocol.

7.2.2 How Staking Bolsters Network Security

Staking offers the most resource and energy-efficient option for aligning incentives, distributing rewards directly to the validators and delegators responsible for securing the chain. As a token holder for any PoS protocol, you hold both a portion of ownership of the protocol and a part of a system used to maintain the protocol. Let us take a practical example to illustrate this. For malicious actors to control the network, they would need to gain control over 51% of the circulating supply of tokens in a particular network.[1] As the proportion of tokens being staked increases, orchestrating such an attack becomes increasingly challenging.[2]

7.2.3 Rewards versus Yield

When evaluating the different ways to generate additional returns in the crypto space, it is essential to understand the fundamental differences between staking and yield-generating activities.[3] The term *yield* in traditional finance refers to the income returned on an investment, such as the interest received from holding a bond or dividends from shares. This concept has been extended into the world of cryptocurrencies, particularly in the context of lending and liquidity provisioning. However, staking fundamentally differs from these activities, and as such, cannot be categorized as generating yield in the same way.

---

1   See "Ethereum Proof-of-Stake Attack and Defense" (2023).

2   At > 50% of the total stake, the attacker could dominate the fork choice algorithm. In this case, the attacker would be able to attest with the majority vote, giving them sufficient control to do short reorgs without needing to fool honest clients. A "reorg" is a reshuffling of blocks into a new order, perhaps with some addition or subtraction of blocks in the canonical chain. The honest validators would follow suit because their fork choice algorithm would also see the attacker's favored chain as the heaviest, so the chain could finalize. This enables the attacker to censor certain transactions, do short-range reorgs, and extract maximum MEV by reordering blocks in their favor. The defense against this is the huge cost of a majority stake (as of June 2023 just under $19 billion USD), which is put at risk by an attacker because the social layer is likely to step in and adopt an honest minority fork, devaluing the attacker's stake dramatically.

3   See Thakur (2022b).

Lending

In crypto lending, token holders loan out their tokens to other users, platforms, or protocols in return for interest. This interest is typically represented as an Annual Percentage Yield (APY), akin to the interest earned on a traditional bank deposit. The yield or interest earned from lending is the return on the investment risk taken by lending out the tokens, which could include counterparty risk, platform risk, and market risk. Contrary to protocol staking the token lenders give up control and custody of their assets during the lending period.[4]

Liquidity Provisioning

Liquidity provisioning in Automated Market Makers (AMMs), like Uniswap or SushiSwap, is another yield-generating activity in the crypto space. In this case, token holders deposit their assets into a liquidity pool, facilitating trading on the platform. In return, they receive a portion of the trading fees, based on their share of the liquidity pool. Like lending, liquidity providers bear the risks of impermanent loss and smart contract exploits.

Protocol Staking

In contrast, staking involves participating in a network's consensus mechanism by locking up tokens to support the operations of a blockchain network, such as transaction validation and governance. The rewards received for staking are not interest or yield. They are incentives provided by the network to encourage participation and secure the blockchain.

In staking, unlike lending or liquidity provisioning, token holders retain control and custody of their assets. Their tokens are not given as a loan or deposited into a pool in exchange for trading fees. The rewards generated from staking are consensus mechanism generated and directly tied to network participation rather than a return-on-investment risk. Additionally, staking does not expose the holder's assets to the same level of risk as lending or liquidity provisioning. Although there is still risk involved—such as the risk of slashing in case of malicious actions or network downtime in some protocols—it is generally lower when delegating to a reputable Staking-as-a-Service (StaaS) provider.[5]

4 See Thakur (2022a).
5 See Section 7.6, "Understanding Staking Risks."

7.3 The Origin and Mechanism of Staking Rewards

When we talk about protocol staking, one of the most enticing aspects that often comes up is the concept of staking rewards. But where do these rewards come from and how do they work? It is essential to understand that if you do not know where the rewards are coming from, there is a good chance you are paying the rewards. So, let us unravel the mystery behind protocol staking rewards.

Staking rewards primarily originate from two sources:

Inflationary Rewards: To motivate token holders to stake their tokens, most PoS protocols incorporate an inflationary design. This design allows the distribution of newly minted tokens to those who stake. In other words, by staking your tokens, you become eligible to receive a share of the new tokens created by the protocol. The staking reward is therefore more a compensation for the value-reducing effect of an increasing number of tokens than a real additional return. In short, it is correct to say that the one who stakes tokens does not win, but the one who does not stake tokens loses.

Transaction Fees: Along with these newly minted block rewards, users staking their tokens also collect a portion of the fees generated from transactions on the protocol. Transaction fees on platforms like Ethereum are aptly named "gas." You can think of smart contracts running on the Ethereum network like a car, and just as a car needs fuel to get around, Ethereum transactions need "gas" to cover the operating costs of the blockchain infrastructure.

Staking Rewards: A Variable Parameter

Rewards are not a constant, varying from blockchain to blockchain. As we have learned, a staker's reward comprises transaction fees and newly minted tokens. For most blockchains, the bulk of the staking rewards stems from new tokens. The blockchain protocol dynamically adjusts this new token supply to incentivize or disincentivize token-holders from staking. This balance is critical because an insufficient number of staked tokens could compromise the network's security, while an excess could result in token hoarding, thereby impeding transaction and trade activities.

7.4 Case Study: Understanding Ethereum Staking Rewards Post-Merge

On September 15, 2022, the Ethereum network witnessed a significant transition known as "The Merge." This event shifted Ethereum from a PoW to a PoS consensus model, merging the Ethereum Mainnet (Execution Layer—EL) and the Beacon Chain (Consensus Layer—CL).

Setting the Stage

Before The Merge, Ethereum's two chains operated separately. Miners received rewards from the Ethereum Mainnet (EL), while validators obtained rewards from the Beacon Chain (CL). However, in the PoS model, validators assumed the responsibilities of miners, and were tasked with proposing blocks and achieving consensus on the state of Ethereum. The requirement for becoming a validator was a stake of 32 ETH.

The Ethereum Merge

"The Merge" refers to the unification of Ethereum's original execution layer (the Mainnet, which has been active since its inception) and its new proof-of-stake consensus layer, known as the Beacon Chain. This pivotal transition did away with the need for power-intensive mining, allowing the network to instead rely on staked ETH for its security. It was, indeed, a significant milestone toward achieving Ethereum's ultimate goals of enhanced scalability, security, and sustainability.

When the Beacon Chain was first introduced, it ran separately from the Mainnet. The Mainnet, with its accounts, balances, smart contracts, and blockchain state, remained secured by proof-of-work, while the Beacon Chain functioned in parallel using proof-of-stake. The Merge marked the moment when these two systems were finally integrated, with proof-of-work being permanently supplanted by proof-of-stake.

7.4.1 Exploring the New Reward Mechanism

With The Merge, validators started receiving rewards from both the EL and the CL. The EL rewards comprised priority fees and MEV. Priority fees are payments from users to validators for ensuring their transactions are included in a block. In contrast, MEV represents the extra profit a validator can make by strategically manipulating the order of transactions within the blocks they produce.

The advent of EL rewards had a profound impact on validator rewards, both in terms of their size and their volatility. The Staking Rewards Rate (STKR) increased significantly after The Merge, from an average of 5.06% before to an average of 5.87% after. This increase is substantial, showing the potential for higher returns for validators in the PoS system.

However, the real game changer seems to be periods of high demand for blockspace. These could be driven by various factors such as the launch of a popular new token, an uptick in NFT trading, or a surge in DeFi applications. The content of Figure 7.1 clearly shows that the first surge resulted from the turmoil at FTX. This was due to a substantial increase in activity on centralized exchanges, including FTX, leading many people to hastily transfer their crypto assets off the exchange and onto the

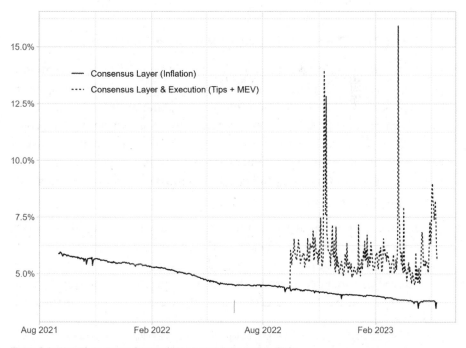

Figure 7.1: MarketVector Figment Ethereum Staking Rewards Reference Rate (STKR)
Source: MarketVector, Figment.

blockchain, thereby causing a significant rise in transaction fees. It's important to note that during times of uncertainty, on-chain activity tends to escalate. Keep in mind that this activity spans across the entire Ethereum network, encompassing not only Ethereum but also all other activities, such as NFTs.

The second notable surge can be attributed to the launch of a new meme coin. This event resulted in a flurry of trading activities and created abundant MEV opportunities, particularly because traders were hesitant to set a low slippage for their orders on decentralized exchanges. It's crucial to understand that when the demand for blockspace intensifies, fees naturally increase, which in turn, boosts the overall staking rewards. During such periods, the annual staking reward rate even shot up to an impressive 16%.

This highlights the fact that for a complete understanding of potential returns, one must consider both the rewards from validating transactions (consensus layer rewards) and the rewards from executing smart contracts (execution layer rewards). These combined rewards could significantly boost the rewards potential for validators, especially during periods of high demand.

7.4.2 The ETH Staking Reward Rate as a Benchmark

In the world of crypto assets, the establishment of an Ethereum staking reward benchmark is crucial for several reasons.[6] One of the most significant is the development of necessary market infrastructure. This benchmark facilitates the creation of a forward rate curve and a discount rate, which are key pillars in traditional finance for the valuation of assets. The application of these elements to digital assets signals a significant advancement in bridging the gap between the worlds of traditional and crypto finance.

Another important aspect is the influence of the benchmark on digital asset valuation. The existence of a staking reward benchmark allows for digital assets to be priced relative to it. This approach offers a more standardized and reliable method of valuation, promoting increased transparency and trust in the crypto marketplace. It's a transformative step

6   The MarketVector Figment Ethereum Staking Reward Benchmark Rate effectively meets this need.

toward bringing consistency to the historically volatile and unpredictable crypto market.

The Ethereum staking reward benchmark also paves the way for the introduction of derivative products, such as fix-to-variable swaps. With these financial instruments, investors can hedge against or speculate on the direction of the staking reward rate. This addition provides more investment options and risk management strategies, thereby enhancing the robustness and depth of the crypto market. The benchmark's establishment is thus not only a significant milestone, but also an essential tool for advancing the integration of digital assets into the broader financial landscape.

7.4.3 The Performance Effect of Staking

From a portfolio management perspective, protocol staking in the realm of crypto assets holds significant potential. Protocol staking acts as a counterbalance to the inflationary rewards inherent in staking protocols, preserving the value of your investment.

Over time, this effect leads to a noticeable divergence between pure price performance and performance that includes rewards. The analogy can be drawn to equity investments where investors seek to benefit not only from the appreciation of the share price, but also from the dividends. Ignoring these dividends, much like neglecting protocol staking rewards, could mean leaving significant returns on the table.

Consider Figure 7.2 as an example. It contrasts the performance of the MarketVector Figment Ethereum Total Return Index, factoring in staking rewards, with Ethereum's standalone price performance. The total return index provides superior results, demonstrating close to a 6% enhanced total return over the specified period. This underscores the potential advantages and significance of employing protocol staking as part of a crypto asset portfolio management strategy.

7.4.4 MEV-Boost: The Catalyst for Increased Staking Rewards

The introduction of an optional piece of software known as MEV-Boost added a new dimension to the Ethereum reward structure from the

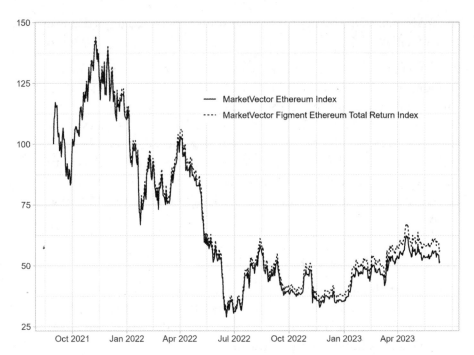

Figure 7.2: The effect of earning rewards.
Source: MarketVector, Figment. The index assumes that 90% of the portfolio is staked. Rewards are restaked on a monthly basis.

validator's perspective.[7] Validators can use MEV-Boost to effectively sell block-space to block builders—specialized actors that optimize blocks for rewards. Block builders create blocks from various sources such as the mempool, private conduits, and MEV searchers.

MEV searchers ("searchers") are looking for MEV opportunities—the inclusion, exclusion, or reordering of transactions for profit. In many instances, searchers are reacting to what they (or more likely their bots) are seeing happening on Ethereum. For instance, a large trade to a DEX could imply many profitable trades from the searcher's perspective. For example, a large trade is likely to push the underlying Automated Market Maker (AMM) pool out of balance and move the price of the traded token away from the market price. This creates an arbitrage opportunity where the searcher buys the undervalued token from the AMM pool and sells it in the market at the higher price making a profit.

7   MEV-Boost is an implementation of proposer-builder separation (PBS) created by Flashbots for the Ethereum proof-of-stake system.

Another such example is that of front-running. The searcher is still taking advantage of the movement in price, but now they are placing a trade in front of the larger trade and selling immediately after, taking advantage of the price movement of the token. This type of MEV strategy has a negative association as it can potentially move the price of the token, and therefore, affects the execution price of the larger trade, that is, the larger trade executes at a more disadvantageous price than it otherwise would have been.

Overall, MEV represents a different reward type that validators can earn on top of the regular transaction fees they receive. However, it is also a source of concern because it can lead to various forms of manipulation and unfairness in the network. After The Merge, blocks resulting from MEV-Boost showed significantly higher rewards for validators.

In summary, The Merge and the consequent introduction of EL rewards have enhanced the appeal of staking on Ethereum. Understanding the reward mechanism and optional pieces like MEV-Boost allows validators to maximize their potential rewards.

7.5 How to Participate in Protocol Staking

For those interested in participating in protocol staking, there are three primary roles you can assume: a delegator, a validator, or an integrator. Each role has its unique characteristics and responsibilities within the proof-of-stake ecosystem.

7.5.1 The Role of a Delegator

Delegators, also referred to as *stakers*, are token holders who lock up their digital assets and delegate them to a validator. The act of delegating can be likened to signaling that the validator you are staking with is a trustworthy actor. In return for this act of trust, you share in their "good acting." This process is known as delegating stake because you are delegating your stake weight to the validator. However, it is crucial to understand that this does not involve sending your tokens to the validator. Protocol staking is noncustodial, which means you or your custodian retain custody of your tokens throughout the entire process. Being a delegator is a relatively passive role. For locking up your tokens to enhance network security, you are rewarded with a share of network fees and new token issuances. This system ensures that the incentives of the token holders align with those maintaining the network. Thus, network security is improved while participants are incentivized for their contributions.

7.5.2 The Role of a Validator

Being a validator is a more complex role and involves various nuances that can vary from one blockchain to another. As a validator, you are required to run specialized software, known as a node. It is this network of nodes that constitutes the blockchain, validating on-chain transactions, and maintaining the necessary infrastructure to run PoS protocols.

As a validator, you will need to self-stake or receive delegations of digital assets to your validator node to enter the active set for most blockchains. As mentioned before, staking is noncustodial, meaning that receiving delegations does not signify receiving tokens. Your validator node should remain online, updated, secure, and honest. By *honest*, we mean you should be a good actor in the network, maintaining uptime and avoiding illicit activities such as double-signing transactions.

The stake that validators put in serves as the mechanism through which the network promotes security and the availability of the validator nodes. It also encourages honest participation in the network. This process plays a crucial role in incentivizing the permissionless, decentralized, and trustless nature of the ledger.

In exchange for their efforts and the risks they shoulder, validators receive rewards from network fees, new block issuances, and reward optimizations like MEV. These incentives help maintain a healthy network by rewarding those who keep it secure and operational.

7.5.3 The Role of an Integrator

The opportunities for becoming an integrator have expanded greatly, covering a broad spectrum that includes asset managers, exchanges, marketplaces, custodians, fund products, foundations, wallets, and much more. Integrators play a pivotal role in staking by simplifying its complexities and nuances, and in return, they share the rewards with their customers.

Running validators can be nuanced and challenging. Given this, many integrators choose to collaborate with service providers that specialize in staking. These service providers are well versed in the complexities of staking and offer a whole toolbox to assist integrators in launching their services faster.

7.6 Understanding Staking Risks

In the world of crypto, staking rewards are largely dependent on validator performance. The concept of staking revolves around validators, and their performance directly influences the returns from staking. Therefore, understanding the risks associated with staking is crucial.

7.6.1 The Concept of Slashing

One of the significant risks in staking is the possibility of slashing. This is an event where the validator forfeits a defined portion of staked tokens due to inadequate performance or specific violations. The forfeited tokens are typically either burned, redistributed to other stakeholders, or sent to the network's treasury.

There are two main actions that may trigger slashing: downtime and double signing. These events are monitored in most PoS networks, each with its unique combination of slashing parameters and varying degrees of severity.

Downtime and Its Implications

Downtime is gauged based on the liveness of the validator. If the node responsible for signing transactions remains inactive for a specific duration—determined by the network parameters—it is considered inactive.

An inactive validator loses out on block rewards. After a specific idle period, the validator might be subject to slashing, resulting in a permanent loss of stake. Furthermore, this could potentially lead to the validator's suspension from the validator set. The downtime could be triggered by the node's cloud infrastructure going down or if the software becomes out of sync.

Double Signing and Its Consequences

Double signing is a graver offense, punished more severely by the protocol. It involves the signing of two blocks at the same block height. It could occur when an adversarial validator attempts to attack the network or due to a poorly set up redundant infrastructure, leading to one key signing the same block twice.

7.6.2 How to Choose a Reliable Validator for Optimal Staking Returns

In the realm of blockchain staking, the performance of your chosen validator plays a pivotal role in determining your rewards. Thus, selecting a reliable validator is a crucial decision that requires careful thought and understanding. This chapter will guide you through some critical considerations when choosing a validator for your blockchain staking needs.

Key Considerations for Choosing a Validator

- Service Level Agreements (SLAs): A strong validator will have robust SLAs in place, indicating their commitment to maintaining an optimal level of service. Check if your potential validator's SLAs are comprehensive and align with your expectations.
- Coverage: When staking, there are inherent risks such as missed rewards, downtime penalties, and double-sign slashing. However, a reliable validator will have multiple coverage sources in place to mitigate these risks and provide compensation if certain events occur. Trust in a proven validator to ensure your safety and maximize your rewards.
- Trustworthiness: It is essential to choose a validator that has earned the trust of its users. This can be assessed through user reviews, their track record, and their responsiveness to user queries.
- Security Prioritization: A validator should prioritize security to protect your staked tokens from potential threats. Check if your potential validator has implemented robust security measures to keep your investment safe.
- Reward Distribution: Last, consider if the validator's reward distribution is fair for the work they are putting in. While validators are entitled to a portion of the rewards for their service, this amount should be reasonable and not overly dilute your staking returns.

Remember, the success of your staking endeavor is tied to your validator's performance. Therefore, understanding staking risks and making an informed decision while choosing a validator is critical to securing your investment and optimizing returns. Take your time to assess potential validators using these considerations and choose one that best suits your staking objectives.

7.7 Liquid Staking Protocols

Liquid staking protocols are a type of DeFi service that allows users to stake their crypto assets in a PoS network while maintaining liquidity. These protocols provide a bridge between the staking mechanism, which usually requires the staked assets to be locked and therefore illiquid, and the DeFi ecosystem, which thrives on the free movement and utilization of assets.[8]

7.7.1 How Liquid Staking Protocols Work

Here is a generalized process of how liquid staking protocols work:

1. Staking: Users stake their tokens through the liquid staking protocol. This involves locking up the tokens in a smart contract or wallet.

2. Issuance of staking derivatives: The protocol issues a new token, often referred to as a staking derivative, to the user. This token represents a claim on the staked assets and any rewards they may generate.

3. Liquidity: These staking derivatives can be freely traded or used in other DeFi applications, providing liquidity to the user.

4. Rewards: As the original staked tokens earn staking rewards (e.g., through block validation in the PoS network), these rewards accrue to the staking derivatives. The user can claim these rewards by redeeming or selling their staking derivatives.

5. Redemption: When the user wants to unstake their tokens, they can return the staking derivatives to the protocol, which will then release the original staked tokens (plus any earned rewards) back to the user.

---

[8] Many validator nodes require your tokens to be locked up for a designated amount of time. For example, staking ATOM will result in a 21-day lock-up period while SOL delegation requires around a 48-hour unbonding period.

The primary advantage of liquid staking protocols is that they enable users to participate in staking (and earn rewards) while also being able to use their staked assets in other ways, such as lending, borrowing, trading, or yield farming in the DeFi space. This can lead to more efficient capital utilization and potentially higher returns for users.

7.7.2 The Risk of Liquid Staking Protocols

Liquid staking protocols introduce additional layers of complexity and potential risks compared to traditional staking or staking as a service.[9] First, there's smart contract risk. Liquid staking protocols rely on smart contracts to issue and manage staking derivatives, and any bugs or vulnerabilities in these contracts could put users' assets at risk.

Second, there's market risk associated with the staking derivatives themselves. The value of these derivatives can fluctuate based on supply and demand dynamics in the market, and this could lead to a situation where the derivative trades at a discount or premium to the underlying staked asset. Third, there is the risk of impermanent loss if users provide liquidity for staking derivatives in a liquidity pool. If the price of the staking derivative and the paired asset diverges significantly, users may end up with less of one or both assets when they withdraw from the pool. In general, while liquid staking protocols offer the advantage of liquidity and additional opportunities, they also come with a higher level of risk compared to protocol staking. Therefore, users should carefully consider their risk tolerance and perform thorough due diligence before participating in these protocols.

7.8 Conclusion

Staking allows participants to collect rewards that at least should offset the negative impact of a growing supply of tokens. If investors opt not to stake, they risk losing value due to dilution. This implies that staking is more a way of maintaining one's share in a network's total token supply than a way to generate real returns. Apart from the monetary side of the equation, by staking, token holders actively contribute to the security and

---

9   See "Liquid vs. Illiquid Staking—What Is Better?" (2021).

functionality of the blockchain network, thereby playing a crucial role in the growth and stability of the cryptocurrency ecosystem.

Acknowledgments

We would like to express our gratitude to the people at Figment, a foremost provider of staking as a service. Their contribution to this chapter, in the form of expertise, detailed insights, and comprehensive data, has been indispensable. The depth of understanding we have been able to impart about staking has been greatly enhanced by their assistance. We appreciate their commitment to furthering knowledge within the blockchain industry and their invaluable support in ensuring the accuracy and comprehensiveness of this work.

7.9 References

"Ethereum Proof-of-Stake Attack and Defense." (2023). Ethereum.Org. https://ethereum.org.

"Liquid vs. Illiquid Staking—What Is Better?" (2021). Staking Rewards. November 24, 2021. https://www.stakingrewards.com/journal/liquid-vs-illiquid-staking-what-is-better/.

Thakur, Nikhil. (2022a). "Protocol Staking—The Optimal Rewards Generating Opportunity." *Figment* (blog). August 1, 2022. https://figment.io/protocol-staking-the-optimal-rewards-generating-opportunity/.

Thakur, Nikhil. (2022b). "Protocol Staking Is Not an Investment Product and Rewards Are Not 'Yield' (and Why This Matters)." *Figment* (blog). August 9, 2022. https://figment.io/protocol-staking-is-not-an-investment-product-and-rewards-are-not-yield-and-why-this-matters/.

8 Index Investments

"...an index-driven strategy may not be the best investment strategy ever
devised, the number of investment strategies that are worse is infinite."
John Bogle (2017)[1]

8.1 Theory Underlying the Case for Index-Based Investments

In the investment realm, the shift toward "passive investments" through index products and ETFs has grown significantly over the past 15 years, but the origins of indexing go back more than 50 years, to the beginning of the 1970s, with academic roots stretching even further than that. A deep foundation of more than 60 years of academic research undergirds index investment theory and practice.

University of California economist Edward Renshaw and student Paul Feldstein jointly published an article outlining the concept of an index fund. This article, titled "The Case for an Unmanaged Investment Company," appeared in the *Financial Analysts Journal* in 1960.[2] Renshaw and Feldstein highlighted the two main arguments favoring simple index funds: lower costs and the provocative question of whether it was more reasonable to accept the overall market return instead of chasing uncertain additional returns. This groundbreaking idea faced many critics, but academic and practical evidence of the logic of indexing continued to build.

In 1965, Paul Samuelson published his paper on the information inherent in stock prices. He stated that "the intrinsic value of stocks is nothing more than their market price at any moment."[3] In other words, the only price at which equilibrium between buyers and sellers is reached is the market price.

Samuelson's work was built on by the Efficient Market Hypothesis (EMH), a theory coined by Eugene Fama in 1970. This concept gave rise to the philosophy that is foundational to indexing, one which is as simple as it

---

1 See Bogle (2017).
2 See Renshaw and Feldstein (1995).
3 See Samuelson (1972).

was revolutionary. The logical progression was to manage the controllable variables by dampening risk through diversification, while minimizing transaction costs.

Two primary arguments support index-based strategies. First, the efficiency and cost savings of this approach is undeniable, beginning with the massive savings for institutional investors since the advent of cap-weighted equity indexing 50 years ago in 1973.[4]

The foundation of academic research continued to support the case for passive investing. Aside from the previously mentioned work, Random Walk theory, beginning with Maurice Kendall in 1953, which was further elaborated by Eugene Fama in his 1965 paper "Random Walks in Stock-Market Prices," culminating in 1973 when Burton Malkiel published the first edition of his classic book *A Random Walk Down Wall Street*."[5]

The case for why pension funds, endowments, Sovereign Wealth Funds, and other sophisticated institutional investors use index funds is strong. One investment executive at a large U.S. state pension fund listed at least six advantages of index-based strategies:

- Lower management fees.
- Lower transaction costs.
- Delivery of market returns with a highly transparent process.
- Facilitation of precise asset exposure.
- Risk control of the total investment portfolio.
- Fewer managers to hire and monitor.[6]

The second argument, which despite overwhelming evidence continues to be debated by numerous active managers, is crystal clear: academic and industry studies demonstrate that passive products outperform most active funds in the long run, taking costs into account. This is most elegantly expressed by William Sharpe as the "Arithmetic of Active

---

4   In a study conducted in 1998, "25 Years of Indexing: An Analysis of the Costs and Benefits" by PricewaterhouseCoopers, the authors estimated that the total savings of U.S. institutional tax-exempt investors ranged between $81 billion and $105 billion since the launch of the first cap-weighted equity index fund in 1973. These savings include transaction costs, management fees, and the performance difference between index and active strategies. They similarly estimated that then "current" annual savings for investors were between $14 billion and $18 billion. See PriceWaterhouseCoopers (1999).

5   See Malkiel (2016).

6   See Schoenfeld (2004).

Management." Brilliant in its clarity and simplicity, it was based on plain logic with no reliance on complex financial concepts of fancy equations replete with Greek symbols.[7] It simply proved that the average active dollar has to produce a performance identical to the average indexed dollar before costs and fees.

Moreover, the impact of taxes can be particularly challenging for active managers with high turnover. Often, the significant theoretical outperformance of some strategies doesn't translate into meaningful results in practice, once costs and taxes are considered. Actual outperformance after expenses occurs, though infrequently. Much like competitive sports, achieving a top position isn't a mass-produced outcome, but is instead the product of effective processes and strict discipline.

In general, investors' focus should not be on the choice between active and passive investing, but how to use them together. As one consultant summarized the issue, while commenting on another study showing active management's challenges in outperforming index-based strategies, stated, "The problem isn't about 'active' versus 'passive' investing, but rather, it's about emotional versus long-term disciplined investing. In the absence of appropriate personal or systematic guidance and education, it's both natural and regrettable that investors depend on emotions instead of an efficient process."[8]

8.1.1 The Development and Expansion of Index Funds

Based on applying this theory into practice, the first equity index fund was launched on July 1, 1971.[9] It was developed by the financial analysis department of Wells Fargo Bank (which eventually became Barclays Global Investors), led by John McQuown, Willliam Fouse, and James Vertin, and tracked a relatively cumbersome equal weight NYSE Composite Index. The catalyst and first client was Charles Schwayder, son of the head of the Samsonite Corporation, whose pension fund allocated $6 million to the strategy.

---

7 See Sharpe (1991).

8 Quote by Greg Patterson, The Advisory Group LLC "DALBAR Study Update Confirms Investor Behavior Problems," February 2007.

9 See Schoenfeld (2004).

Despite initial resistance to Wells Fargo's pioneering index fund launched in 1971, other asset management companies such as American National Bank (now part of Northern Trust) launched a cap-weighted fund tracking the S&P 500, and Wells Fargo launched its first S&P 500 fund that year too.

However, private investors could not yet invest in index funds. MIT economist Paul Samuelson publicly criticized this limitation and expressed hope that it would change soon. As expected, some employees of banks and asset management companies had a different opinion on the matter:

"I hope the damn things fail because if they don't, it's going to mean the jobs of a lot of good analysts and portfolio men."[10]

An unnamed analyst at a Boston bank (November 1975)

A mere two weeks after the anonymous bank employee's statement, Vanguard launched the first index fund under John Bogle's leadership, who had since embraced passive investing. The concept was slow to catch on, but this launch marked the beginning of an ongoing success story for private investors, eventually leading to the development of small-cap index mutual funds, international index funds, fixed income index funds, and ultimately, index-tracking exchange-traded funds (ETFs).

The original intent behind index-tracking funds was to provide a straight-forward and cost-effective way for all investors to invest in a broad stock market. The creation of the first index mutual fund widely available to individual investors is generally attributed to John Bogle of Vanguard. In 1976, the company introduced the "Index Investment Trust" (now known as the "Vanguard 500 Index Fund"), the first index fund available to the public. However, it is important to note that the concept had been conceived by others many years prior. Bogle was initially against passive investing in the early 1960s, and even wrote an article arguing for active fund management, titled "The Case for Mutual Fund Management," published in the *Financial Analysts Journal* under the pseudonym John B. Armstrong.[11]

Since then, index mutual funds, institutional index comingled funds, equity index futures and options, index swaps, and ETFs have brought

---

10 See Mihm (2016).
11 See Armstrong (1960).

myriad "pure passive" and index tools to investors. The first ETFs were designed with this goal in mind, revolutionizing the trading of fund shares. Investors could now buy and sell an entire index like a stock on the exchange, a significant milestone in the capital market's evolution. An entirely new investing philosophy has grown around indexing, and fundamentally changed how sophisticated investors look at markets. This philosophy is an interesting mix of faith in efficient markets, sober examination of the facts of performance attribution, and a good dose of common sense.[12]

As equity index products proliferated, their use, together with active strategies, became seamlessly blended, even as debates over "active versus passive" continued to rage in the financial media and the boardrooms of investment committees. However, the constant interplay between academia and practitioners only resulted in even more innovations, including "smart beta" indexes, sophisticated ETF rotation strategies, and deeper penetration of indexing around the world's equity markets.

The growth of index-based strategies has been profoundly valuable to institutional and individual investors alike—for the simple reason of better long-term returns and substantially lower costs.

From our perspective, the "index versus active debate" was obsolete even 20 years ago when *Active Index Investing* was published. And, in fact, the indexing revolution was just starting in 2004, even after 30 years of indexing.[13]

The innovation certainly did not stop with passively tracking equity indexes or stock index products for tracking. In fact, equity indexing established a foundation for indexing in a wide range of asset classes over the course of the last four decades, culminating with the advent of digital asset indexes and indexing in the late 2010s. Over the course of the 1980s and 1990s, indexing rapidly spread to other asset classes, starting with fixed income indexes in the mid-1980s. Indexing physical assets, whether commodities or real estate also became possible, and has grown in popularity and efficiency.

---

12 See Schoenfeld (2004).
13 See Schoenfeld (2004).

Real Estate indexing began in the 1970s, with a pioneering effort by the National Association of Real Estate Investment Trusts with its NAREIT index. Several major REIT index families were in play by the early 2000s, and scores more by this decade.

Benchmark indexes for broad-based commodities were launched by the Commodities Research Bureau (CRB) in 1958, with investable futures-based index launched in 1986. Since then, other indexes such as S&P/ GSCI and the Dow Jones Commodity Index, along with a wide range of specialized indexes, have been developed and now are the basis for ETFs and index derivatives.

Digital assets indexes of cryptocurrencies were first introduced in the second half of the 2010s. In 2017, "MVIS"—MarketVector's predecessor—launched a family of digital asset indexes, which this chapter discusses.

8.1.2 Active Choices for Passive Investors

Even for those who advocate passive investment products, active decisions are inevitable, and in fact, both natural and highly beneficial

Asset allocation—whether using active or passive products within individual asset classes—requires deliberate choices. As a result, one can find portfolios consisting entirely of passive products or a mix of active and passive products. In fact, with the advent of financial advisors' and wealth managers' increased use of ETFs and model portfolios, it is arguable that a majority of investors are using "Active Index" approaches, whether they fully-acknowledge it or not.

As noted in *Active Index Investing*, "The use of index products can be as active as the investor wants it to be. Active and sophisticated decision-making by investors undergirds their use of index-based products and strategies. Investors who choose an index-based approach in no way abdicate the quest for outperformance. In fact, integrating indexing and active strategies within a total portfolio approach allows them to better segment the beta or market exposure from their sources of alpha or excess return."

Furthermore, many investors still rely on active managers in more illiquid asset classes, such as high-yield corporate bonds or emerging market equities, as they expect the active approaches to exploit inefficiencies in these segments. However, even in inefficient asset classes, the results do not always meet expectations. For example, the percentage of emerging market equity funds that underperform their benchmarks is shockingly high—data from the well-regarded S&P Index Vs Active Scorecard (SPIVA) shows that more than 85% of active emerging market funds underperform the S&P/IFCI Composite Index over the 10-year period ending December 2022.[14]

Passive, index-based investors also make active, fundamental decisions that influence their capital growth, even without incorporating active products. One such decision is selecting the indices on which the products used are based. While this may seem simple, the reality is more complex. Index providers offer numerous products that closely represent the performance of specific market segments, but the range of indexes has become vast and continues to grow.

For example, the "U.S. equities" category can be interpreted in various ways. Consider the S&P 500: although this U.S. stock index comprises only 44% of all stocks from the more comprehensive MSCI USA, it accounts for about 88% of the total market capitalization of the U.S. stock market. While this index's performance is representative of the overall market, it doesn't necessarily reflect the performance of the "median U.S. stock." If companies with lower market values significantly outperform the heavyweights, this index presents a negatively skewed representation of all stocks' performance. Conversely, if the larger stocks perform much better, the result is a positive distortion.

The size effect should not be underestimated as sometimes only a few individual stocks lead to a substantial increase in the index.[15]

Aside from the aforementioned distortions, market capitalization-based weighting has two primary advantages. First, this approach is pragmatic. Apart from the regular replacement of some index members, which follows specific rules set by the index provider, such an index doesn't require any position adjustments. If a stock's market value changes, the security's share changes accordingly. Second, an index with a weighting methodology based on its constituents' market capitalization essentially acts as a trend follower for the stocks it contains. Investors are increasingly

---

14 See "SPIVA® U.S. Year-End" (2022).
15 See Alquist, Israel, and Moskowitz (2018).

invested in securities with rising market values. Stocks moving toward lower valuations gradually leave the index.

"But don't small stocks perform better in the long run?" some may ask, referencing the "size effect" according to Fama and French. In some cases and time periods, this assumption holds true. However, investors should avoid generalizations. Figure 8.1 illustrates a comparison between a small-cap and a large-cap ETF and the overall U.S. market.

Over extended periods, allocating shares with low market capitalization can have a positive impact. However, there may be intermittent, prolonged periods with sometimes significantly weaker performance for smaller stocks, which can negatively affect investor patience and lead to emotional decisions. Those who happen to enter the market at an unfortunate point may quickly experience considerable price drops. These drops are often more severe for small stocks than for their larger counterparts, increasing the risk of impulsive decisions. Even a single overreaction triggered by

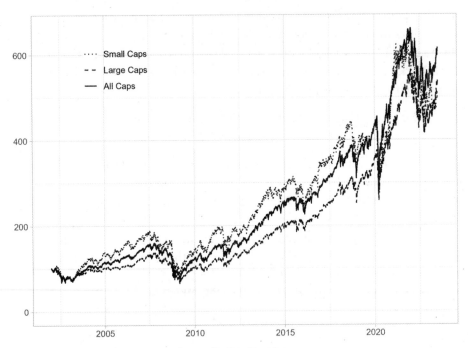

Figure 8.1: Development of U.S. large- and small-cap equities. Data: NorgateData.com.

mental stress can cause more financial damage than can be offset over the years by the potential additional return on smaller shares.

There is a wide range of possible weighting approaches. Many approaches are well conceived and have a complex appeal to investors. For example, there are fundamental weighting methods based on key figures such as companies' sales. Simple equal weighting is also described as advantageous in numerous publications. The chart in Figure 8.2 shows the performance of the U.S. total market compared to an ETF that weights stocks equally. Since corresponding ETFs were launched later, the history does not extend as far back as with funds based on standard indexes.

The result is sobering (see Figure 8.2). What reads well and sounds plausible in numerous publications does not materialize in reality for investors. Apart from the lagging performance compared to a simple index, there are further disadvantages to such strategies. The regular weight adjustments of the individual securities cause considerable transaction costs. In addition, the tax burden for investors increases.

Figure 8.2: Development of an equal weighted versus a market cap weighted U.S. stock Index. Data: NorgateData.com.

In a vacuum, there is much to be said for an equally weighted index of medium-sized and large companies. In practice, however, this often looks different in many cases over the long term. When selecting an index as a basis for long-term capital investment, investors should take the preceding points into account. Investing in the overall market may sound overly simplistic to many, but it is not easy to beat over the long term. A major reason for the disappointing performance of many equity strategies that deviate from market capitalization is the significant increase in the efficiency of liquid markets. The excess returns that can still be achieved today are significantly lower than in the past. In segments with less transparency and low liquidity, however, the situation is different. There, even simple active strategies can lead to notable outperformance.

Many institutional investors, such as pension funds, endowments, and large family offices, have therefore switched to using passive products for allocation to predominantly highly liquid and transparent markets, while still preferring to use active managers where there is still an expectation that there is something to be gained in prospective alpha relative to the additional costs of active strategies.

Among the asset classes where we anticipate that there will still major inefficiencies for the foreseeable future are digital assets. Yet despite anticipation of inefficiencies, index-based allocation via "Active Indexing," can play a major role for implementing both passive and actively oriented strategies in crypto assets.

8.1.3 Establishing Clear Standards for Greater Transparency

The initial step in digital asset allocation often leads investors to the most well-known asset, Bitcoin. Those who seek not only a single asset, but also appreciate risk diversification for smaller portfolio positions typically turn to investable indexes. Although there are currently more funds and indices than individual stocks in the stock market, the realm of digital asset indices is still in its infancy, with strong growth momentum.

Standardized indexes play a crucial role in enhancing transparency, with standardization and the establishment of easily understood categories being vital prerequisites. The commodity market exemplifies the transition from unregulated, simple bilateral trade to a highly standardized and efficient markets.

Modern commodity trading brings to mind forward or futures trading on terminal exchanges. Efficient systems, including clearinghouses, allow for transactions with standardized contracts. However, well before these computerized marketplaces, societies participated in relatively organized exchanges of animals, agricultural commodities, and later, processed goods like fabric.

Over 6,000 years ago, the Sumerians were already involved in organized raw material trade. Centralized, uniform exchange methods were introduced in various civilizations at an early stage. Gold, silver, and cowrie shells are some of the most well-known examples.

Throughout the Middle Ages, gold became an almost universally accepted standardized medium of exchange. In the early 16th century, the first stock exchanges emerged in Europe, including the Amsterdam Stock Exchange in 1530. Prior to trading shares, commodities were traded on this exchange, with market participants able to do more than just buy and sell. Forward trading and optional transactions flourished alongside short selling. By the end of the century, stock exchanges had spread across Europe.

Similarly, the world's first true futures exchange—the Dojima Rice Exchange—was established in 1730 in Osaka, Japan.[16]

North America joined the international commodity exchanges with the founding of the Chicago Board of Trade (CBOT) in 1864. Regulatory advancements, such as the Commodity Exchange Act of 1930, expanded the range of tradable commodities. This seemingly simple step required extensive standardization of newly traded commodities. Assessable quality characteristics, ratios, and scales had to be established. The successful creation of standardized contracts led to the breakthrough of commodity trading on futures exchanges. Commodities attracted not only producers and consumers, but also investors seeking a new liquid asset class, portfolio diversification, inflation protection, or speculative opportunities.

The increasing interest of nonspecialized investor groups who wanted a quick overview of the entire segment led to the creation of the first commodity index. In 1934, the U.S. legislature prompted the calculation of the Commodity Price Index, reflecting the price development of 22 commodities divided into categories. Six years later, the index was made

---

16 JPX (Japan Stock Exchange) website, www.jpx.co.jp.

public and eventually became part of the broader Producer Price Index (PPI) published by the Bureau of Labor Statistics. Today's popular commodity indices, such as the S&P GSCI or the CC-CRB Commodity Index, are provided by commercial providers and often serve as the basis for exchange-traded commodity products.

The success story of commodities highlights the significance of standardization, categorization, and development of benchmarks for the breakthrough adaption of an asset class. Not all investors are interested in the specifications of individual assets.

For volatile asset classes—especially like crypto—index strategies that rebalance regularly have the added benefit of capturing mean-reversion, essentially selling high and buying low.

Many investors use indexes with the primary aim to map an asset class as a whole and must consider whether a passive or active orientation best achieves this goal. However, even for investors with an active orientation, investors require a benchmark to classify the performance and risk profile of a chosen strategy. Essentially, as with the asset classes that have preceded them, the case for an active index approach to crypto is as strong as for equities or fixed income—and ultimately, will have multiple dimensions, including active benchmark choice and the active use of index products for everything from broad-based asset allocation to short-term tactical trading.

Consequently, creating a range of indexes for digital assets—both "pure passive" and strategy indexes that represent an element of "active indexing"—is an essential prerequisite for the success of this new asset class among institutional investors, and will facilitate adaption and implementation by these same investors.

8.2 Digital Asset Indexing

As the digital asset space continues to mature, the demand for better benchmarks and tools to track the performance of various crypto assets has grown. Digital asset indexes are at the forefront of this development, offering market participants a means of gauging the overall health of the market and comparing the performance of specific assets against the broader ecosystem. In this chapter, we delve into the market structure of the crypto landscape and explore the challenges faced by index providers in this new asset class.

8.2.1 Crypto Market Structure: Key Features

For those acquainted with traditional financial markets, it is essential to look at the characteristics of the cryptocurrency market structure, its trading venues, and how it diverges from other well-established financial markets. Within the expanding cryptocurrency landscape, there are currently over 300 spot exchanges and more than 30 derivatives exchanges for trading cryptocurrencies. This means that there is no definitive market price or the concept of a "consolidated tape." Furthermore, the quality of exchanges varies considerably in terms of operational aspects, the regulations they are subject to, their compliance, governance practices, platform security and stability, and the overall robustness of their trading volume, liquidity, pricing, and range of instruments available.

In response to these challenges, several cryptocurrency price aggregator platforms have emerged to provide a unique price indication from these exchanges. Naturally, these aggregators differ in their selection of exchanges for pricing (ranging from one to all), as well as the type of pricing they offer. Among price aggregators, volume-weighted average pricing (VWAP), time-weighted average pricing (TWAP), median-based variations, and fair market value (FMV) pricing are all accessible. Last, due to the lack of a standard identifier (ticker) for each asset across exchanges, price aggregators must employ a robust solution to address the data challenges. Given the overview of the market structure, we can identify the following key features that characterize the crypto ecosystem:

Decentralized and Fragmented: The crypto market is spread across various platforms, including centralized exchanges (e.g., Coinbase, Binance), decentralized exchanges (e.g., Uniswap, SushiSwap), and over-the-counter (OTC) trading desks. This fragmentation presents challenges in terms of liquidity, pricing, and data aggregation.

24/7 Trading: Crypto markets operate continuously, without any breaks, weekends, or holidays. This creates a need for round-the-clock monitoring and reliable infrastructure to ensure accurate index calculation and dissemination.

Evolving Regulatory Landscape: The legal and regulatory environment surrounding cryptocurrencies is in flux, with varying degrees of clarity across jurisdictions. This can create uncertainty and potential road-blocks for index providers and market participants.

Wide Variety of Assets

The crypto ecosystem comprises thousands of assets with varying levels of liquidity, market capitalization, and underlying technology. Selecting and weighting these assets in an index can be a complex task.

8.3 The Importance of Exchange Vetting and Clean Prices for Institutional Investors

Author: Marco Manoppo

In 2019, the infamous digital asset exchange, QuadrigaCX, closed its doors following the mysterious death of its founder. Thousands of investors lost their digital assets, valued at over $169 million, as the private keys to the exchange's wallets were supposedly known only by the deceased founder. The QuadrigaCX debacle underlines the critical importance of a well-vetted and transparent digital asset exchange.

The rapid growth of the digital asset ecosystem has given rise to concerns about the legitimacy and reliability of such exchanges. In a landscape marked by light regulations and high volatility, investors must conduct their due diligence when choosing a platform to trade digital assets. One of the key steps in this due diligence process is exchange vetting, a rigorous evaluation of an exchange from both quantitative and qualitative perspectives. This chapter aims to walk you through the importance of exchange vetting, its key components, and how a lack of it led to the downfall of FTX, a once prominent digital asset exchange.

Exchange Vetting: Why Is It Important?

Exchange vetting is important to determine if an exchange is acting in the best interest of its users. A variety of factors contribute to the need for exchange vetting, including:

- Lightly regulated environment: The digital asset space is still relatively new and oversight varies widely across jurisdictions.

- Low barriers to entry: The rapid growth of the digital asset space combined with low barriers to entry has led to a proliferation of exchanges globally.
- Illegitimate trading volumes: Some exchanges falsely claim substantial trading volumes, which may give an inaccurate impression of their importance in the market and available liquidity.

8.3.1 Key Exchange Vetting Factors

When evaluating an exchange, institutional market participants should consider a series of key factors. Here are some examples:

Trade and Order Book Data

Trade and order book data serve as critical indicators of market integrity. Analyzing patterns across historical trade and order book data sets can provide insights into potential market "wash trading" or "spoofing" practices. Let's delve into these a bit further:

- Wash trading involves a trader or a group of traders buying and selling the same asset to create the illusion of activity or liquidity. In the context of digital asset exchanges, a wash trader might simultaneously buy and sell the same cryptocurrency to artificially inflate trading volume and manipulate prices. This deceptive practice can mislead other traders into making decisions based on false market signals.
- Spoofing, on the other hand, involves placing large buy or sell orders without intending to fill them. These orders are usually canceled before they can be executed. The purpose is to create a false impression of the demand or supply of a digital asset, thereby manipulating the price. A spoofer might, for example, place a large sell order to create an illusion of increased supply, which can cause others to panic and sell, driving the price down. The spoofer can then buy the asset at a lower price.

In Figure 8.3, we compare Bitcoin trades from the first seven days of February 2022 across two vetted exchanges (Gemini and Liquid) and two other centralized exchanges (BTSE and Hopex) that didn't pass our stringent vetting process. The vetted exchanges display the anticipated pattern: the direction of the previous transaction (buy or sell) often indicates the direction of the next transaction, which ultimately influences asset price

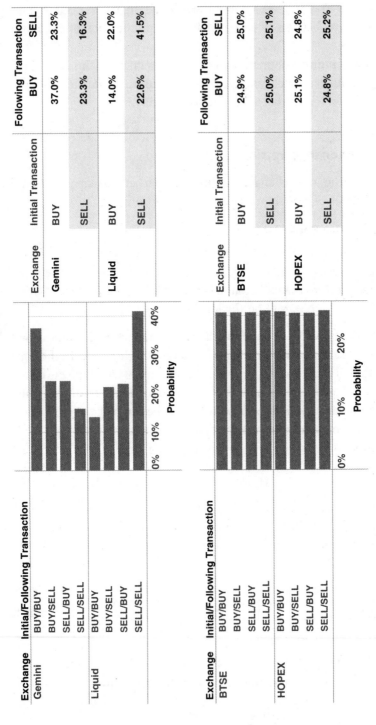

Transaction Independence for Bitcoin Trades Across Exchanges
10/01/2022 - 10/05/2022

Exchange	Initial Transaction	Following Transaction	
		BUY	SELL
Gemini	BUY	37.0%	23.3%
	SELL	23.3%	16.3%
Liquid	BUY	14.0%	22.0%
	SELL	22.6%	41.5%

Exchange	Initial Transaction	Following Transaction	
		BUY	SELL
BTSE	BUY	24.9%	25.0%
	SELL	25.0%	25.1%
HOPEX	BUY	25.1%	24.8%
	SELL	24.8%	25.2%

This chart represents observed data across a selection of active centralized crypto exchanges.

Figure 8.3: Buy-sell permutations.
Source: Digital Asset Research.

fluctuations. In contrast, the other exchanges in this comparison demonstrate a uniformly random pattern. In other words, the likelihood of buying or selling Bitcoin at any given moment on these platforms is akin to a toss of a coin.

Corporate Organizational Structure

The credibility of a digital asset exchange is inextricably linked to its corporate structure and ownership. A comprehensive evaluation should consider the experience and expertise of the management team, the team's past performance, and any potential conflicts of interest. For example, an exchange with opaque ownership that is composed of complex offshore entities might indicate that the exchange is trying to obfuscate information.

Financial Health

Evaluating an exchange's financial health, including its balance sheet, reserves, insurance policies, and independent audits, is paramount for institutional market participants who are assessing an exchange for counterparty risk.

Governance and Compliance

Examining an exchange's Know Your Customer (KYC) and Anti-Money Laundering (AML) protocols, and other compliance-related policies is crucial. Weak KYC and AML policies invite money laundering.

Comprehending a trading platform's market surveillance strategies and systems is beneficial for determining their effectiveness in thwarting potential market manipulations. Similarly, understanding a platform's policies on conflicts of interest can shed light on their efficacy in appropriately managing any discrepancies between their operations and associated entities.

8.3.2 The Downfall of FTX

FTX, once a prominent digital asset exchange, became insolvent due to mismanagement and irresponsible organizational practices.

Background

FTX was a major player in the digital asset market. It had rapid growth and acquired a significant portion of the digital asset trading volume market share. However, the exchange's expansion came at a cost, as it turned out that the exchange did not uphold best practices. These and other issues eventually led to FTX's downfall.

Factor Contributing to FTX's Downfall: Inadequate Management of Rapid Growth

As the exchange's user base grew, it disregarded standard practices in managing customers' assets, which led to an asset-to-liability mismatch. When FTX customers lost confidence in the exchange and withdrew their capital, FTX did not have enough assets on hand to honor withdrawals, causing the company to file for bankruptcy.

How Exchange Vetting Could Have Helped

Key areas where vetting could have been beneficial include:

- Conflicts of Interest: A comprehensive review of FTX's business could have shown that the exchange had used its own token, FTX Token (FTT), as collateral at inflated values.
- Verifying Transparency: Assessing the level of transparency provided by FTX, including its financial health, security practices, and risk management, would have allowed investors to make more informed decisions about the platform's trustworthiness.

Conclusion

The downfall of FTX serves as a cautionary tale for institutional digital asset investors on the importance of a robust exchange vetting process.

By thoroughly examining factors such as security measures, regulatory compliance, and transparency, investors can better identify potential risks and red flags associated with digital asset exchanges.

8.4 Pricing: The Foundation of Capital Markets

Institutional market participants venturing into the digital asset space require "clean" digital asset pricing data to make informed decisions, manage risk, and comply with regulatory requirements. That is, pricing data which has not been manipulated. Despite the importance of accurate pricing data, institutions face challenges in obtaining reliable and trustworthy data, which emphasizes the need for transparent pricing methodologies.

Accurate pricing forms the bedrock of capital markets. A wide range of activities in the financial space require clean pricing data, including:

- Indexes and benchmarks.
- Portfolio valuation.
- Research and back testing.
- Policy and regulatory decisions.
- Fraud and investigations.

8.4.1 Challenges in Digital Asset Pricing

In traditional markets, price discovery is relatively easy due to the presence of primary listing exchanges and well-established price reporting mechanisms. However, obtaining accurate pricing data in the digital asset market presents unique challenges.

Digital assets are the only asset class that combines multidisciplinary fields with open-source principles. Anybody can create a new digital asset, and the assets trade 24/7, 365 days. These assets are also natively digital, which means that they are cross-border in nature.

As a result, digital asset markets are fragmented, leading to new challenges.

Hundreds of Exchanges

Unlike U.S. equities, which have only a few major venues (like the NYSE and NASDAQ), crypto has hundreds of trading venues, each with its own markets and practices. There are hundreds of crypto exchanges globally as of May 2023, many with little transparency around governance and compliance.

Decentralized Platforms

In crypto, there are also decentralized applications that can power peer-to-peer transactions, creating what is known as DEXs. DEXs are fully managed by code and can run on their own via smart contracts on the blockchain. DEX users are not forced to complete any KYC/AML and are able to conduct direct transactions "on-chain" without going through any centralized counterparties. There are hundreds of DEXs, which further fragment and affect the quality of crypto asset prices.

FX Rate Discrepancies

Additionally, as digital assets are traded globally, they are exposed to various FX rates (see Figure 8.4). Crypto exchanges around the world support trading pairs in their local currencies. This means that capital control rules applied in different countries will affect crypto asset prices. The most famous example of this is the price premium that Bitcoin has in South Korea, which is known as the "Kimchi Premium." Bitcoin sometimes trades at a higher price in South Korea because of the country's capital control rules, which limit cross-border flow of the Korean Won.

Even recently, the Kimchi Premium phenomenon has impacted a high-demand asset. Aptos, a new Layer-1 blockchain valued at $4.5 billion, recently launched its APT token. The price of APT on Korean exchanges (Korbit and Upbit) was considerably higher than U.S.-based exchanges (Binance.US and Coinbase).

8.4.2 Transparent Pricing Methodologies

To ensure accurate and reliable digital asset pricing data, it is essential to have transparent pricing methodologies. Institutional market participants should seek pricing sources that provide clear information on how their prices are derived.

Figure 8.4: Price differences due to FX rate discrepancies.
Source: Digital Asset Research.

Rigorous pricing methodologies should eliminate the impact of:

- Fraudulent or manipulated prices: The inclusion of prices from exchanges that engage in fraudulent activities or allow market manipulation can distort an asset's price.
- Extreme market phenomena: Digital asset markets are known for their volatility and the occurrence of extreme market phenomena, primarily because the asset class itself and the associated market infrastructure are relatively young. The price of an asset on a single exchange can disconnect from the broader market. One recent example is the discrepancy in the price of TRX on the now defunct FTX exchange versus the broader market. It occurred when the founder of TRX, Justin Sun, stated the following: "We will do everything we can to protect our users, including exchange all #TRX, #BTT, #JST, #SUN, #HT on the FTX platform at a 1:1 ratio," This statement caused the price of TRX on FTX to surge by more than 4,000%. Ensuring that one has a proper pricing data provider is crucial to understand what happens in the crypto market during extreme market phenomenon (see Figure 8.5).
- Exchange infrastructure: The reliability of crypto exchange infrastructure has not always been guaranteed, even for the most prominent exchanges (see Figure 8.6). A notable incident occurred on February 22, 2021, when the price of Ethereum (ETH) on Kraken temporarily deviated from the overall market for approximately 15 minutes before realigning with broader market trends.

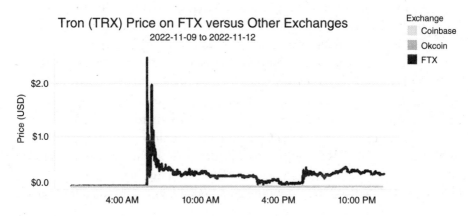

Figure 8.5: Extreme market phenomena.
Source: Digital Asset Research.

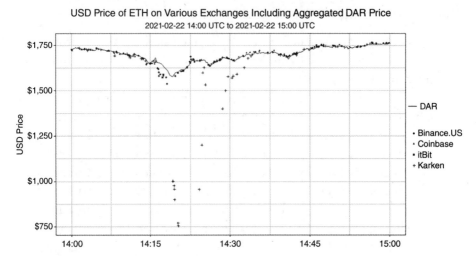

Figure 8.6: Unreliable exchange infrastructure.
Source: Digital Asset Research.

8.4.3 How to Solve It?

Institutional investors engaging in the digital asset landscape must adhere to optimal practices to guarantee the precision and dependability of pricing data. A comprehensive pricing methodology, such as the one that includes a five-step process: vetting, qualifying, aggregating, cleaning, and calculating, could serve as a useful model.[17]

Initially, the process involves scrutinizing over 450 exchanges using both quantitative and qualitative criteria. After this meticulous examination, only a handful qualify as reliable pricing sources. Next, the trade and order book data from these selected exchanges are inspected for any indications of market manipulation. Following this, the trade data is consistently monitored and aggregated, incorporating alerts, updates, news, and performance metrics that could potentially affect the exchange's status. During the cleaning phase, outliers are systematically eliminated to uphold price integrity and safeguard against undue influence from extreme market phenomena. Finally, a volume-weighted or time-weighted average price is calculated from the most liquid pricing pairs, offering a dependable and "clean" pricing benchmark for digital assets. Following such a rigorous method allows institutional investors to

---

17 Vetting process taken from Digital Asset Research, https://www.digitalassetresearch.com/diligence-exchange-tokens-counterparties/.

reliably base their investment decisions and risk management strategies on clean prices. To guarantee accurate and reliable pricing data, thorough vetting of exchanges and pricing sources is essential.

Institutional investors should give preference to pricing sources that exhibit transparency in their methodologies and show commitment to providing accurate, reliable data by considering various unique factors of digital assets.

8.5 Moving Out the Risk Curve—The Benefits of Investing in a Multi-Token Index

It is widely acknowledged that a diversified portfolio containing risky assets can potentially yield higher returns for a given level of risk compared to what individual assets could offer on their own. Digital assets, particularly Bitcoin, have emerged as the top-performing asset class in 8 of the past 10 years. However, the significant volatility associated with these assets remains a barrier for many investors, who perceive price fluctuations as a disadvantage rather than a beneficial attribute.

8.5.1 Low Survival Rates Have Been a Constant in Financial Markets

In 1956, Ford Motor Company's highly anticipated IPO was so massive, valued at $658 million, that it required the collaboration of major Wall Street firms and most of the minor ones. Goldman Sachs led the way, with over 200 banks and brokers listed as underwriters.[18] Interestingly, by the time Goldman Sachs went public in 1984, it was the only bank or broker from that prospectus still in existence. This highlights the volatile nature of financial markets and the difficulty in picking the survivors in equities.

History has repeatedly taught us this lesson: canal stocks, railroads, automobiles, radios, dot-coms—the successful investments are always significantly outnumbered by the unsuccessful ones. It is a challenging task to invest in even the most established and reliable companies. Professor Richard Foster from Yale University reports that the average lifespan of a firm listed in the S&P 500 index of top U.S. companies has fallen

---

18 See Rosevear (2019).

significantly in the last century. In the 1920s, companies remained in the index for an average of 67 years. However, today, this average lifespan has dropped down to just 15 years.[19] It is reflecting the natural process of business cycles, mergers and acquisitions, bankruptcies, and other factors that affect the composition of the index over time. When it comes to crypto investing, choosing the survivors becomes an even more challenging task.

8.5.2 Why a Naïve Buy-and-Hold Approach Does Not Work in Crypto

Investing in a token and holding it for the long term might appear simple, but it poses a greater challenge than most investors realize. These tokens can be equated to startups, as many lack a historical background and have either underdeveloped or nonexistent minimum viable products. A more cautious tactic could involve buying the highest market cap tokens and retaining them indefinitely. But is this really the guidance we should abide by? Let us scrutinize the top 10 tokens throughout time (Table 8.1).

Apart from Bitcoin, the composition of even the top 10 tokens is unstable. Even if we consider a larger universe, the situation does not get better. Of the top 50 coins in 2015, 34 are not even in the top 500, 16 of them have become so small and insignificant that they are not able to be traded on any mainstream exchange today, and 11 do not even exist anymore. This has all taken place in just eight years.

The challenge lies in the fact that, although some might argue that it was apparent that those early tokens failed due to unsound protocols. But this is an example of hindsight bias as assessing this at an early stage is no easy task. If you were to examine the white papers of those early 2014 protocols, they all appeared promising. Consider NXT as an example. NXT was marketed as a cutting-edge blockchain network designed to improve the functionality of emerging cryptocurrencies like Bitcoin, Ethereum, and others. Issues such as scalability and efficiency, which remain buzzwords even today, were associated with popular cryptocurrencies. Another example is Peercoin, a protocol employing a proof of stake consensus algorithm. This is an important technological step, as evidenced

---

19 See Lam (2015).

Rank	2015	2016	2017	2018	2019	2020	2021	2022	2023
1	Bitcoin	Bitcoin	Bitcoin	Bitcoin	Bitcoin	Bitcoin	Bitcoin	Bitcoin	Bitcoin
2	XRP	Ethereum	XRP	XRP	Ethereum	Ethereum	Ethereum	Ethereum	Ethereum
3	Litecoin	XRP	Ethereum	Ethereum	XRP	XRP	BNB	BNB	BNB
4	Ethereum	Litecoin	Bitcoin Cash	Bitcoin Cash	Bitcoin Cash	Litecoin	Solana	XRP	XRP
5	Dash	Monero	Cardano	EOS	Litecoin	Bitcoin Cash	Cardano	Terra	Cardano
6	Dogecoin	Ethereum Classic	Litecoin	Stellar	EOS	BNB	XRP	Cardano	Dogecoin
7	Peercoin	Dash	IOTA	Litecoin	BNB	Chainlink	Terra	Solana	Polygon
8	BitShares	MaidSafe	NEM	Bitcoin SV	Bitcoin SV	Cardano	Polkadot	Avalanche	Solana
9	Stellar	NEM	Dash	TRON	Stellar	Polkadot	Avalanche	Polkadot	Polkadot
10	MaidSafe	Steem	Stellar	Cardano	TRON	Stellar	Dogecoin	Dogecoin	Litecoin

Table 8.1: Top 10 tokens by year as of April 20, 2023. Data: MarketVector.

by Ethereum switching its consensus mechanism from proof-of-work to proof-of-stake just in 2022. But being ahead of the time did not help Peercoin. Thus, the question arises: who can accurately assess a coin's validity? The average investor is certainly not equipped to make that determination.

Understanding a token's protocol and investment potential can be daunting. Consequently, many investors resort to a faith-based approach, believing in the potential of crypto without knowing which specific assets to choose. A common strategy is to invest in a handful of crypto assets, hoping that a few significant winners will compensate for the inevitable losers. Just hold, or HODL,[20] them, and all will be fine. But selecting a well-rounded portfolio of the top number of altcoins may prove challenging. Some cryptocurrencies, such as Dogecoin and Shiba Inu, are often viewed as joke or meme coins, while others, like Ethereum Classic, Bitcoin Cash, and Litecoin, are deemed "zombies" that persist despite losing relevance. Furthermore, numerous altcoins remain relatively unknown, with their investment potential being largely speculative. Is it better to invest solely in Bitcoin? As the highest-ranking coin with the most extensive decentralization and a long-standing reputation, Bitcoin is an attractive option. However, for those new to investing, the uncertainty can be daunting. Why shouldn't a meme coin excel or an antiquated legacy token be hindered from making a comeback? Conversely, the mere fact that a protocol is novel does not guarantee it will outshine its competitors. When choosing coins, it is important to remember that we cannot assume we know better than the rest of the market, as evidenced by the findings in behavioral finance literature. This is why it is incredibly challenging for an individual to accurately choose the most suitable token.

8.5.3 Beyond Bitcoin

Bitcoin, the largest token by market cap, has seen its dominance decline over time, as shown in Figure 8.7.[21]

This ratio refers to the proportion of Bitcoin's market capitalization relative to the aggregate market capitalization of all cryptocurrencies. The

---

20 *HODL* is a term used in the cryptocurrency community that stands for "Hold on for Dear Life." It refers to the practice of holding onto a cryptocurrency, like Bitcoin or Ethereum, despite market fluctuations, with the belief that its value will increase over time. It originated from a misspelling of "hold" in a forum post and has since become a popular investment strategy among crypto enthusiasts.

21 Bitcoin dominance is a measure of how much of the total market cap of crypto is comprised of Bitcoin.

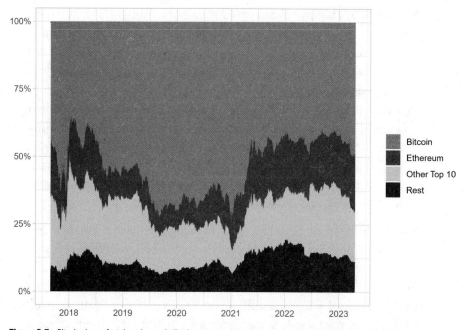

Figure 8.7: Bitcoin share of total market capitalization compared to other coins as of April 20, 2023. Data: MarketVector.

current 49% ratio suggests the existence of other viable use cases. There are multiple factors contributing to this progression:

Proliferation of Altcoins: The emergence of a multitude of alternative cryptocurrencies, commonly referred to as altcoins, has played a significant role in the decline of Bitcoin's dominance. With unique features and applications, these digital assets have attracted investments, thereby increasing their respective market capitalizations and diluting Bitcoin's relative share.

Technological Advancements and Innovations: Certain newer tokens have addressed the inherent limitations of Bitcoin's technology, including transaction processing speed, scalability, and energy efficiency. Consequently, investors and users have diversified their portfolios to include these technologically advanced digital assets, contributing to the decrease in Bitcoin dominance.

Institutional Diversification: Financial institutions have increasingly broadened their cryptocurrency investments beyond Bitcoin. By allocating funds to a variety of digital assets, these institutions have contributed to the expansion of altcoins' market capitalizations, resulting in a diminished Bitcoin dominance.

Market Speculation: The cryptocurrency market is characterized by a high degree of speculation. Investors constantly seek opportunities to profit from promising projects and technological breakthroughs. As a result, capital inflows into altcoins have surged, expanding their market caps and reducing Bitcoin's dominance.

Growth of Decentralized Finance and Non-Fungible Tokens: The rapid expansion of decentralized finance (DeFi) platforms and non-fungible tokens (NFTs) has further impacted Bitcoin's market share. DeFi and NFTs, built predominantly on platforms like Ethereum, have attracted significant investment and interest, spurred the growth of platform-owned tokens, and reduced Bitcoin's dominance.

It is crucial for institutional investors to recognize that a decrease in Bitcoin dominance does not inherently imply a decline in the digital asset's value or significance. The overall cryptocurrency market continues to expand, with Bitcoin maintaining its position as a major participant. By understanding the factors driving this shift, investors can better navigate the evolving landscape of digital assets and make informed decisions regarding portfolio diversification. This trend is consistent with a logical rationale. The potential market cap for a store of value use case, which is Bitcoin's primary narrative, is smaller than the potential market cap for various digital applications running on alternative base layer blockchains. A similar phenomenon can be observed in traditional finance, where gold, as a store of value, has a significantly lower market cap (10 trillion USD) compared to global listed equities (over 100 trillion USD).

8.5.4 Variability in Returns

Digital assets exhibit significant differences in returns due to their varying operational fields and maturity levels. To obtain a comprehensive understanding without depending on a random selection of coins Table 8.2 features exemplary returns of single assets and sectors.

The returns of different category indexes exhibit considerable variability, with no consistent leaders. The top index in one quarter seldom remains in the lead during the subsequent quarter. It is accurate to describe this as a "random walk" environment, posing a significant challenge for investors who opt for a single coin or active approach. Return rankings lack consistency, and the dispersion of returns among categories is substantial.

Q4-2020	Q4-2021	Q4-2022	Q1-2023
Bitcoin 163.2%	Media & Entertainment 62.0%	Ethereum −11.7%	Bitcoin 72.0%
Ethereum 103.1%	Exchanges 43.2%	Bitcoin −16.1%	Small-Cap 67.3%
Top 10 93.1%	Ethereum 25.6%	Top 10 −17.9%	Infrastructure Applications 58.7%
Smart Contract Platforms 73.0%	Mid-Cap 14.9%	Exchanges −19.1%	Smart Contract Platforms 53.6%
Mid-Cap 40.9%	Infrastructure Applications 13.6%	Infrastructure Applications −23.4%	Ethereum 53.1%
Small-Cap 37.2%	Small-Cap 12.9%	Smart Contract Platforms −28.8%	Top 10 52.3%
	Top 10 12.4%	Decentralized Finance −30.4%	Decentralized Finance 42.4%
	Bitcoin 10.5%	Small-Cap −33.5%	Media & Entertainment 41.4%
	Smart Contract Platforms 9.9%	Mid-Cap −39.6%	Mid-Cap 32.0%
	Decentralized Finance −9.0%	Media & Entertainment −49.5%	Exchanges 29.5%

Table 8.2: Exemplary quarterly returns of digital asset indexes as of March 31, 2023. Data: MarketVector.

The top 10 index, representing the 10 largest cryptocurrencies by market capitalization, performs consistently well compared to other sectors. This suggests that investing in the top 10 index may offer a more stable, albeit still relatively volatile, investment option compared to the broader market. The case for focusing on the top 10 index as an initial investment lies in the fact that these cryptocurrencies have more established networks, higher liquidity, and stronger support from the crypto community. Additionally, they are more likely to have a diversified range of use cases and applications, which may contribute to their longer-term growth potential.

8.5.5 The Correlation of Large-Cap Crypto Assets

In the early stages of crypto markets, retail investors were the driving force behind the crypto trading ecosystem, resulting in unpredictable price movements for cryptocurrencies. However, with the entrance of institutional investors and their significant trading volumes, the correlation between assets appears to have increased.

When evaluating the long-term correlation coefficients of the current top 10 crypto tokens, not every coin exhibits a strong correlation with others (Table 8.3). Aside from the Bitcoin-Ethereum pair, correlations appear to be moderately strong. Dogecoin stands out for its relatively low correlation to other tokens.

As the crypto asset domain continues to mature, it is plausible that correlations between crypto assets might decrease, driven by factors such as regulatory clarity, improved market infrastructure, and a better understanding of the distinct use cases for various crypto assets. A higher dispersion among different crypto assets should be expected in the future.

Is a correlation coefficient between 0.3 and 0.8 too high for a diversified group of tokens? When comparing the correlation coefficients of large crypto tokens to those of major components in an equity index like the S&P 500, the figures are strikingly similar. To illustrate this point, we can compare the 90-day rolling correlations of Bitcoin with the largest crypto assets and Apple with the largest components of the S&P 500 (see Figure 8.8).

The resemblance between the correlations of large-cap crypto assets and large-cap stocks is remarkable. Ultimately, shared factors influence this emerging asset class, including regulation, liquidity, adoption, and institutionalization. Interestingly, the largest stocks in the S&P 500 primarily

	ADA	AVAX	BNB	DOGE	DOT	ETH	LTC	SOL	BTC
ADA		0.51	0.83	0.26	0.78	0.42	0.41	0.79	0.46
AVAX	0.51		0.27	0.64	0.66	0.63	0.25	0.79	0.31
BNB	0.83	0.27		0.20	0.64	0.27	0.41	0.66	0.43
DOGE	0.26	0.64	0.20		0.35	0.59	0.25	0.56	0.13
DOT	0.78	0.66	0.64	0.35		0.68	0.65	0.80	0.76
ETH	0.42	0.63	0.27	0.59	0.68		0.66	0.63	0.70
LTC	0.41	0.25	0.41	0.25	0.65	0.66		0.43	0.74
SOL	0.79	0.79	0.66	0.56	0.80	0.63	0.43		0.46
BTC	0.46	0.31	0.43	0.13	0.76	0.70	0.74	0.46	

Table 8.3: Correlation matrix of well-known crypto assets (as of April 30, 2023. Correlation coefficient based on monthly returns since September 1, 2020).
Source: MarketVector.

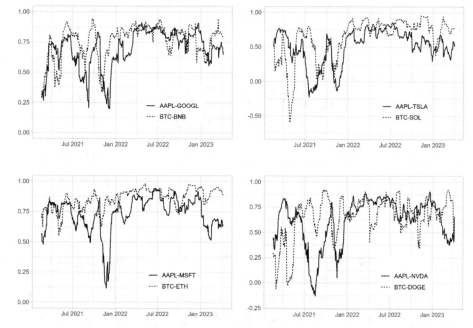

Figure 8.8: Comparison of rolling correlations of stocks and cryptos (correlation based on 90 days, as of April 16, 2023). Data: MarketVector.

consist of tech equities. Consequently, it is reasonable to assume that the correlation among different crypto tokens mirrors that of equities within the same sector. Examining bank stocks or consumer discretionary stocks would likely yield a similar range of correlation ratios. However, negative correlations within the crypto space, akin to those between oil stocks and tech stocks, are yet to emerge.

As the fundamental factors defining this asset class become more established, such as regulatory frameworks, tax structures, and investment infrastructure, the distinctions between the use cases of various crypto assets should become increasingly pronounced and comprehensible. For example, Bitcoin should not be linked to an exchange token like Binance, which in turn, should not be associated with an oracle like Chainlink.

8.6 Crypto Indexing: Can Traditional Strategies Translate to the Fast-Paced Digital Asset Market?

The current crypto market is often compared to the late 1990s dot-com boom and bust. If you had invested in a basket of the top 20 internet companies from 1998, you would have seen many failures, but Microsoft and

Amazon would have more than compensated for those losses. The question is, can the same strategy work in the crypto market?

8.6.1 The Market-Cap-Weighted Index: An Active Decision

A market-cap-weighted index, in contrast to a static buy and hold strategy, is a dynamic approach to portfolio management. This approach automatically adjusts the portfolio composition based on market capitalization, effectively rebalancing as the market fluctuates. As a result, this type of index is inherently an active solution. Its ongoing adaptation can be compared to a slow trend-following strategy, as both seek to capitalize on the prevailing trends in the market.

In the fast-paced world of crypto investing, a regular review of the market-cap-weighted index can offer several advantages. By reassessing the index's composition at regular intervals, investors can stay in tune with the market's fluctuations and respond accordingly. This approach ensures that the portfolio remains aligned with the most relevant assets, capturing the returns of the broader market rather than relying on the performance of a select few tokens.

While the market-cap-weighted index may not deliver the astronomical returns of a 100× token, it offers a more stable and consistent performance. By automatically adjusting to the shifting landscape, this approach minimizes the risk associated with choosing individual tokens, thus providing investors with a reliable and diversified exposure to the crypto market. Moreover, the market-cap-weighted index mitigates the fear of missing out on major gains by incorporating the top-performing assets as their market capitalization increases. This enables investors to participate in the market's growth without the need to meticulously monitor individual tokens or make constant buy and sell decisions.

8.6.2 Diversification Is King

So, what does this all mean for investors? One approach is to focus on a top 10 index as an initial investment. A top 10 index includes the 10 largest and most established cryptocurrencies, providing a good balance between potential returns and risk. Investing in such an index can take advantage of the strong performance of individual cryptocurrencies while also benefiting from diversification across the sector.

In this chapter, our focus is on the MarketVector Digital Assets 10 Index, (MVDA10) a modified market-cap-weighted index that tracks the performance of the 10 largest and most liquid digital assets. The component weightings have a 30% cap, allowing for increased diversification, as Bitcoin and Ethereum can constitute over 90% of a 10-token basket. The index is reviewed monthly, enabling new tokens to enter and exit on a monthly basis. Its history extends back to the end of 2014, providing a sufficiently long time series for analysis.

We compare the MVDA10 to a static buy-and-hold basket that begins with the same allocation as the MVDA10 but then remains unchanged. During the period under consideration, several significant events occurred, including multiple bull and bear markets, the implosion of Terra Luna, the insolvency of the 3AC hedge fund, and the FTX debacle. It is worth noting that the MVDA10 had an investment in Terra Luna, making it particularly intriguing to examine the index's behavior during this period.

Figure 8.9 demonstrates that the MVDA10 significantly outperformed the static buy-and-hold portfolio. This return is accompanied by marginally

Figure 8.9: Cumulative returns of an index and a static portfolio from December 2014 to March 2023 (start value indexed at 100).
Source: MarketVector.

lower volatility, and in risk-adjusted terms, the Sharpe Ratio is also higher. The primary advantage of such an index concept is its ability to capture the crypto market return consistently. Investors do not need to concern themselves with token selection, which provides considerable relief and presents a straightforward, robust strategy to implement.

Upon examining the final composition of the static portfolio, it is evident how risky this asset class can be. As discussed in the valuation chapter, this asset class is akin to investing in startups. From the initial 10-token investment, it is reasonable to say that, from a practical perspective, the portfolio is primarily invested in Bitcoin and Litecoin. All other tokens have nearly zero weight and can therefore be disregarded.

In contrast, the MVDA10 still comprises the top 10 tokens by market cap, providing a significant advantage in terms of future return potential. The static portfolio, however, relies heavily on the performance of just two coins. While it is likely that Bitcoin will remain relevant in the coming years, the same cannot be confidently said for Litecoin. It is possible that in another decade, the static buy-and-hold investor will be left with only Bitcoin (see Table 8.4). This means that the investor's success will be dependent on a single coin, while the index will remain diversified and capture the overall crypto market returns, regardless of what transpires over the next 10 years.

Ticker	Name	Static buy-and-hold initial allocation	Static buy-and-hold final allocation
BTC	Bitcoin	30.00%	64.57%
LTC	Litecoin	25.56%	31.65%
PPC	PeerCoin	4.72%	0.07%
USNBT	NuBits	0.84%	0.00%
XPY	PayCoin	30.00%	0.00%
NMC	NameCoin	2.72%	0.11%
NSR	NuShares	1.55%	0.09%
FTC	FeatherCoin	0.38%	0.01%
DASH	Dash	3.93%	3.28%
XPM	PrimeCoin	0.30%	0.24%

Table 8.4: Composition and Weightings (initial allocation as of December 30, 2014. Final allocation as of March 18, 2023). Source: MarketVector.

8.7 Refining Crypto Asset Portfolios: Risk Parity and Beyond—Exploring Advanced Indexing Strategies in Crypto

By Gregory Mall, CFA, Head Investment Solutions AMINA, formerly SEBA Bank AG, and Rohan Misra, CFA, FRM, CEO AMINA India

Gregory Mall has many years of experience in portfolio management and managing digital assets on a discretionary basis. At AMINA, he is responsible for the product structuring of ETPs, AMCs, and structured products as well as for the management of discretionary mandates. Prior to joining AMINA, he worked as a multi-asset fund manager at Credit Suisse. Mall holds a Master's degree in Economics from the University of St. Gallen (HSG) and is a CFA charterholder.

Rohan Misra is the CEO at AMINA India. Rohan brings 15 years of investment management experience spanning quantitative research and analytics, systematic trading, and risk management. Misra holds a Bachelor's degree in Electronics and Communications Engineering from the Indian Institute of Technology Roorkee, is a CFA charter holder, and a Certified Financial Risk Manager. Before joining AMINA, Misra worked at Credit Suisse and Infosys Technologies.

The realm of crypto indexes, though teeming with potential, requires careful navigation for a secure and efficient investment experience. From universe selection to compliance and market structure to liquidity, there are essential factors that can shape the outcome of investments in this sector.

Several indexes apply seemingly straightforward criteria to define their index universe, leading to an inclusion of a diverse range of coins. While this can bring exposure to potentially lucrative opportunities, it can also lead to the inclusion of coins with lower liquidity, questionable security, or unclear token issuance mechanisms, thereby increasing tracking error and idiosyncratic risk.

Many crypto indexes employ the market capitalization-based weighting methodology, stemming from the capital asset pricing model and the efficient market hypothesis.[22] While these principles have their limitations

---

22 See Al-Yahyaee et al. (2020); Tran and Leirvik (2020).

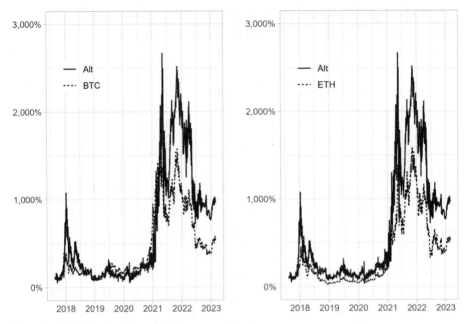

Figure 8.10: Performance comparison of alt coins[23] versus Bitcoin and Ethereum.
Data: Coinmarketcap.com, SEBA Bank AG.

in the crypto universe, it is important to highlight the utility of market cap weighting as a starting point for investing in cryptocurrencies. This approach mirrors the broad market consensus on a coin's value, and it inherently provides exposure to established players such as Bitcoin and Ethereum, delivering a beta strategy that forms the backbone of many portfolios.

However, it is also true that a strict adherence to market cap weighting may limit exposure to altcoins, potentially affecting portfolio diversification due to the high concentration of the crypto market. Refining index weighting schemes therefore could present additional opportunities for capturing the potential alpha of alt-coins over extended investment periods (Figure 8.10).

8.7.1 An Innovative Weighting Concept

The AMINA Crypto Asset Select Index (AMINAX, formerly SEBAX) addresses the issues previously highlighted by implementing an alternative

---

23 The alt-coin performance is calculated by subtracting the market caps of BTC and ETH from the total market capitalization.

weighting methodology aimed at increasing the exposure to alt-coins (Table 8.5) in a systematic and controlled manner The final weight of each constituent in the index is the average of its market capitalization weight and its "risk-parity" weight within the eligible list of index constituents. The risk-parity approach weights index constituents in inverse proportion to their risk so that the risk contributions from each constituent are equal. Periodic rebalancing results in increasing exposures to constituents with lower risk and decreasing exposures to constituents with higher risk (Table 8.6).

Risk-parity outperforms the capitalization-weighted index of the same constituents over the full market cycle. The alternative weighting approach results in more balanced weights, and is therefore better positioned to

Symbol	Market-Cap Weights	Risk-Parity Weights	SEBAX Weights (average)
BTC	64.0%	18.6%	41.3%
ETH	28.3%	15.3%	21.8%
ADA	1.9%	12.8%	7.3%
LTC	1.0%	13.6%	7.3%
DOT	1.1%	11.9%	6.5%
MATIC	1.6%	10.7%	6.1%
AVAX	0.9%	10.0%	5.4%
SOL	1.2%	7.2%	4.2%

Table 8.5: Introducing a controlled altcoin bias through risk-parity.
Source: SEBA Bank AG, as of 28.02.2023.

	90d volatility	Risk-parity weight
SOL	124%	7.2%
AVAX	94%	10.0%
MATIC	74%	10.7%
DOT	73%	11.9%
ADA	66%	12.8%
LTC	57%	13.6%
ETH	51%	15.3%
BTC	43%	18.6%

Table 8.6: Risk-parity weights are inversely proportional to the risk.
Source: SEBA Bank AG, as of 28.02.2023.

capture significant performance run-ups in small-cap cryptocurrencies during up-trending market periods while suffering drawdowns similar to the cap-weighted ones during down-trending market periods. Crypto run-ups, while extreme, are quite short-lived—making it almost impossible to time these markets. The SEBAX weighting scheme provides a more balanced exposure across constituents of different market caps, and therefore can capture significant upside as and when a bull run manifests (Figure 8.11).

The alternative weighting approach also strikes a balance between the performance surplus and the increase in volatility. Figure 8.12 displays the annualized return, volatility, Sharpe ratio since index inception with SEBAX, risk-parity, and market-cap weighting methodologies. The SEBAX index demonstrates a significantly higher return versus a market-cap-weighted index and only marginally higher volatility resulting in a higher risk-adjusted return since inception. It also demonstrates a better return, volatility, and risk-adjusted return profile when compared to a risk-parity-weighted-only portfolio.

Our results show that the SEBAX combination creates a more robust and diversified portfolio in most scenarios and significantly decreases volatility as well as drawdowns versus a pure risk-parity approach. The improved performance from the alternative weighting techniques is not a free lunch. A higher allocation to crypto assets with smaller market

Figure 8.11: Different weighting schemes applied to small-cap crypto assets.
Source: SEBA Bank AG.

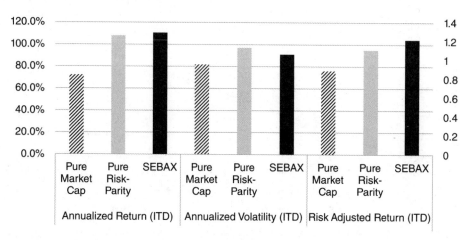

Figure 8.12: Performance and risk stats for market-cap, risk-parity, and blended methodologies (01.01.2017–28.02.2023).
Source: SEBA Bank AG.

caps comes with lower liquidity, and therefore, potentially higher trading costs. We have employed portfolio construction rules to mitigate the impact of these tradeoffs, by limiting and/or controlling constituent participation.

The index performs particularly well versus the broad market (measured by the Bitwise 10 index) and versus Bitcoin during bull market phases while experiencing similar drawdowns. The index has slightly higher volatility versus Bitcoin over an entire market cycle, but compensates the investor with a significantly higher return. Figure 8.13 shows the monthly performance of SEBAX versus Bitcoin and the broad market (proxied by the Bitwise 10 Index). Dots that are on the diagonal line indicate performance in line with the benchmark. As one can easily detect there are more dots above than below the line. Most of the dots that are significantly above the line are in the northeastern quadrant, indicating that the bulk of the relative outperformance stems from bull markets.

Unsurprisingly, this is also reflected in a long-term performance comparison versus Bitcoin (Figure 8.14).

8.7.2 Index Inclusion beyond Quantitative Criteria

Although the SEBAX index is a passive index governed by the rules defined in the publicly accessible index guide, we want to emphasize the

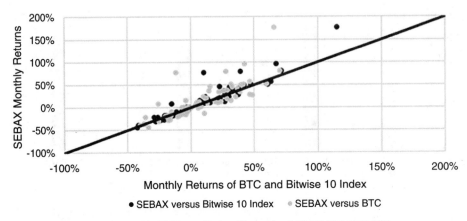

Figure 8.13: Relative performance of the SEBAX versus Bitcoin and the broad market (01.01.2017–28.02.2023).
Source: SEBA Bank AG.

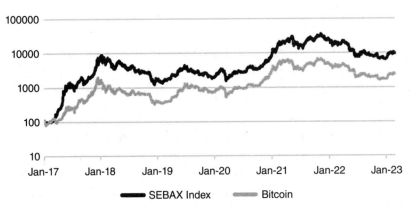

Figure 8.14: SEBAX versus Bitcoin (01.01.2017–28.02.2023).
Source: SEBA Bank AG.

element of filtering the index universe. While most of the eligibility criteria are quantitative by nature (i.e., market cap, liquidity) some rules are more qualitative and require a certain amount of discretion. For example, it is clearly stated in the index guide that:

> *"Crypto assets that do not pass the Index criteria related to technical maturity and safety are excluded. These include factors such as the degree of blockchain network decentralization, main-net stability, quality of development team, community involvement, etc. of the underlying blockchain."*

These factors are harder to quantify and require a significant collaborative effort on MarketVector's and AMINAs side with research, blockchain engineering, custody, and the asset management team all involved. We only include coins that have passed our stringent due diligence process and are compliant with the FINMA guidelines on KYC/AML.

8.8 Benchmark Rates: Safe against Manipulation?

8.8.1 Why Do You Need an Index for a Single Token?

In contrast to traditional assets, whose trading in any particular asset tends to be limited to just a few exchanges, digital assets can trade across hundreds of venues, all of which have markets that fluctuate independently based on order flows. While it is profitable for arbitrageurs to keep these differences in check across the ecosystem, temporary price differences persist. Sometimes, large orders on any exchange can drive significant relative price differentials in the same asset when compared to other exchanges, a phenomenon that happens more frequently during times of market stress.

As a result, even the basic question "what is the price of bitcoin today" is not easy to answer, which is why using an index or aggregated price provides a better answer than simply picking the last traded price on a specific exchange. These benchmark reference prices have been crafted for investors who express concerns over potential price manipulation and the potential for exchange failures. Benchmark reference prices are particularly favored in the resolution of financial derivatives and in the computation of a fund's net asset value (NAV). A reliable, regulated, and universally acknowledged reference point for leading digital currencies creates a more secure and trustworthy environment.

The creation and maintenance of such reference rates, however, are not without challenges. This section dissects the methodology behind the MarketVector Bitcoin Benchmark Rate (BBR) and MarketVector Ethereum Benchmark Rate (EBR), exploring how they compare to standard cryptocurrency indexes. We delve into the use of volume-weighted medians and the technical challenges encountered by data providers. Furthermore, through a series of case studies, this chapter demonstrates the resilience of the BBR index in withstanding market shocks and anomalies. Using time series from CCData, we will simulate intraday variations of these reference rates during significant events such as the Bitfinex Flash Crash and other market dislocations. These simulations underscore the robustness of the BBR and EBR, and their efficacy in mitigating manipulation.

8.8.2 Understanding the Bitcoin Benchmark Rate

The Bitcoin Benchmark Rate (BBR) serves as an important tool for understanding the market value of Bitcoin. The BBR's design prioritizes accuracy, reliability, and resilience against market manipulation. To understand this tool better, let us break down its methodology into digestible components:

The Calculation Methodology

Medians over Averages

Imagine you are trying to find the middle value in a series of numbers. An average would consider all values equally, but what if there is a single extraordinarily high or low number? This could skew your average, creating a less accurate representation of the "middle" value. Here's where medians come in handy. Medians help us pinpoint the middle value, minimizing the influence of extreme values, or "outliers." In terms of BBR, medians ensure that the price reflected is less affected by any extreme Bitcoin prices on a particular exchange.

Volume-Weighting of Medians

The utilization of volume-weighting in calculating medians serves to neutralize the effect of numerous smaller trades that might skew a median that does not account for volume. Unlike a traditional median, a volume-weighted median incorporates a weighting element—in this instance, the size of the trade—into its computation, thus providing a more comprehensive analysis.

Understanding Medians and Volume-Weighted Medians

Median: A *median* is the "middle" number in a sorted list of numbers. To find the median, you arrange your numbers in order from smallest to largest. If you have an odd number of observations, the median is the middle number. If you have an even number of observations, the median is the average of the two middle numbers.

This contrasts with the *mean* (commonly referred to as the "average"), which is determined by summing all numbers and then dividing by the total count of numbers. The median is less influenced by outliers (values that are extraordinarily high or low) and offers a more precise depiction of the "central" point of your data.

Volume-Weighted Median: A *volume weighted median* is a statistical measure used to find the midpoint value in a set of data that's been sorted in ascending order, where the weightings are determined by associated volumes. For a list of prices, each paired with a particular volume, the prices are first sorted from smallest to largest.

The volumes paired with these prices represent their respective weights. The volume weighted median is identified as the first price at which the cumulative volume (from smallest price to that point) constitutes 50% or more of the total volume. This ensures that half of the volume is concentrated at or below this price, providing a median measure that is influenced by the volume associated with each price, rather than just the prices themselves.

20 Equal Partitions: Imagine trying to understand the weather in your city. If you only look at the temperature at noon, you would miss out on the cooler morning and evening temperatures. The same principle applies to understanding Bitcoin's price. The BBR divides one hour into 20 equal parts or "partitions." It then calculates the median price in each of these partitions (Figure 8.15).

This method ensures that the final rate is not overly influenced by the price at a particular time and provides a more comprehensive view of the market conditions throughout the day. Large-scale individual trades typically have a marginal impact on the index level, as they merely alter the volume-weighted median for that partition. Similarly, a series of trades happening within a brief time frame would only affect the volume-weighted median of the partitions in which they took place. This process is repeatedly done in real-time every 15 seconds, on a rolling one-hour period.

The BBR's methodology is carefully designed to capture a reliable picture of Bitcoin's price. By incorporating medians, volume-weighting,

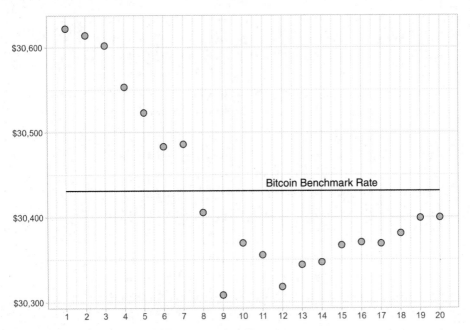

Figure 8.15: Bitcoin Benchmark Rate: Example with 20 partitions and the 4 p.m. ET closing time fixing on BTC-USD.
Source: MarketVector, CCData.

and partitioning, the BBR ensures a fair representation of Bitcoin's price. Manipulating such a rate would require significant resources and effort, making it a robust tool against market manipulation.

8.8.3 A Robust Data Set

The quality of data inputs for benchmark reference rates in the cryptocurrency domain is of paramount importance. Choosing the appropriate sources of data can greatly influence the integrity and reliability of the indexes. A careful selection of exchanges whose prices should be included into the index calculation is a vital first step. The amount of trading volumes an exchange has is another important factor. Finally, limiting the markets to USD pairs is also important.

Exchange Selection

Bitcoin trading is a broad, dynamic field, featuring numerous markets and exchanges worldwide. However, with variations in trading volumes and practices, not all exchanges are created equal and they vary significantly in terms of regulatory compliance, security measures, and liquidity.

This disparity emphasizes the importance of selecting the right exchanges when trading or developing a pricing index. Furthermore, the chosen exchanges must effectively address market manipulation, liquidity, pricing, and arbitrage concerns. Therefore, it is vital that traded volume is not the sole criterion for exchange inclusion. The adoption of a listing framework can significantly curtail the instances necessitating operator intervention. Both the EBR and BBR are dependent on the top five exchanges, as rated based on the Exchange Benchmark Report authored by CCData.[24]

USD Pairing

The BBR is specifically designed to minimize vulnerability to temporary price swings and outlier prices. As such, the BBR only includes trades executed between BTC and USD. It does not use alternate currency pairs or crypto-to-crypto pairs, and does not include transactions involving USDT or other stablecoins into the BTC-USD order book. This approach ensures the stability of the reference rate, as the U.S. Dollar, a government-issued currency, offers a level of stability and confidence that cryptocurrencies or stablecoins may not provide. Moreover, USD pairing is more familiar to most people, making the index more accessible to a broader audience.

8.8.4 Case Studies

In the following, we discuss case studies that demonstrate how the Bitcoin Reference Rate can tackle some of the challenges that the crypto markets can face at times.

The Bitstamp Bitcoin Flash Crash

One of the prevailing mistakes in the trading world is the so-called "fat-finger" error, where a trader accidentally enters an incorrect trade (usually when entering the desired trade quantity for a transaction) due to a typing error. These blunders can trigger flash crashes, which are sharp, sudden market downturns that retrace back to previous price levels very quickly once the market realizes that the move was due to a trading error rather than an exogenous event.

---

24 See https://ccdata.io/research/exchange-benchmark-rankings.

A case in point is the Bitcoin flash crash on May 17, 2019. This crash was induced by a hefty sell order that may have been submitted erroneously. The repercussions were particularly severe on Bitstamp, the exchange from which the order originated, and the Bitcoin price on Bitstamp fell precipitously compared to other exchanges.

As can be seen in Figure 8.16, the BBR remained stable due to its extensive computation window, accurately tracked the market price, and excluded the extraneous downward movement on Bitstamp.

The Binance.US Flash Crash

On October 21, 2021, a sudden flash crash on the Binance.US Exchange led to a drastic plunge in Bitcoin's price, where it tumbled from $66,000 to $8,000 and then swiftly rebounded back to $65,000 within a matter of seconds (Figure 8.17). This event was reportedly triggered by a glitch in the trading algorithm of a significant institutional investor. The tremors from the flash crash on Binance.US were felt across other Bitcoin markets, clearly showing that an anomaly in a specific exchange does not exist in a vacuum. Yet, during this time of heightened volatility, the BBR remained

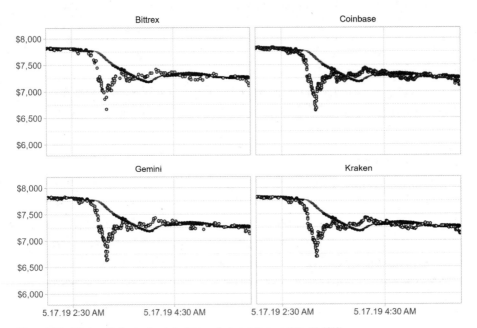

Figure 8.16: BBR versus. Exchange prices during Bitstamp flash crash (Data as of May 17, 2019). Source: MarketVector, CCData.

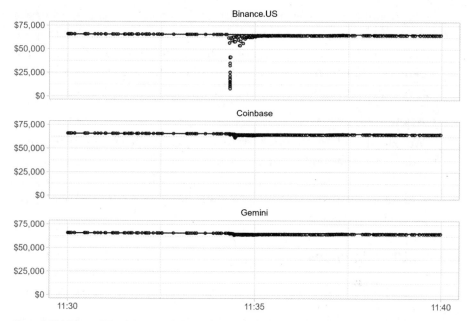

Figure 8.17: Binance.US Flash Crash: Exchange quotes (dots) compared Bitcoin Benchmark Rate as of October 21, 2021. Data: MarketVector, CCData.

entirely unaffected. Within a short span of time, all exchanges resumed trading in congruence with the BBR Index.

Inconsistencies in pricing are a notable feature of cryptocurrency markets, rendering the use of price feeds from a single exchange precarious for calculating portfolio worth and settling contracts. Those who calculate benchmark rates should construct their methodologies to withstand market dislocations and failures robustly.

8.9 Conclusion on Index Investments

This chapter has delved into the structure, application, and implications of digital asset indexes, demonstrating their value in providing a comprehensive view of the broader market trends.

Digital asset indexes play a crucial role in helping investors mitigate risk. They allow for a diversified exposure, which can help insulate against the extreme price volatility often witnessed in individual digital assets, and allow investors to apply traditional risk management techniques.

The rise of digital asset indexes also underscores the maturation of the digital asset ecosystem. As these instruments continue to evolve, they are likely to foster greater institutional participation, promote market transparency, and enhance the accessibility of cryptocurrencies for a broader spectrum of investors.

Acknowledgments

We extend our heartfelt gratitude to the people at CCData, a leading provider of accurate and actionable digital asset data. Their contribution to this chapter, in the form of detailed intraday tick data, in-depth insights, and comprehensive market information, has greatly enriched our analysis of flash crashes.

8.10 References

Alquist, Ron, Ronen Israel, and Tobias J. Moskowitz. (2018). "Fact, Fiction, and the Size Effect." *The Journal of Portfolio Management* 45.

Al-Yahyaee, Khamis, Walid Mensi, hee-un Ko, Seong-Min Yoon, and Sang Hoon Kang. (2020). "Why Cryptocurrency Markets Are Inefficient: The Impact of Liquidity and Volatility." *The North American Journal of Economics and Finance* 52

Armstrong, John B. (1960). "The Case for Mutual Fund Management." *Financial Analysts Journal* 16(3): 33–38.

Bogle, John. (2017). "The Little Book of Common Sense Investing."

Lam, Bourree. (2015, April 12). "Where Do Firms Go When They Die?" *The Atlantic*. https://www.theatlantic.com/business/archive/2015/04/where-do-firms-go-when-they-die/390249/.

Malkiel, Burton G. (2016). *A Random Walk Down Wall Street: The Time-Tested Strategy for Successful Investing*. Norton & Company.

Mihm, Stephen. (2016, September 6). "The Secret History of Index Mutual Funds." *InvestmentNews* (blog). https://www.investmentnews.com/the-secret-history-of-index-mutual-funds-69099.

Patterson, Greg. (2007). "DALBAR Study Update Confirms Investor Behavior Problems." https://advisorygroupsf.com/wp-content/uploads/2013/02/AGSF-DALBAR2006StudyResults.pdf.

PriceWaterhouseCoopers. (1999). "25 years of Indexing: An Analysis of the Costs and Benefits."

Renshaw, Edward F., and Paul J. Feldstein. (1995). "The Case for an Unmanaged Investment Company." *Financial Analysts Journal* 51(1): 58–62.

Rosevear, John. (2019, January 16). "63 Years Later, What Can Investors Learn from Ford's 1956 IPO?" The Motley Fool. https://www.fool.com/investing/2019/01/16/63-years-later-what-can-investors-learn-from-fords.aspx.

Schoenfeld, Steven A. (2004). "Active Index Investing: Maximizing Portfolio Performance and Minimizing Risk Through Global Index Strategies."

Samuelson, Paul Anthony. (1972). "Proof That Properly Anticipated Prices Fluctuate Randomly." *The Collected Scientific Papers of Paul A. Samuelson*; vol. 3, Cambridge, Mass. [u.a.]: MIT Press, pp. 782–790. ISBN 0-262-19080-x.

Schoenfeld, Steven A. (2004). *Active Index Investing: Maximizing Portfolio Performance and Minimizing Risk through Global Index Strategies*. Wiley Finance.

Sharpe, William F. (1991). "The Arithmetic of Active Management." *Financial Analysts Journal* 47(1): 7–9.

"SPIVA® U.S. Year-End." (2022). S&P Dow Jones Indices. https://www.spglobal.com/spdji/en/spiva/article/spiva-us/.

Tran, Vu Le, and Thomas Leirvik. (2020). "Efficiency in the Markets of Crypto-Currencies." *Finance Research Letters* 35.

9 Outlook: Navigating the Future—The Expansive Potential of Digital Assets

> "The most transformative financial development I've seen in the last two decades is the ATM. It truly benefits people by eliminating the need to visit a bank, providing genuine convenience. Can you name another innovation as influential to the individual as the ATM, which is more of a mechanical breakthrough than a financial one?"
>
> Paul A. Volcker

In the sphere of finance, groundbreaking change has been overdue. Despite the internet's integration into nearly every aspect of our existence, shifts within the conventional banking industry have been modest. The most dramatic changes have unfolded within the realm of online brokerage. The number of trading platforms for individual investors has surged, leading to a significant reduction in costs and an increase in speed, bolstered by the buzz around stocks at the start of the new millennium.

The Long-Awaited Innovation

Many other everyday activities have also evolved. Instead of using a paper form, initiating a money transfer via smartphone increases efficacy for all parties involved. However, this change is not a technological marvel worthy of a Nobel Prize. Anyone who has ever sent money overseas is familiar with the outdated sensation of high costs and slow speeds, reminiscent of the dial-up internet era. Other industries have been significantly reshaped by technological change, clearly illustrated by the media and communication sectors. The financial sector still has much catching up to do, and the window of opportunity for true innovation remains wide open.

A significant hurdle to a quicker, more affordable, and concurrently, secure financial system is the reliance on numerous middle persons. This issue was identified by Milton Friedman as far back as 1999 when he stated, "What's lacking, but will soon emerge, is a reliable form of e-cash—a way to transfer funds on the internet from person A to person B, with neither knowing each other, similar to handing over a $20 bill with no record of its origin."

This observation could have been taken directly from Satoshi Nakamoto's white paper. The innovation it encapsulates is a decentralized financial system that eliminates the need for intermediaries and does not require mutual trust among participants—precisely what blockchain technology provides. Therefore, the invention of the blockchain is a giant step in the direction of such a system, revolutionizing how we think about and manage money.

Don Tapscott, a distinguished Canadian academic, co-founder of the Blockchain Research Institute, and author of several books on how emergent technologies impact business and society, presents an intriguing perspective. He views the internet as a conduit for information, while blockchains serve as a network of value.

There can be a debate over distinguishing *information* and *value* since digital assets are fundamentally information controlled by cryptographic access, to which users assign value. However, Tapscott's classification does not delve into these technical nuances. Instead, it offers an application-oriented viewpoint, positioning the two technologies in terms of their practical uses and benefits to users.

The potential to generate digital assets, which can be distributed freely and moved almost effortlessly across a decentralized network, opens the door to unprecedented opportunities. We are poised for an even greater surge in automation, an acceleration of the Internet of Things (IoT) growth, and a rise in truly autonomous computer programs. These programs will possess value they can utilize within both traditional and burgeoning marketplaces.

Nevertheless, it is uncertain which blockchain protocols will strike the ideal balance of resilience and adaptability for their specific objectives and eventually come out on top. This ambiguity, however, is the lifeblood of innovation, promising a future where the utilization of blockchain technology becomes a norm rather than an exception. However, what remains unarguable is the profound influence of blockchain-based applications on nearly all economic sectors.

The Inevitable Transformation

The trends of digital transformation and automation show no signs of ceasing or reversing. Instead, they will continue to broaden, progressively influencing economically vital areas like our monetary system. Karl-Heinz

Land, an author and consultant, encapsulates this trend neatly: "Everything that can be digitized, networked, and automated, will be."[1]

Investors need to critically analyze which entities will profit from these potential developments and which will falter. However, it is crucial to avoid hasty conclusions. Those who prematurely predict the downfall of banks and other financial service providers may be overlooking the significant role of personal relationships in this sector.

Yes, blockchains enable secure transactions even between parties lacking mutual trust, but that does not negate the value people place on trust. In fact, in a largely automated and anonymized environment, personal relationships gain even greater importance. Banking, at its core, remains a "people's business."

While the significance of trust remains, numerous processes will undergo profound transformation. This change will demand more from both the infrastructure and the employees of financial service providers. Financial institutions can seize the opportunities presented by this new technology. They can achieve economies of scale and reap the benefits of more efficient processes provided by external service providers.

The key is to embrace this change sooner rather than later, to preempt rather than react. As a wise Chinese proverb reminds us "Dig the well before you are thirsty."

Embrace Change!

Not too long ago, the world of one generation closely resembled that of the preceding one. With the advent of industrialization and the flourishing of natural sciences, however, we have witnessed remarkable advances in technology. Although these advancements often brought about significant economic and social shifts, time and again, the tireless efforts of researchers, developers, and engineers have led to monumental and consequential technological strides. One need only reflect on the discovery and utilization of antibiotics, the progress in agriculture, or the revolution in transportation to appreciate the transformative power of innovation.

---

1   See Land (2018).

Capital markets, too, have seen innovations that have significantly propelled the real economy. A prime example is the futures markets, which have accomplished great strides through standardization and the establishment of clearing houses. However, these advances rest on foundations laid centuries ago. The Dojima Rice Exchange in Japan began trading rice contracts as early as 1710. Since then, a plethora of improvements have been made within individual asset classes, with the central objective always being the pursuit of optimal standardization and the creation of liquid and efficient trading platforms. The global foreign exchange market serves as a classic illustration. Dominated by telephone trading just a few decades ago, the landscape was dramatically reshaped by electronic, and subsequently, algorithmic trading.

Currently, we are witnessing another evolutionary leap with blockchain-based applications. They carry the potential for sweeping changes, marking the next frontier in the continuous journey of financial innovation. The evolution triggered by Bitcoin in 2009 has demonstrated tremendous momentum. The heart of this transformation is not the multitude of digital tokens—many of which will fade while a few will persist. Instead, the essence of change is a vibrant ecosystem of small enterprises powered by highly motivated individuals, along with those who dare to innovate within traditionally structured organizations. This transformative wave is not emanating from a single location. It is not a worldwide campaign by a local investment bank. It is a global collaborative and competitive effort, with teams scattered across North and South America, Africa, Asia-Pacific, and Europe. They are pushing the boundaries of this new technology at a remarkable pace.

Apart from the technological advancement itself, time is the greatest ally of change. People acclimate to change. For a prolonged period, gold-backed currencies were the norm, and the concept of accepting unbacked paper as currency seemed unimaginable. Today, the situation has flipped. The use of fiat money is so ingrained in our everyday lives that questions challenging its permanent existence often seem outlandish.

The question that should be at the forefront for both private and institutional investors is not whether the price of a specific digital asset will increase or decrease tomorrow. The crucial question is how prepared they are to professionally incorporate digital assets into their asset allocations.

In an increasingly competitive environment, it is unwise to delay this preparation, especially when others are aggressively pursuing it.

People often struggle to foresee the long-term implications of ongoing changes, and this challenge amplifies when the development is in its nascent stages. New concepts often seem puzzling, and the unavoidable initial hiccups and failures linked to any innovative idea are swiftly seized on as reasons to view the entire venture skeptically or even negatively. This was no different during the early stages of the internet and the World Wide Web, or when Jeff Bezos launched an online platform for book sales.

Who buys books on the internet, right?

9.1 Reference

Land, Karl-Heinz. (2018). *Erde 5.0: Die Zukunft Provozieren.* Future Vision Press.

About the Authors

Martin Leinweber

Martin Leinweber, a seasoned finance professional and Digital Asset Product Strategist at MarketVector Indexes, is at the forefront of developing and popularizing innovative strategies in the crypto asset space. His expertise is solidified by his near two-decade tenure in portfolio management, overseeing equities, fixed income, and alternative investments in some of Germany's most prominent institutional asset management firms. Throughout his career, he has catered to an array of institutional investors, such as insurance companies, pension funds, and sovereign wealth funds. Leinweber, a CFA Charter holder with a Master's in Economics from the University of Hohenheim, co-authored the pioneering *Asset-Allokation mit Kryptoassets: Das Handbuch* (Wiley Finance, 2021), the first guide to integrating digital assets into conventional portfolios.

Jörg Willig

As a director and Head of Portfolio Management at a distinguished private bank, Jörg Willig is responsible for managing funds for both institutional and private clients. With over two decades of experience, he has successfully navigated various market regimes using systematic asset allocation strategies. Willig's career includes the notable position of Head of Fixed Income Markets at Germany's largest quantitative asset manager as well as other key roles at high-ranked asset management institutions. He co-authored the influential book *Asset Allokation mit Kryptoassets* (Wiley Finance, 2021), which charted new paths for integrating digital assets into traditional portfolios. Willig's academic background comprises a diploma in Business Informatics from the University of Hamburg.

Steven A. Schoenfeld

Steven Schoenfeld is the Chief Executive of MarketVector Indexes, a leading global index and data provider for global equities, fixed income, and digital assets. Previously, he was the Founder of BlueStar Indexes, which was acquired by MarketVector in 2020. Schoenfeld is a 40-year veteran of the investment management industry, having served in senior fiduciary positions at Northern Trust, where he oversaw more $300 billion in global equity and bond portfolios, and at Barclays Global Investors (now Blackrock), where he managed more than $70 billion in international equity index funds and ETFs. Prior to these positions, he led the team at the World Bank/IFC that developed the first investable Emerging Market indexes, and traded Japanese stock index futures at the Singapore Exchange.

Schoenfeld is the editor of *Active Index Investing* (Wiley Finance, 2004), co-author of *The Pacific-Rim Futures and Options Markets* (McGraw-Hill, 1992), and co-founder of ETF.com. He has a B.A. from Clark University, was a Fulbright Scholar in Economics at the National University of Singapore, and earned an M.A. from the Johns Hopkins School of Advanced International Studies (SAIS).

Index